# Teach them to speak

a language
development
programme
in 200 lessons

Gordon
McGregor
Shiach

Principal
Donaldson's School
for the Deaf
Edinburgh

Ward Lock
Educational

ISBN 0 7062 3089 2 hardbound
ISBN 0 7062 3090 6 paperback

First published      1972
Reprinted            1973
Reprinted            1974
Reprinted            1977
Reprinted            1978
Reprinted            1981

Set in 10 point Apollo
by Yendall and Company Limited
and printed by
Hollen Street Press Ltd, Slough
for Ward Lock Educational
47 Marylebone Lane,
London W1M 6AX
A Pentos Company
Made in England

# Contents

Preface 5

1 The rationale of
the programme 7

2 The materials 17

3 The daily class
lessons 33

Index 254

For my family, friends, teachers
and bank manager—to all of
whom I am indebted.

# Preface

This book has been written in an effort to help teachers develop the oral language skills of their pupils. The lessons are intended for an age group of approximately four to seven year olds so the materials, procedures and classroom practices detailed will be appropriate for

1 the normal class of first year and second year infants
2 some groups of slower learning children or culturally disadvantaged children in their third and fourth year of primary schooling
3 some groups of children in schools for the educationally subnormal
4 some groups of children in schools for the severely subnormal
5 partially hearing children
6 immigrant children
7 preschool playgroups and nurseries.

Many of the materials and procedures recommended are the type which the average mother would find useful in entertaining and educating her own preschool children.

Probably few readers of this book will have had formal instruction in language development, but such preparation is not essential in order to use the procedures recommended. However, familiarity with the rationale supporting the procedures should help the teacher to grasp the point of the lessons better and also to appreciate generally how valuable it is for a child to have a well developed linguistic ability. The phrase 'well developed linguistic ability' means the child's ability to

1 understand simple instructions quite readily
2 express in words what he is doing at any time in the classroom or what he is looking at
3 describe activities that have gone before, and outline orally what he plans to do
4 describe pictures, objects and actions
5 pay particular attention to crucial words in a sentence
6 structure his own oral language according to the grammatical conventions used in school.

Chapter one therefore presents the rationale of the programme and outlines some of the many investigations on the role of language. A study of this chapter will indicate the influence which language has in stimulating growth, promoting social interaction and influencing how a child will see and hear what goes on around him.

Chapter two lists the materials required for the programme. Some of these will already be available in schools and so need not be specially bought; others can be made easily and cheaply by the class and the teacher; others will need to be collected and prepared for whichever style of presentation the teacher prefers. A *few* of the materials will have to be bought, but the cost will not be great; any items which do have to be bought can in any case be used outside the programme.

Chapter three, the most important section of the book, contains the daily class lessons—enough for an entire school year. Each lesson indicates the materials to be used each day, the procedures to follow and is designed to last twenty to thirty-five minutes depending on the size of the class or group. Although designed with a class size of thirty-five in mind, the lessons can be used for smaller classes, groups and individual tuition.

The selection of materials or procedures enables the lessons to be used in classes of wide ranging ability and ages. Obviously the skill of the individual teacher will be extended in such situations but it is precisely on the skill, expertise, insight and enthusiasm of the teacher that the procedures depend.

The aim is to encourage the child to respond orally—quickly and in a well structured manner. The teacher must therefore take account of the individual differences among her children and adjust her questioning and expectations to the assessed level of each child in her class. The aim is also to improve the language skills of each and every child. Here the teacher must exercise care in drawing out the timid, duller and nonresponding child, and tactfully prevent the enthusiastic brighter child from usurping an undue proportion of time and attention.

To use the lessons effectively, the teacher's preparation should include

1 familiarity with the studies outlined in chapter one
2 preparation and collection of sufficient materials
3 quick reading of a sample of the daily class lessons to give an indication of their style
4 general familiarity with the work to be covered four to five weeks ahead
5 more detailed familiarity with the daily lessons to be covered in the week immediately ahead
6 complete familiarity with the daily lesson to be covered so that materials are at hand and reference to the book is only exceptionally required.

# 1 The rationale of the programme

As mentioned previously, this chapter will outline a sample of the literature concerning the role of language as follows:

1 a classic study by A Luria which examines the impact of artificially hastened speech acquisition on the behaviour of children who have linguistic retardation
2 a more structured example of the impact of language on how children perceive simple pictures
3 the contribution of Vygotsky
4 the effects of verbal mediation intrusion in a task of discrimination learning by children
5 an outline of Bernstein's study on class differences in language
6 the differences shown up by deaf and hearing children
7 summary and short discussion.

First the work of A R Luria. In his view the study of language and its development is the key to our understanding of vital problems in human intellectual growth. He believes the mastery of language extends the scope of learning and control of the environment. In the study to be outlined below[1] on the development of speech of identical twins, the findings illustrate clearly the role of language in social interaction, improving understanding, governing and directing action and in promoting the growth of realistic concepts. The growth of the child's mental activity is seen to take place in certain determined social circumstances, between mother and child, between the child and his peers and between the teacher and child. Through this medium of actual communication and interaction with the environment the child acquires from adults the experience and knowledge of previous generations. From birth the child learns through language about the objects surrounding him, their similarities and differences, their relationships, their functions. This whole process of the transmission of knowledge and the formation of concepts through adult influence constitutes the central process of the child's intellectual and linguistic development.

The acquisition of a language system involves the reorganization and constant restructuring of all the child's basic mental processes. Language creates new forms of attention both to visually and orally presented material; it facilitates memory and promotes imagination in thought and action. The attachment of a word to a corresponding object in the external world is itself of value, but it also allows the child to abstract and isolate the necessary features which identify that object. It enables him to generalize about these perceived features and so categorize, classify and order. The immediately perceived, concrete and direct experience becomes symbolized and a system is applied for easier reference and recall.

The actual task of studying the interrelations between speech and mental processes gives rise to practical difficulties. One of the best ways—the way to be outlined below—is an investigation of retardation in the development of the child's speech processes. In such cases an artificially hastened acquisition of speech may lead not only to language enrichment but also to a substantial reorganization of the child's mental development and behaviour. That is, if the child's speech activity can be changed in a relatively short time it becomes possible to investigate variations in mental processes which arise as a direct consequence of this speech development.

. . There is a tendency for retardation of speech to occur when twins grow up together. It may be reasonably assumed that this is largely caused by the fact that they are not faced with the objective necessity for transition to speech communication so frequently as other children.

Two such twins were Yuria and Liosha G. Their speech was retarded, primitive and largely autonomous and they both exhibited complex phonetical impairment. Neither had speech until around two years of age. Between the ages of two and three they could say *mama* and *dada* and could make sounds to each other at age four. By the age of five they knew a small number of words. From detailed observations of their speech it was clear that 75 per cent of their language consisted of their own names; words of common speech denoting objects constituted a small proportion of their expressions. They still distorted many words and used a host of autonomous words. Their speech gradually acquired meaning only in a concrete, active situation. One and the same word might possess an entirely different meaning in different situations. Only an insignificant proportion of the twins' speech consisted of grammatically developed and structured sentences.

The twins gave no indication of being mentally retarded; both were cheerful, energetic and efficient and displayed affability and cooperation when placed in the kindergarten. Previously they had played mostly with each other since they could not readily understand other people's speech and vice versa. However their play was primitive and monotonous. They could not build with blocks and their attempts at painting and drawing were below their age level.

Two factors were seen as preventing the development of good language —first the twin situation, and second their phonetical impairment.

The twins were separated and one of them (Yuria) was given additional speech training. The experimental method called upon the twins to name objects, to actively answer questions, repeat complete phrases and structured sentences and describe pictures and actions.

The impact of this enforced separation was quite startling and took effect within a three month period. An increase in common and comprehensible words and a decrease in distortions was noticed. Running commentary and narrative and descriptive speech began to play a more significant part. Their understanding of extraneous speech, tied to the concrete immediate situation, fell into the background. Yuria, who was given special speech training, improved to the extent that only 40 per cent of his speech remained autonomous. The rest of their language, however, was more meaningful. And in addition to all this, and after only a three month period, their lexicology and grammar approximated to the normal speech of their counterparts.

After a ten month period their autonomous speech had virtually disappeared. Yuria remained ahead of his twin but both had improved so much that the results indicated that special speech training had played only a subsidiary role. The most formative influence had been the direct speech communication forced by the separation.

But what about the most important question—how did this acquisition of a language system influence the structure of their mental activity?

Generally there was an immediate and self perpetuating all round improvement in their play and constructive activity. They could draw, paint, play games, use objects, invent stories. They were able to model and cut paper shapes. They were able to formulate the aims of their activity verbally. The whole structure of their mental life was changed.

These improvements took place within such a short time that maturation played only an insignificant role. It seems justifiable to conclude that improvements in the productive activity of both twins took place in close connection with the acquisition of language and this introduced new potential for the organization of the children's mental life.

The method and conclusions of Luria's study reflect the basic principles of Soviet psychology—the child's mental activities are conditioned from the beginning by his social relationships with adults, through which he acquires new knowledge, new modes of behaviour. The vehicle in these relationships is primarily language. The child's behaviour—i.e. how he sees, touches, feels objects and hears sounds, how he organizes his world verbally and internally—is influenced by his mother naming and describing objects, and descriptions of his and her own actions.

In the studies outlined below we shall again see how language influences a child's perception of things, this time in a more structured artificial but no less real setting.

The following two 'pictures' are presented to an infant.

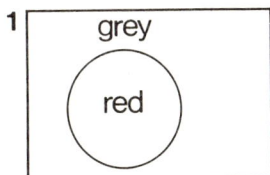

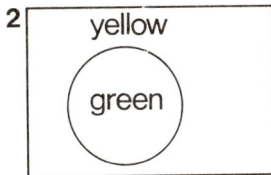

He is instructed to squeeze a balloon with his right hand for picture 1 and with his left hand for picture 2. This task he easily learns to do.

It is simple to determine which element of each picture the child is responding to—the circle or the background. Picture 1 is replaced by a third picture.

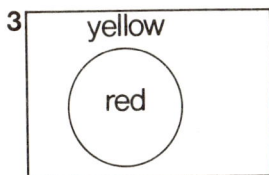

Notice the red circle is taken from picture 1 and the yellow background from picture 2. The child still squeezes with his right hand for this replacement picture 3 and his left hand for picture 2. It is the circle therefore to which he is responding.

It is quite possible to alter the determining strengths of the circle and background simply by introducing language. We can draw attention to the background using speech and instruct the child to squeeze his right hand for the grey background and his left hand for the yellow background. However the results of this intrusion of speech vary with age. With three to four year olds the circle remains the stronger element. Even four to five year olds find it difficult to adapt. But five to seven year olds begin to react to the background, which speech has made the stronger element.

An extension of this study indicates even more strongly how speech can modify further the relative strength of two such elements or stimuli. In the above study the circles were replaced by aeroplanes, with yellow and grey remaining as background colours.

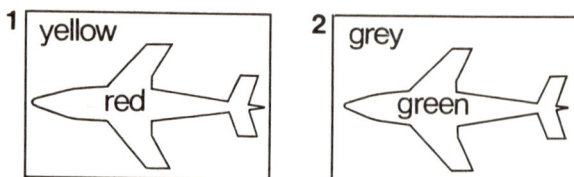

Instructions given by the investigators indicated yellow as good flying weather and grey as prohibitive flying conditions. By this meaningful verbal intrusion the backgrounds, the naturally weaker stimulus, took on as much importance as the figures of the aeroplanes, the naturally stronger stimulus, and even children as young as three and four learned to react to them largely because their attention and thought processes had been influenced by language.

Studies with children even younger than these indicate that if 'the word' is supplied or suggested then a learning task becomes easier.

Children aged twelve months to thirty months were presented with two boxes—a green box, which was empty, and a red box containing sweets. The children were called upon to select the correct box (obviously the red one which contained the sweets). They were being asked, in fact, to learn which box contained the sweets. Surprising as it may seem, this was found to be a difficult task for these young children to learn and even when apparently learned their later selections were easily upset. Without 'the word', and without drawing the children's attention to the fact that red meant sweets, the task was not at all easy. Predictably the picture changed completely when the experimenter named the colours for the children; the relationship between red and sweets became established three times quicker and the relationship was not easily upset. This simple but striking example shows once again the power of the word on children's attention, perception and learning.

To sum up, the introduction of a word can help a child learn or solve a problem. The child has been supplied with a tool which allows him either to focus his attention more easily on the significant element of a problem, or to shift his attention to another element. Language allows him to think out a problem or learn a task verbally; it permits circuiting of mental processes, a shorthand method of thinking. The adult supplies a key, a technology for thinking through language, and the child can be actively taught much earlier.

Other Soviet psychologists have been in the vanguard in investigating the role of speech in thought, and L S Vygotsky[2] was among the first to express the view that speech plays a decisive role in the formation of mental processes. He believes thought and language have different genetic roots and develop along different lines quite independently. Prespeech thought development has been corroborated by experiments with infants; the intellectual reactions of the young infant may be rudimentary but they are independent of speech. Preintellectual speech roots are manifested in the child's babbling, crying and vocalizing, which serves more as a release or social function. Vygotsky's contribution to the study of the relationship between speech and language is the discovery that around the age of two the development curves of thought and speech, till then largely separate, meet and join to initiate new forms of behaviour. Speech serves intellect as thought begins to be spoken. It is not suggested that thought cannot exist without language or speech; rather that language and thought develop separately at first then interrelate and develop intertwined.

The investigation outlined below is in line with the conclusions reached by Vygotsky which are set out in the previous sentence. It was directed by H H and T S Kendler,[3] and similar experiments have been conducted on students, young children, rats and rhesus monkeys.

The subjects were presented with the following two sets of stimuli and had to learn to discriminate between them.

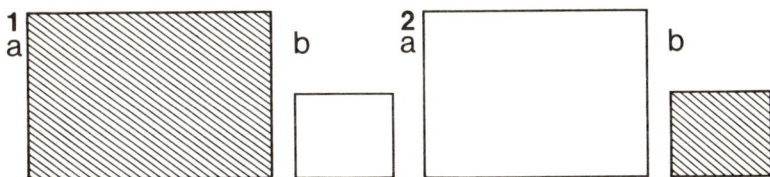

The basis on which they were required to choose at this stage was size, not colour—that is the subjects were required to respond to the large rectangle, lettered a in the diagram.

Once this basis for response was firmly established the experiment moved on to a second stage with two substages. In substage 1 the subjects were again required to respond on the basis of size, but this time on the basis of small size. Thus when presented with stimulus 1 they were required to respond to figure b, and similarly in figure 2. This change in required response is termed a reversal shift as the dimension to which they were to respond was reversed from large to small.

In substage 2 the subjects were required to respond on the basis of another dimension—colour. Thus when presented with figure 1 they should learn to respond to a, and with figure 2 they should respond to b. This change in required response is called a nonreversal shift.

Predictions as to which of these two shifts, reversal or nonreversal, would be easier depends on how we feel the subjects learn the initial task. Are there differences between the human, speaking, subject and the non-human, nonspeaking subject?

Assuming an approach by the subjects which does not rely on verbal mediation, we would have to predict that a reversal shift should be more difficult than a nonreversal shift because the reversal shift requires the subject to replace a response which has previously been consistently encouraged by a response that has been consistently discouraged. In a nonreversal shift previous training has encouraged responses to the new dimension equally often—half the time the required response has been to colour and half to size.

However if we assume the subjects' approach does include verbal mediation our predictions will be different. For subjects who can and do use verbal mediation, a reversal shift will be acquired more easily than a non-reversal shift because in a reversal shift the initial dimension—size—maintains its importance, and so also does the mediated verbal response. In a nonreversal shift the previously acquired verbal mediation is no longer relevant and must be replaced (by colour). It is this replacement which makes the task more difficult.

Several experiments to test these predictions have been conducted using rats (who do not use verbal mediation) and college students (who, it must be assumed, do use verbal mediation). The predictions for both groups are confirmed. Rats find reversal shifts more difficult than nonreversal shifts, and students find reversal shifts easier.

This difference between verbally mediating students and nonverbally mediating rats prompted investigation with children to determine how they would react. Results suggested that between three and four years of age children respond in a way not unlike rats in that they find nonreversal shifts easier than reversal shifts; between the ages of five and seven children divide fairly evenly in which they find easier. It would seem that increasing maturity and facility with language leads to increases in the proportion of children whose peformance seems to be determined by some verbal mediating system.

Further investigations along these lines with children ranging from three to ten years of age do not point to a perfect relationship between response and verbal behaviour. But trends heavily suggest that the development of the verbal process is intimately related to the development of the general ability to relate words to actions. It is therefore suggested that a measurable transition from the behaviour typical of rats in the learning situation to a higher level more typical of adults is a function of increasing age and this development is linked with language. However we cannot be as dogmatic as the above passage would indicate in describing the nature of the mediational process which seems to develop around age five. The investigator himself seems to prefer a process which includes verbal mediation but there are other possibilities.

Further experiment along the procedures already described shows that enforced verbalization relevant to the learning task makes the reversal shift easier than the nonreversal shift, even for four year old children, pointing again to the value of language in a learning task and especially to the effectiveness of artificially hastened acquisition or use of verbal tools. Similar enforced relevant verbalization did not make the reversal shift any easier for seven year old children which suggests that the latter are verbalizing anyway. Furthermore, enforced verbalization which is irrelevant disrupts the performance of seven year old children much more than it does four year old children, suggesting again that the older children have come to depend very much on their verbal mediation.

Bernstein's sociological analyses of class differences do not explain why these differences have the effects they do have, nor does Bernstein claim they do.[4] His very valuable work merely enumerates the various styles of language which accompany social class, not why these styles should help or hinder. Bernstein's thesis is that social relationship acts upon and develops the language style which is eventually used; people from different classes develop different language styles which influence intellectual growth and performance in school to a large extent.

Bernstein isolates several factors in the middle class environment which determine a language style which is much more formal than that of the working class child. Generally the middle class child is treated as an individual with a definite social status. He or she, as a person, is the subject of comment and opinion. He is oriented to certain values which are made verbally explicit and he is encouraged by verbal persuasion to make a personal adjustment to these values. Pressure is put on the child to avoid direct expression of hostility, i.e. he is encouraged to express his feelings verbally. The middle class situation supplies constant verbal explanation of why the child does or shouldn't do things. The tendency is to verbalize and interpret his own motives and feelings for him. In fact most aspects of his behaviour are articulated with subtleties of meaning delineated and used constantly. Stress is given to differentiating means from ends; deferred gratification is suggested; distinctions are made between objects and classes of objects; objects and actions are seen not in isolation but as relationships. This style of language tends to promote abstract thinking.

Generally the middle class home promotes a formal language. The grammatical order of words in a sentence is emphasized and the child learns meaning from this conventional sequencing. There is a wide use of subordinate conjunctions, modifications of sentences and meaning contained in sentences. A wide range of propositions and conjunctions, adjectives and adverbs is used. General expression of individual feeling and intention is encouraged and frequent use of the pronoun 'I' and impersonal 'one' or 'it' allows abstract thought. The ability to use passive and modal verbs such as 'may have been' allows use and understanding of subtle changes of meaning. What develops is what Bernstein calls an elaborated code as opposed to a restricted code.

A similar analysis of working class language reveals that there is not the same stress on individuation, nor the same comment on the child as an individual. The child is regarded more as merely a member of the family group where the social structure is geared to maximum group solidarity with shared ideas, attitudes and assumptions. The need for articulation does not exist to the same extent as in the middle class environment since group solidarity does not need personal individual observation. Individual response may even be suppressed, while the language developed is geared to increase concensus and agreement. Subtle distinctions are not made; large areas of feeling and human expression are not put into words; objects within categories are not described in detail, nor are categories broken down and built up again. The means-end chain is not found so frequently—emphasis is on the present, the concrete, the immediate with little attention paid to sequence and relationship. Explanations of actions or situations, and relationships between sets of objects are ignored. Thinking tends to be concrete, tangible and is not elevated to the abstract level.

The sentences used tend to be short with little subordination, and infrequent use of common conjunctions. The use of adverbs and adjectives is limited. Qualification, if any, comes from a restricted and unspecific group of expletives like 'nice' and 'big'.

The words 'it' and 'one' are rarely used since there is no need to objectify human experience. There is minimal logical thinking, discussion or sustained thinking. Statements are given as reasons and reasons, if given, are not explicit. The child is not really able to understand why and why not, nor is he able to explain why and why not.

Sentence tags such as 'isn't it' and 'you know' will be used. These are designed and used to elicit agreement and if repeated can have a restricting influence on conversation. Statements will be made to encourage agreement.

How far do these different language codes affect the child's response to schooling? The middle class child accustomed to and competent in the use of the elaborated code will tend to adapt more readily and the school will reinforce those habits he has learned at home. He will tend to be more curious and have greater logical powers. His 'good' behaviour will be all the more likely because of the satisfaction he finds in school and his co-operation will be enlisted much more readily. He will tend to misbehave less frequently and respond in a more positive way if 'checked' because of his lower guilt barrier. He has this low guilt barrier because since infancy reasons and feelings promoting acceptable social behaviour will have been expressed and inculcated verbally.

The working class child with his restricted code will face many difficulties in the school where the elaborated code is used. He will be asked to elaborate feelings, ideas, opinions and reasons verbally. And he is just not used to doing this. His capacity for generalization and abstraction will not have been developed. He may fail to see the relevance of school. He will lack motivation or involvement and his general behaviour will reflect this attitude. For example he may have difficulty entering into relationships with his peers or teachers and his higher guilt barrier will not respond to reasoned argument.

Bernstein's analysis, outlined above, seems to suggest two policies: the need, often expressed, for more free nursery schools; more satisfactory procedures for teaching language systematically from the day the child enters primary school. The school must be concerned with teaching a universalistic, explicit, elaborated code to free the child with the restricted code from his language style by which he has been socialized and which controls and restricts his thinking, observations and behaviour.

The studies of language outlined above might lead the reader to conclude that language equals thought or that there can be no thought without language. Indeed a more exhaustive sample of the literature would reveal that such an extreme position has been taken by psychologists. J B Watson advocated a behaviourist point of view—'what psychologists have talked of as thought is nothing but talking to ourselves'.[5] The linguist and anthropologist Whorf concluded from his cross cultural studies that 'what we think is determined by the language we use'.[6]

These extreme positions are not really tenable in the light of evidence. Language does not appear to make many areas of learning discrimination tasks and problem solving easier. Language obviously has a beneficial influence but adequate performance cannot be said to be dependent on it. Activities and thinking simply become easier when relevant verbal associations are available.

The extreme position is easily discredited. It is widely recognized that there are specific brain centres associated with language. In the light of the original extreme view, a brain damaged subject should be bereft of the power of thought, if he has lost the power of language. This hypothesis is not supported by the evidence. Patients suffering from aphasia do often show disturbed thought but the relationships between thought and language disturbance are not usually commensurate with one another.

Similarly thought processes may be damaged while language remains fairly intact.

There is also evidence of rational thinking in organisms which do not have language. In addition to the work of Vygotsky mentioned previously, there is in fact a glut of evidence from studies on apes and infants which demonstrates that rational thought takes place without language.

Another interesting area is the studies on deaf-mute children. Although deaf people do have language, as a group they are below the standard of the general population in their linguistic competence. Is their thinking likewise below the standard of the general population? Furth compared the performance of deaf-mute children and normal children on various problems.[7] The tests used in the investigation were obviously nonverbal. Both deaf and hearing children of eight years of age have a word for 'same', so they should not differ in a task of learning sameness of figures (illustrated below), and in fact they don't.

sameness

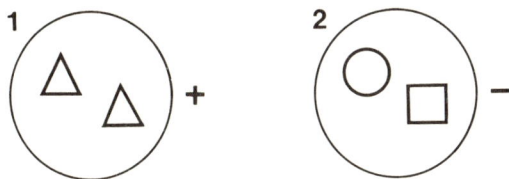

But the word 'symmetry' is not yet known by either group. Therefore in a task of learning symmetry of figure as illustrated below there should again be no difference between the two groups, and there isn't.

symmetry

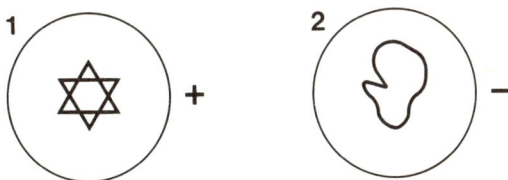

However the word 'opposite' is known by hearing children but not by deaf children in this age group. There should be, and is, a difference in a nonverbal task involving the concept 'opposite'. But although there is a difference at age eight, there is no difference if a group of sixteen year old deaf children are compared. And, interestingly, the process of learning 'opposite' in deaf children is similar to that of mentally defective children.

Some confusion about the role of language enters the scene in a classifying task. In a picture-sorting task, deaf children aged eight were noticeably worse than hearing children, which seems strange. Does classification of oranges and apples and similar pictures depend on verbal labels? Again, in a task to test their ability to conserve weight, eight year old deaf children were considerably below the standards of the general population.

So it appears that there are differences between deaf and hearing children and this we would really expect. What is confusing is that these differences appear on tasks in which language does not seem to play an important part.

15

And sometimes, to add to the confusion, no differences at all are measured on tasks which seem more language-based, like symbolic learning and transfer of learning tasks.

The picture presented is not as straightforward as the earlier passages of this chapter may have led the reader to believe. We seem unable to pinpoint accurately situations and activities where language is essential. Perhaps it may turn out that linguistic competence is less important than is generally assumed—perhaps not.

Whatever the outcome of future investigations, too much reliable evidence points to the importance of an adequately developed linguistic competence for us to ignore the message. Indeed teachers and psychologists are increasingly convinced that language has a key role to play in almost every human activity and especially within the school classroom. Improved procedures are urgently needed to promote the more efficient use and growth of language as a decoding and encoding device. The earlier in a child's school career an attack is made, the greater benefit to the child and the less the waste of time, energy and resources. It seems incredible that relatively little time is given to a graded, systematized programme of language development when so much other learning, especially of the basic skills, depends on the easy flow of instructions. I hope that this book will make some contribution towards filling this glaring gap (not just at primary level) in what is taught and learned in our schools.

*References*

1   A R Luria *The role of speech in the regulation of normal and abnormal behaviour* (Pergamon 1961)
2   L S Vygotsky *Thought and Language* (Wiley 1962)
3   H H and T S Kendler 'Vertical and horizontal processes in problem solving' in *Psychological Review* 69
4   B Bernstein *Class Codes and Control* (Routledge and Kegan Paul 1971)
5   J B Watson *Behaviourism* (Routledge and Kegan Paul 1925)
6   B L Whorf *Language, Thought and Reality: Selected Writings* (Wiley and Chapman Hall 1956)
7   H G Furth *Thinking without Language* (Collier-Macmillan 1966)

# 2 The materials

**Picture cards**

This type of material may be collected or bought by the class teacher and pupils. The material will be displayed (either held up by the teacher or on an easel) to the class so the pictures should be sufficiently large (250mm × 300mm) and simple for the essential details of each picture to be seen clearly by the whole class. The pictures should preferably be coloured.

*Animals*

| | | |
|---|---|---|
| 1 cats—variety | 32 cheetah | 67 octopus |
| 2 dogs—variety | 33 rhino | 68 seahorse |
| 3 hamster | 34 brown bear | 69 shark |
| 4 mouse | 35 eagle | 70 whale |
| 5 puppies—variety | 36 polar bear | 71 porpoise |
| 6 kittens—variety | 37 seagull | 72 dolphin |
| 7 horses—variety | 38 owl | 73 sea snake |
| 8 cows—variety | 39 albatross | 74 crab |
| 9 pig | 40 hawk | 75 penguin |
| 10 sheep | 41 sparrow | 76 puffin |
| 11 goats—variety | 42 starling | 77 otter |
| 12 calves—variety | 43 blackbird | 78 rat |
| 13 lamb | 44 robin | 79 salmon |
| 14 rabbit | 45 thrush | 80 pike |
| 15 hare | 46 crow | 81 swordfish |
| 16 deer | 47 ostrich | 82 tuna |
| 17 ponies—variety | 48 parrot | 83 goldfish |
| 18 tiger | 49 budgerigar | 84 angelfish |
| 19 tiger cub | 50 stork | 85 spiders—variety |
| 20 lion—male and female | 51 pheasant | 86 ladybird |
| 21 giraffe and young | 52 grouse | 87 daddy-long-legs |
| 22 seal | 53 peacock | 88 ant |
| 23 walrus | 54 pigeon | 89 cockroach |
| 24 monkeys—variety | 55 woodpecker | 90 centipede |
| 25 elephant and young—Indian and African | 56 cuckoo | 91 grasshopper |
| | 57 worm | 92 moth |
| 26 kangaroo and young | 58 earthworm | 93 butterflies—variety |
| 27 camel | 59 adder | 94 housefly |
| 28 dromedary | 60 python | 95 bee |
| 29 gorilla | 61 cobra | 96 wasp |
| 30 leopard and young | 62 boa constrictor | 97 caterpillar |
| 31 wildcat | 63 anaconda | 98 goose |
| | 64 turtle | 99 duck |
| | 65 tortoise | 100 snail |
| | 66 hedgehog | |

*Articles of clothing*

| | | |
|---|---|---|
| 1 shoes—variety | 4 sandals—variety | 7 trousers |
| 2 boots—variety | 5 socks | 8 shorts |
| 3 slippers—variety | 6 stockings | 9 skirts |

| | | |
|---|---|---|
| 10 dresses | 14 jackets | 18 coats |
| 11 frocks | 15 cardigans | 19 sports clothes |
| 12 blouses | 16 gloves | 20 hats and headgear, |
| 13 jerseys | 17 suits | all sorts |

*Occupation cards*

| | | |
|---|---|---|
| 1 milkman | 20 nurse | 39 glazier |
| 2 butcher | 21 teacher | 40 artist |
| 3 baker | 22 clerk | 41 painter and |
| 4 plumber | 23 typist | decorator |
| 5 joiner | 24 bricklayer | 42 actor and actress |
| 6 electrician | 25 slater | 43 musician |
| 7 janitor | 26 policeman | 44 orchestra |
| 8 grocer | 27 lawyer | conductor |
| 9 coalman | 28 traffic warden | 45 tailor |
| 10 miner | 29 lollipop man | 46 shoemaker |
| 11 factory worker | 30 pilot | 47 fishmonger |
| 12 farm worker | 31 soldier | 48 car mechanic |
| 13 bus driver | 32 sailor | 49 steelworker |
| 14 engine driver | 33 fisherman | 50 roadsweeper |
| 15 taxi driver | 34 radio announcer | 51 banker |
| 16 shop assistant | 35 TV announcer | 52 newspaper worker |
| 17 housewife | 36 road workers | 53 dentist |
| 18 doctor (GP) | 37 gardener | 54 hairdresser |
| 19 surgeon | 38 potter | |

*Shops and public entertainments and institutions*

| | | |
|---|---|---|
| 1 supermarket | 14 florist | 28 hotel |
| 2 greengrocer | 15 jeweller | 29 garage |
| 3 fishmonger | 16 dressmaker | 30 church |
| 4 butcher | 17 toy shop | 31 hospital |
| 5 furniture | 18 sports | 32 fire brigade |
| 6 radio and | 19 book shop | 33 town house |
| television | 20 restaurant | 34 school |
| 7 newsagent | 21 theatre | 35 university |
| 8 tobacconist | 22 cinema | 36 multistorey car |
| 9 furrier | 23 library | park |
| 10 shoe shop | 24 zoo | 37 airport |
| 11 interior decorator | 25 circus | 38 harbour |
| 12 post office | 26 park | 39 fairground |
| 13 hairdresser | 27 museum | 40 sports stadium |

*Family relationships*

| | | |
|---|---|---|
| 1 mother | 7 sister | 13 girl |
| 2 father | 8 brother | 14 baby |
| 3 grandmother (2) | 9 cousin | 15 friend |
| 4 grandfather (2) | 10 niece | 16 pet |
| 5 uncle | 11 nephew | 17 neighbour |
| 6 aunt | 12 boy | 18 colleague |

*Shape cards*

| | | |
|---|---|---|
| 1 horizontal line | 3 diagonal line | 5 cross (St George) |
| 2 vertical line | 4 cross (St Andrew) | 6 circle |

| 7 square | 9 heart | 11 star |
| 8 diamond | 10 ellipse | 12 rectangle |

*Furniture and house*

| 1 table | 14 sofa | 27 garage |
| 2 chair | 15 television | 28 garden |
| 3 armchair | 16 radio | 29 attic |
| 4 stool | 17 radiogram | 30 hall or lobby |
| 5 highchair | 18 bookcase | 31 door |
| 6 carpet | 19 heater | 32 window |
| 7 bed | 20 kitchen | 33 wall |
| 8 dressing table | 21 scullery | 34 roof |
| 9 wardrobe | 22 dining room | 35 stair |
| 10 tallboy | 23 lounge | 36 bannister |
| 11 cooker | 24 bedroom | 37 landing |
| 12 washing machine | 25 toilet | 38 sideboard |
| 13 refrigerator | 26 bathroom | |

*Number cards*

1 the numbers 1 to 20 on separate cards
2 cards illustrating various objects in groups of 1 to 10

*Tools and utensils*

| 1 knife | 29 rake | 57 hairdryer |
| 2 fork | 30 trowel | 58 tap |
| 3 spoon | 31 flower pots | 59 jug |
| 4 kettle | 32 wheelbarrow | 60 bottle |
| 5 saucepan | 33 lawnmower | 61 fork (garden) |
| 6 frying pan | 34 garden shears | 62 hose |
| 7 toaster | 35 scissors | 63 sewing machine |
| 8 teapot | 36 vacuum cleaner | 64 mirror |
| 9 cup | 37 brush, short handle | 65 washing powder |
| 10 saucer | 38 brush, long handle | 66 soap |
| 11 dinner plate | 39 shovel | 67 towel |
| 12 soup plate | 40 watch | 68 bath |
| 13 drinking glass | 41 clock | 69 sink |
| 14 milk jug | 42 alarm clock | 70 light bulb |
| 15 sugar bowl | 43 pen | 71 oil lamp |
| 16 butterdish | 44 pencil | 72 tray |
| 17 jam pot | 45 typewriter | 73 matchbox |
| 18 condiment containers | 46 Biro pen | 74 pencil sharpener |
| 19 tablecloth | 47 crayon | 75 glue |
| 20 telephone | 48 book | 76 iron |
| 21 letter | 49 paper | 77 ironing board |
| 22 screwdriver | 50 newspaper | 78 clothes line |
| 23 hammer | 51 comic | 79 clothes pegs |
| 24 nail | 52 rubber | 80 needle |
| 25 pliers | 53 tape measure | 81 thread |
| 26 saw | 54 drawer | 82 musical instruments |
| 27 axe | 55 tin opener | — variety |
| 28 spade | 56 meat mincer | |

*Means of transport*

| | | |
|---|---|---|
| 1 legs | 8 train | 15 scooter |
| 2 horse | 9 plane | 16 tank |
| 3 mule | 10 boat | 17 submarine |
| 4 camel | 11 ship | 18 spaceship |
| 5 car | 12 bus | 19 tractor |
| 6 lorry | 13 bicycle | 20 ambulance |
| 7 van | 14 motorcycle | |

*Sports and games equipment*

| | | |
|---|---|---|
| 1 football | 8 cricket stumps | 15 hockey stick |
| 2 rugby ball | 9 tennis racquet | 16 nets and posts |
| 3 cricket ball | 10 table tennis ball | 17 shin pads |
| 4 tennis ball | 11 table tennis bat | 18 skis |
| 5 shuttlecock | 12 bathing costume | 19 ski sticks |
| 6 skittle | 13 flippers | 20 springboard |
| 7 cricket bat | 14 goggles | 21 swimming pool |

## Narrative pictures and posters

This type of material can also be collected from magazines, newspapers etc. There are several sources of commercially produced posters which come with educational journals or which are produced for special subjects such as history, geography, nature or science.

*Posters depicting*

1 winter scenes: the human activities and animal activities and changes in scenery associated with winter
2 summer scenes
3 autumn scenes
4 spring scenes
5 boys and girls arriving at school
6 street scenes
7 zoo scenes
8 supermarket scenes
9 bus scene
10 living room scene
11 kitchen scene
12 classroom scene
13 fire scene
14 storm at a harbour
15 flooding in the countryside or farm
16 bonfire night
17 puppet show at the seaside
18 children's playground in city
19 a building site
20 hospital ward
21 Christmas party
22 a parade
23 a circus
24 characters from television with whom the children are familiar (e.g. Dougal and Dylan of the *Magic Roundabout*)
25 characters and stories with which the children are familiar (from nursery rhymes and fairy tales etc)

## Sources

Colour pictures may be cut from weekly and monthly magazines of all sorts; the Sunday supplements are especially good. Catalogues are helpful; these can be obtained from large stores and from trading stamp companies. Pictures from calendars are good; picture postcards can sometimes be used.

Many specialty stores and organizations hand out free pamphlets and brochures for advertising purposes:

1 travel agents, tour operators, national tourist offices
2 ironmongers
3 paint, wallpaper and linoleum dealers
4 furniture manufacturers and retailers

| | | |
|---|---|---|
| 5 car dealers | 9 florists and seed | 14 clothing stores |
| 6 china manufacturers | merchants | (men's, women's, |
| and retailers | 10 linen suppliers | children's) |
| 7 crystal and glassware | 11 uniform suppliers | |
| manufacturers and | (including | |
| retailers | armed services | |
| 8 cutlery | tailors) | |
| manufacturers and | 12 sports goods | |
| retailers | 13 toy shops | |

Many associations, societies, embassies etc provide free brochures, pamphlets, wallcharts and so on to schools for educational purposes. See *Treasure Chest for Teachers* (The Schoolmaster Publishing Company, first published 1960, latest revision 1971) for a list of services.

## Colour cubes

Colour cubes can be used to teach colour, sequencing from oral and visual instructions from left to right, to promote memory, and to encourage the children's skill in following simple instructions. A set of the eight basic colours (green, red, blue, black, white, brown, yellow, orange) is required for each child. The objects should be such that they can be clipped or stuck together so that a chain can be formed. In addition two other colour sets of similar objects but each of increasing size should be obtained. These three sets will be used to teach the concepts biggest, bigger, big, longest, longer, long etc. (Invicta of Leicester supplies this equipment).

## Hand puppets

Three hand puppets (one for each new term of the academic year) should be acquired. There are many fairly cheap but beautifully produced puppets available commercially. A puppet for each term is needed whom the children will associate only with the language programme. He will be used only by the class teacher (except in exceptional cases) to attract the children's attention and to help the more timid child to join in. It is best to choose a puppet with some eccentricity (three ears, one big eye right in the middle of his forehead or a compound of human/animal features) and give it a catchy name—say Yogi Bear.

## Objects

The following items of fruit and vegetables are readily available commercially and are fairly inexpensive. They will be used in several learning tasks detailed in the daily class lessons.

| *Fruit in plastic* | *Vegetables in plastic* |
|---|---|
| 1 apple | 1 potato |
| 2 orange | 2 tomato |
| 3 banana | 3 onion |
| 4 pineapple | 4 cauliflower |
| 5 grapefruit | 5 leek |
| 6 plum | 6 cabbage |
| 7 peach | 7 lettuce |
| 8 coconut | 8 turnip |
| 9 lemon | 9 carrot |

21

Plastic models of items of furniture are available as kits for furnishing dolls houses. These kits are usually comprehensive and cover most rooms of the average house. In addition to the objects already listed the class teacher will need to collect miscellaneous items of different functions, size, shape, colour, texture and weight, most of which will be readily available in schools e.g. rubbers, pencil sharpeners etc.

## Tape
Many tapes and records of songs, stories, rhymes and rhythms are available commercially. However, apart from the question of cost, teachers may feel that they can quickly produce a tape or series of tapes better suited to their own style of presentation, and to the taste and interest level of their children. The teacher can record the occasional song or tune from a radio or recorded presentation and then have the children sing along or sing the songs chosen with only piano accompaniment on the tape. Any teacher who cannot play the piano could enlist the help of a colleague.

The taped songs and music will be introduced at the beginning and end of several of the daily class lessons. The tape should include progressively more difficult rhythms which the children will be asked to repeat by clapping their hands or their pencils.

No tape should be used for longer than two or three minutes at any one time. The aim is to give the teacher a moment of rest, and to introduce a focus of attention other than the teacher or puppet.

The children should also be encouraged to record their own voices while they recite rhymes, sing songs and converse casually either as groups or individuals. A pretape and post tape could be used to evaluate the changes that have taken place during the year.

## Matching shapes and pictures
The shapes used in class should be cut out of fairly thick cardboard. Each child will need two sets of every shape:

| | |
|---|---|
| 1 triangle | 5 cross (St George) |
| 2 square | 6 cross (St Andrew) |
| 3 circle | 7 heart |
| 4 diamond | 8 rectangle |

The size of the square should be around 50mm × 50mm, with the other shapes corresponding. Details of how to use the material are included in the daily class lessons. The pictures, which can be drawn or bought, should be simple stick figures or live drawings depicting simple actions.

## Manikin
Various types of manikin are available commercially but again this is the sort of material which can be made by the class or class teacher. A model of a man is needed, cut in such a way that his hands, arms, feet etc can be easily detached from the display board. The aims of the lessons in which the manikin is used are explained in the daily class lessons.

## Nursery rhymes and songs
Teachers tend to assume, possibly because of their own background, that the children in their class will be familiar with a wide range of nursery

rhymes and songs. This may not be the case. With both parents either at work or with interests outside the home, and with the all pervading television, many children do not get the opportunity to hear nursery rhymes. Therefore the opportunity must be provided in school.

Nursery rhymes are of course pure fun. But they have enormous value in terms of teaching language: through them the child can learn the rhythm of our language; he will be introduced to novel words and structures; the similarities and differences between words are reinforced; he will derive satisfaction from repeating them and adapting them himself.

The teacher will be in the best position to evaluate the taste and interest level of individuals in her class. The following list gives a very wide sample which should appeal to an ability range of three to eight. These nursery rhymes and songs should be spoken by the teacher as often as she feels the children are willing to listen. Opportunity should be given for the class as a whole, and individuals, to repeat them. Once any rhyme is mastered by the children or child the teacher should make sure that the child actually understands the words and meaning of the rhyme so as to avoid the amusing mistakes that occur when the child repeats a series of sounds but has no real understanding of what he is parroting, for example 'Gladly the cross-eyed bear'.

Above all the fun and enjoyment of the rhymes should be emphasized.

1 Lavender's blue
2 Old King Cole
3 There was a crooked man
4 Mary had a pretty bird
5 The bells of London
6 If all the world were apple pie
7 Which is the way to London town?
8 How do you like to go up in a swing?
9 Rock a bye baby
10 Diddle diddle dumpling, my son John
11 Monday's child
12 Jack be nimble
13 Little Boy Blue
14 Old Mother Hubbard
15 Baa baa black sheep
16 Simple Simon
17 Mary, Mary, quite contrary
18 Humpty Dumpty
19 One, two, buckle my shoe
20 Goosey Goosey Gander
21 There was an old woman who lived under a hill
22 Bobbie Shaftoe
23 Hey diddle diddle
24 Little Miss Muffet
25 Little Jack Horner
26 Little Polly Flinders
27 Polly put the kettle on
28 Rub a dub dub
29 Pussy cat, pussy cat
30 Tom, Tom the piper's son
31 The owl and the pussy cat
32 Jack and Jill
33 Sing a song of sixpence
34 Here we go round the mulberry bush
35 I saw a ship come sailing, come sailing on the sea
36 I love little pussy
37 What are little girls made of?
38 The house that Jack built
39 There was an old woman tossed up in a blanket
40 Boys and girls come out to play
41 Tom he was a piper's son
42 Little Betty Blue
43 See saw Margery Daw
44 A diller, a dollar, a ten o'clock scholar
45 Daffy Down Dilly
46 Jack Sprat
47 Ding dong bell
48 A robin and a robin's son
49 The north wind doth blow
50 Fiddle de dee, fiddle de dee, the fly shall marry the bumble bee
51 Hickory dickory dock
52 Three young rats
53 Ring a ring o' roses
54 Cock robin

55 Six little mice sat down to spin
56 Bye baby bunting
57 This little pig
58 Little Jenny Wren
59 Twinkle twinkle little star
60 One misty moisty morning
61 The queen of hearts
62 Little Bo Peep
63 I had a little pony
64 Hark, hark, the dogs do bark
65 Pat a cake, pat a cake
66 I had a little nut tree
67 There was an old woman who lived in a shoe
68 Three blind mice
69 Mary had a little lamb
70 Hot cross buns

71 Wynken, Blynken and Nod
72 Wee Willie Winkie
73 Hector Protector
74 Rain rain go away
75 The old woman's three cats
76 Come let's to bed
77 Roses are red
78 The grand old Duke of York
79 Fee fi fo fum, I smell the blood of an Englishman
80 Punch and Judy
81 Doctor Foster
82 Twelve days of Christmas
83 The death and burial of Cock Robin
84 Tweedle Dum and Tweedle Dee
85 Rain on the green grass

86 Davy Davy Dumpling
87 Jeremiah
88 Ladybird
89 The owl
90 London Bridge is falling down
91 The candle (Little Nancy Sitticoat)
92 Teeth (thirty white horses)
93 The egg (In marble walls as white as milk)
94 The robin (I'm called by the name of a man)
95 Boots (Two brothers are we)
96 Trees (In spring I look gay)
97 Moses supposes his toeses are roses

# 3 The daily class lessons

**General instructions on the use of the daily class lessons**
The following instructions are intended more as guidelines than rigid directions.

The aim of the programme is to improve the linguistic performance of all the children in the class. With an anticipated class register of more than thirty children, obviously some control and structure must be placed on a class lesson. However the language lessons will, it is hoped, be conducted more in the spirit of a game so that the teacher and children may relax and, above all, enjoy what they are doing.

A structured but informal class arrangement is best for most daily class lessons. The children should be asked to sit cross-legged on the floor in the shape of a crescent so that as many as possible are close to the teacher, who may sit on a chair or stand, but at all times her face should be above the level of the heads of the children. She may find it convenient to have a small table beside her with whatever materials she requires prepared and ready at hand.

The class lessons should take place at the same time or as near the same time as possible each day : perhaps after some strenuous activity like games or playtime.

Although the class lessons are designed to last around half an hour, the teacher should not feel at all bound to stay within this period and should extend it as she feels is necessary provided the class interest level remains high.

The materials, procedures and questions in the daily lessons have been designed so that the majority of the children will meet with early success and then by very small steps be extended in their linguistic development. The emphasis is on constant revision, repetition and, occasionally, drill. The quick pace of the lesson and energy of the teacher are crucial to avoid the lessons becoming dull. It should be made clear to the children from the very beginning that they will all be called upon in each lesson to respond in some way. And, of course, the greatest care must then be taken to ensure that they *are* called upon to respond in each lesson.

The following excerpt from an imaginary class lesson might illustrate some of the principles on which the teacher should base her own approach. The class are seated on the floor in the shape of a crescent. The teacher sits sufficiently close to them to be able to make personal contact with each child, but sufficiently far away to maintain contact with the whole class. On the small table beside her she has arranged a selection of animal cards (cat, dog and mouse) and has placed the tape recorder with tape set at the nursery rhyme *Six little mice sat down to spin*. To end the lesson she plans to have the puppet 'McSporran' ask some of the children about their pets.

Teacher:    Right then children, it's language time! (*she displays the picture of the dog*) What do we call this?
Class together:    Dog. Bow-wow. It's a dog. Doggie.
Teacher:    Yes, it's a dog, isn't it? What is it, Tony?
Tony (*a very dull boy*):    *no response*
Teacher (*without waiting too long*):    It's a dog *and continuing* Peter, what else can you tell me about this dog?

Peter (*average boy*):   It's brown.

Teacher:   Yes, it's a brown dog, isn't it? *and continuing* Jane, what else can you tell me about this brown dog?

Jane (*bright girl*):   It's got a tail and it's big.

Teacher:   Yes, it's got a tail and it's big. It's a big brown dog with a tail. *and continuing* Mary, can you tell me what we've learned so far? What have I just said about this dog?

Mary (*dull girl*):   It's a brown dog. *Pauses*

Teacher:   What else? It's got a . . . . ?

Margaret (*dull girl*):   tail.

Teacher (*quickly*):   Yes, good Margaret. It's a big brown dog with a tail. *continuing* What else can we see in this picture? What else has the dog got? (*indicating that this is a question addressed to the whole class*)

Jean (*bright*):   It's got four legs.

Teacher (*quickly and intent on injecting pace into the question and response situation*):   Yes, it's got four legs. (*emphasizing 'four legs' by lifting her voice*)

Peter (*average*):   It's got ears.

Teacher:   Yes, it's got two ears, and . . . . *and pointing to Miriam*

Miriam (*dull*):   It's got a tongue.

Teacher:   Yes, it's got a tongue and its tongue is hanging out, isn't it? *and to Tim* What do you call these on its face, Tim? *as she asks the question she points first to the dog's eyes, and then to her own*

Tim (*dull*):   Eyes.

Teacher:   Yes, we call these his eyes. Good Tim. And this is his . . . . ? (*asking Tim again*)

Tim:   Nose.

Teacher:   And this is his . . . . ? *asking Tony*

Tony (*dull boy*):   Mouth.

Teacher:   Yes, this is his nose, and that is his mouth. So we've learned a lot about this dog, haven't we?

She begins to repeat all that has been learned, indicating by pauses that she wants the class to join in. She looks especially at the dull children, inviting them with her eyes to respond, and she nods as they do. She does not neglect the others, but lets her eyes flow back and forth along the crescent of children, fixing as many as she can with her eyes.

Teacher:   He's a big brown dog. He's got a (*pause*) tail, and he's got four (*pause*) legs, and he's got two (*pause*) ears. And on his face he has two (*pause*) eyes, one nose and and one mouth.

As she speaks she also points to the itemized features with her finger. Then quickly she repeats the story leaving out the connecting words: 'A big brown dog, with four legs, two ears and a tail. He's got eyes, a nose and mouth on his face. Good.'

What has the teacher done in these few minutes?

1  She displays only one stimulus so as not to divert attention.
2  She indicates the start of this special lesson by 'It's language time!'
3  She allows a general free response.
4  She structures the free response to what she considers is the appropriate response.

5 She tries to bring out a dull, timid boy, to reinforce the name given the picture and to indicate that everyone will be asked to respond individually.

6 She does not embarrass the duller boy by waiting too long and is aware of the need to maintain a quick overall pace for the class.

7 She repeats a response, reinforcing and rewarding by 'yes' or 'good'.

8 She structures the single word response into a simple sentence, linking the present response with the past. She modifies and extends responses.

9 She helps the duller children by inviting them to complete a simple sentence, giving some clue to the response required, 'It's got a . . . ?'

10 She summarizes and repeats, invites the class to summarize and repeat, repeats again herself.

This repetition, modification, extension and structuring of response may not come naturally to some teachers. However it is a style that is basic to many of the class lessons and is fairly easy to adopt. The children hear their responses repeated, modified, extended and structured. They will tend to imitate this style, in particular structuring, themselves. In fact this is the basic aim of the programme—to have the children learn by imitation in a formal but relaxed setting.

The same procedure would be used with the pictures of the cat and the mouse. The similarities, differences and relationships between the animals should be pointed out but not in great detail at the first showing. At this time passing mention is enough. Once the three animals have been shown separately they are displayed together and the teacher will repeat for the last time the features and characteristics of each, inviting the class to join in. The children quickly learn the kind of simple responses that are expected of them and the pace of the lesson will be maintained more naturally.

The first activity of the lesson should last between ten and fifteen minutes. The second activity is introduced by the teacher saying 'Now we shall listen to a poem about some mice and a pussycat. Listen.' She plays the tape recording of *Six little mice sat down to spin.* 'Did you like that? Let's listen carefully to it again.' After the second playing she may produce an illustration from her nursery rhyme book so that the children can picture what the poem is about. On this occasion the children can listen and look. But during the first two playings there was no visual stimulation to divide their attention. The teacher should introduce a visual presentation of the poem only after some familiarity with the words has been established. The children are invited to join in the third playing, but very, very quietly. Finally, the teacher rounds off the second activity, 'Good, we'll hear that poem again soon.'

The third activity introduces McSporran. First he will remind the children of what they have been doing.

McSporran:    You have been looking and talking about a picture of a dog, have you?
Class:   Yes!
McSporran:    And a cat?
Class:   Yes!
McSporran:    And a mouse?
Class:   Yes!
McSporran:    And you've just listened carefully to a poem about six little mice, haven't you?
Class:   Yes!

27

McSporran then asks individuals in the class about the dogs, cats and mice with which they are familiar. He asks their names, what noises they make, how many legs, what colour, how big and so on. McSporran then closes language time by asking the children if they would like to listen to the poem again. At the end of the poem he says, 'Goodbye children. I'll see you tomorrow at the same time—language time. Bye bye, and back to your seats—bye bye.' As the children return to their seats, teacher packs away all the materials.

The principles illustrated in this imaginary lesson, summarized below, are put into practice in most of the daily class lessons:

1 An intensive half hour with two or three different activities, each activity focusing on a different source.
2 The principles of repetition, modification, extension and structuring of response are maintained throughout.
3 Questions of an appropriate level are directed to the class as a whole and to individuals.
4 The language lesson is seen to have a definite start and finish, although, of course, the lessons are supplementary to the general language learning that goes on all day.

### General instructions on the separate activities used in the daily lessons
*Vocabulary*

This activity calls upon the class to name animals, articles of clothing, tools, occupations etc. The same question (What do we call this? What name do we give to this?) should be put to different members of the class about the same item so that the not so bright children will be given more than just one opportunity to hear and learn the name. These children should also learn that the same question about the same object will usually be repeated with the hope that this will encourage them to attend to what is going on, rather than opt out. The names given to objects and animals etc should be pronounced clearly by the teacher, and reinforced by asking several members of the class to repeat it quickly.

Structured sentences should always be encouraged, even if it is just a one word response being sought, e.g. after the response 'tiger', the teacher should say 'Yes. It's a tiger, isn't it? Yes, a tiger.'

*Nursery rhymes*

A large number of the daily class lessons use nursery rhymes; the aim is to introduce a wide variety of long and short rhymes from our culture, just for enjoyment. In addition the children are to be encouraged indirectly to remember the titles, the story and the moral of each rhyme. The rhymes will also serve as a model of standard English—the children will absorb the rhythms and patterns of the English language, the vocabulary, the phrases, the rhyming words, the opposites and the language of colour, number and dimension so vital to early learning in the primary school.

Obviously the class teacher is free to include rhymes not recommended specifically by the text and also to omit rhymes which she considers inappropriate.

*Self expression*

The children should be encouraged to practice expressing the simplest of ideas in lucid short sentences. So often young children are unable to elaborate on the simplest idea or, at the other extreme, ramble on in an incomprehensible way. Quantity should not be sacrificed for quality completely at this stage; however the class teacher should take the trouble to encourage and occasionally even insist on several simple short sentences rather than one long rambling one. The nonproductive child should be encouraged to repeat simple sentences prepared on the spur of the moment by the class teacher.

Q   And what did you see at the zoo?
A   No response.
Q   You saw fish, snakes and a parrot?
A   Yes.
Q   Then tell me about it—you went to the zoo yesterday, and you saw some fish, snakes and a parrot. You tell me.
A   I went to the zoo yesterday and I saw some fish and some snakes and a parrot.

In this example the child has been given the means to express himself—the vocabulary, the starting point, the rhythm, the pattern and, most important, the structure. Gradually, as he becomes familiar with the structure of similar responses, he will be able to transfer his knowledge and adapt it to other situations. The adult's job is to supply the basic vehicle of structured language by which the child's thoughts and images can be conveyed and communicated to others.

*Self identity*
A few daily class lessons are given over to having individual children tell (to the teacher, their peers, or the tape recorder) some of the basic facts about themselves. This has both social and practical importance and will help to establish self identity. Ask many young children their name and they give only their christian name; ask their surname and they are mystified. Almost certainly only a small minority know their date of birth. Generally they do not know the number of their house, nor the name of the street in which they live. And few are aware of the physical characteristics which cause them to be differentiated from the class as a whole. These facts must be learned and the earlier the better.

*Rhythm*
Children who have difficulty in listening to and remembering rhythm will have difficulty in learning new words, patterns of phrases and sentences. Practice in simple rhythm reproduction will help to remedy this deficiency and will encourage children to listen attentively, and develop the listening skill basic to all classroom learning.

*Drama*
Although only recommended once in the specific instructions in the daily lessons, nevertheless the class teacher should use her discretion in introducing this activity into the class lesson. It helps to encourage participation and comprehension of, say, a nursery rhyme. It can also be good fun.

*Drawing*
Occasionally the class will be asked to draw (a man, or scenes from a visit to somewhere). The teacher should take as many opportunities as possible to let the class hear directional, positional, colour and shape words in this

activity. When supervising the individual's work, she should encourage the child to describe the picture using these words.

### Family relationships

The aim of this activity (apart from becoming familiar with the appropriate names) is to teach the children their position in relation to their family and hence reinforce their own self identity.

### Stories and questioning on stories

Many children do not have well developed listening skills and often quickly learn that they can opt out of listening in the classroom situation because they know that, either they will not be questioned by the class teacher, or if they fail to respond often enough the teacher will stop questioning them or move on quickly to a child more likely to respond. About 20 per cent of the daily class lessons are designed to remedy this attitude to listening and questioning. The stories are quite short and relevant to the interests and activities of most children. The questions on each story follow a similar pattern and the class should learn in time to anticipate the questions. The teacher should ask several children the same question and call upon individuals to question the responses given by others. In short the class is to be encouraged to remain at a fairly high peak of attention for a long period.

The class teacher is free to lengthen or shorten the stories as she so desires, to include stories she has composed herself, or to repeat stories which the class find difficult or interesting.

### We went to market and we bought . . .

The aim of this game is to encourage children to listen and memorize a connected series of items. One child starts the game by saying 'We went to market and we bought a . . . .' (the blank is filled by an item chosen by the child e.g. pig). A second child then repeats the phrase, including the original item (a pig), and adding a further item and so on. It is left to the discretion of the teacher whether a limit in terms of time or number of items should be imposed.

### Opposites

The concept of 'opposite' is difficult for children to understand. However once mastered it proves useful, and the game is entertaining.

### Sounds

Activities relating to animal sounds and sounds heard in various situations do not often form part of the daily class lessons. As a general rule adults do not use many words to describe the sounds in their world. However the class teacher should again feel free to include as many 'sound' activities as she feels desirable.

### Nonsense

It is important for children to be able to notice how including just one inappropriate word can make nonsense of an otherwise meaningful sentence. The aims of this activity are to develop listening skills, especially in relation to crucial words, and to encourage the class to pay only due regard to structure. Children learn to anticipate words in a sentence and so anticipate meaning from the structure of language. This exercise is designed to temper their anticipatory skill and to exercise their listening, comprehension and critical skills as a balance.

## Classification

Children must learn to group items in their appropriate families and to regroup familiar items according to new criteria. The daily lessons develop higher order grouping and classification. The children must be taught to abstract characteristics from the concrete particular item and relate these abstractions to similar abstractions from other items i.e. classifications according to colour, shape or size (concrete, visual dimensions) are discouraged while abstractions on the basis of function or origin are encouraged.

## Mime

The whole point of the language programme is to help the children put into words the sights and sounds they perceive. They are to be encouraged to see and hear as much as possible, and to break down the general into the particular. Mime will help children to learn to observe more closely the simple actions of everyday life and to break them down into language. For instance, when a child is called upon to mime playing a violin he may not hold it properly, or use only one hand. The teacher should demonstrate a realistic use of such an instrument, emphasizing the use of both hands and proper actions. The teacher should also verbalize the action, asking the child to copy her and if possible to verbalize.

## Similarities and differences

The class are to be encouraged to verbalize the similarities and differences between objects. Young children will find differences between objects easier to see and verbalize than similarities. 'Higher order' differences should be emphasized, i.e. although colour differences may on occasion be higher order, generally they relate to two particular examples of a wider family and, as with size differences, should not be encouraged. An example of the kind of response the teacher should look for is: slipper and boot— one is worn outdoors, the other indoors.

With similarities the same higher order responses are to be encouraged. To say that a plum and a cherry are alike because they both have pips or skin is an acceptable response, but better higher order responses would be that we eat them both, or both grow on trees, or that they are both fruit.

## Descriptive exercises

Looking at pictures, as opposed to listening to stories, forms a large part of the programme. Young children often need to be taught to listen and to hear, and how to look and observe. These basic skills are essential to effective classroom learning. The describing activities aim to give practice in how to look at objects and pictures under guidance from the class teacher. The object or picture will be analyzed generally and in detail and the characteristic features of each abstracted and structured in language.

## Following instructions

Adults who deal with young children know well how difficult children find it to follow even simple instructions, and very dull children soon learn that they can opt out. The games in this activity aim to give practice in following verbal instructions. The instructions are generally very simple and the vast majority of children find little difficulty with them.

*General comments on the class lessons*
Within one class of around thirty children there will be a wide range of language development. The difficulty and interest level of this programme is geared to a comprehensive range of abilities, but there will be occasions when the teacher will feel that certain activities are too difficult or too easy for her particular class or a good proportion of her class. On such occasions the teacher should feel free to adapt the programme to her needs and the needs of her class.

The author would be very happy to receive any constructive criticisms or suggestions which teachers feel would improve the programme, or details of the way teachers have incorporated their own ideas or adapted the lessons to meet their particular needs.

# Daily lesson 1

**Materials**
1 Picture cards—animals (cat, dog, hamster, mouse, goldfish, tortoise)
2 Term one puppet
3 Tape recorder and tape of nursery rhyme (*Six little mice sat down to spin*)

*Vocabulary* Display the pictures of the animals on the easel, or chalk ledge or display board. Initially only one picture should be displayed at any one time. By a question-response procedure establish the name of each item and its distinguishing features. Having gone over the six animals in turn, display them all together and establish again some of the features they have in common and point out features on which they differ. Ask the children to think about physical observable features only; differences and similarities in their food, milieu and habits will be examined later in the programme.

*Listening and rhyme* Play the nursery rhyme having explained that the story is about two of the animals already talked about. Play the rhyme twice. Then discuss it briefly. Display a picture illustrating the rhyme or the pictures of the cat and mouse and invite the children to say or sing the rhyme along with the tape.

*Self expression* Introduce term one puppet. Let him obtain from the children confirmation of what they have been doing. He will then go on to question the children about the pets they have at home or school.

**Note**
Remember that the children's responses have almost always to be 'reflected back' to the children in a structured questioning sentence. If a child is having obvious difficulty expressing an idea, let the puppet help him out by prompting.
Puppet:   Who else has a pet? *Tony puts up his hand* Tell me about it, Tony.
*Tony pauses. He doesn't know where to start. He is confused and approaching embarrassment. The puppet intervenes.*
Puppet:   What sort of animal is it, Tony?
Tony:   A dog.
Puppet:   What's its name, Tony?
Tony:   Roger.
Puppet:   You've got a dog called Roger?
Tony:   Yes.
Puppet:   What does Roger look like, Tony?
Tony:   He's big and black.
Puppet:   Good. So Roger is a big black dog, eh Tony? Perhaps you can tell me more about him later on?

# Daily lesson 2

**Materials**

1 Clothing cards—shorts, skirts, dresses, frocks, blouses, jerseys, trousers, shoes, stockings
2 Puppet
3 Tape recorder and rhyme:
*Diddle diddle dumpling, my son John,*
*Went to bed with his trousers on.*
*One shoe off,*
*One shoe on,*
*Diddle diddle dumpling*
*My son John.*

*Identification*   Introduce puppet. Let puppet explain that he is going to describe several of the class in terms of some article of their clothing. He would like whoever he chooses to stand up and tell him his/her name and age. The puppet must emphasize that he wants this information in a clear simple sentence—'My name is Roger Brown and I'm five years old.' Having involved perhaps a dozen children, let puppet congratulate them and move on.

*Listening, rhyme and clapping*   Let the children hear *Diddle diddle dumpling* once. Clarify the meaning and the objects mentioned in the rhyme briefly by question-response method. Let the children hear the rhyme again, inviting them to clap to the rhythm. Give them whatever instruction is necessary to accomplish this. Let them hear the rhyme again and invite them to clap and speak along if they can.

*Vocabulary*   Display the nine items of clothing one at a time. Establish the name of the article and on which part of the body it is worn.

# Daily lesson 3

**Materials**
1 Two manikins and items to cover main parts of the body—jersey for trunk and arms; trousers for legs; hat for head; shoes and socks for feet and legs
2 Nursery rhyme—*Jack and Jill went up the hill*
3 Clothing cards—jersey, trousers, dress, hat, shoes and socks
4 Blackboard and coloured chalk

*Vocabulary*   Using manikins establish the names given to various parts of the body—head, neck, arms, trunk, legs and feet. Use question-response procedure—'Yes, this is his head, and these are his arms' etc. Use words like 'up here', 'down there', 'above', 'below'. Dress one manikin under the children's directions asking question 'What goes on here?' Dress one boy and one girl. Name them Jack and Jill.

*Rhyme and drama*   Recite *Jack and Jill*. Tell the children you are going to repeat it but this time they are going to act it out. The boys will be Jack, the girls Jill. Emphasize the effort required going up the hill, the slight rest at 'a pail of water', and then Jack falling down with rapid acceleration of Jill behind. Repeat this drama twice. Briefly discuss the rhyme pointing out the parts of the body required in the effort to get up the hill, the fall and the damage done.

*Drawing*   Draw a green hill with a well on top on the blackboard. Draw two stick figures climbing up. Ask the children to return to their seats and draw three pictures: one of Jack dressed, one of Jill and one of the rhyme. Have the pictures of the items of clothing, and the manikins dressed and displayed.

# Daily lesson 4

**Materials**
1 Family relationships cards—mother, father, grandmother, grandfather, brother, sister, baby
2 Nursery rhymes—*Bye baby bunting; Rock a bye baby; Tom, Tom the piper's son*
3 Puppet

*Nursery rhymes*   Let the puppet explain to the children that they are going to be asked about their brothers and sisters—how many, what their ages are and so on. But first they will hear two rhymes about a baby and then a boy called Tom who was the son of a piper. Play each rhyme on the tape twice.

*Vocabulary*   Display all the family relationship cards and have the children discover who's who.

*Self expression*   Have the puppet ask the children about their families and insert the number of brothers, sisters and babies in each family alongside each child's name on a piece of paper or board large enough for permanent display in the classroom. The teacher may feel it worthwhile to have one such 'head count' for brothers, another for sisters and a third for babies.

# Daily lesson 5

**Materials**
None

**Procedure**
Explain to the class that you are going to read them a story called *Shopping*.
Tell them you want them to listen very carefully to the story because you
are going to ask them questions about it afterwards.

### Shopping

John and Betty were brother and sister. They didn't mind shopping too
much as long as it didn't go on too long. Every Saturday morning without
fail their mother would go to this big store that sold almost everything you
could think of. She always took John and Betty along.

They sometimes tagged along close behind her carrying baskets or
pushing a trolley piled high with food, fruit, tin cans, vegetables, biscuits,
washing powder and all sorts of things. Sometimes John and Betty would
arrange to meet their mother at some place like the front door of the store.
She would go off and shop and they would stand munching potato crisps or
sweets, staring at the crowds pushing and rushing about. Sometimes they
would stand beside the rocking mechanical toys at the front door and help
smaller girls and boys off and on the machines. Sometimes, if they had a
little money of their own, they would go on these machines themselves.

Sometimes mother took ages to do her shopping and sometimes she took
what seemed like just a little time. But Betty and John were seldom bored.
There was so much to see and do.

Ask the class if they enjoyed the story and then ask the following questions:
1 What was the name of the story?
2 What were the names of the brother and sister in the story?
3 What did they do every Saturday morning?
4 Who did they go with?
5 How did they help their mother in the shop?
6 Name some of the items that their mother bought.
7 What kind of shop did they go to? Can you guess the name of the shop?
8 If John and Betty didn't help their mother, what four activities did they
  get up to?
9 Did their mother take long to shop?

Ask the class to play a variation on the game 'I went to the market and I
bought . . .' They are to imagine they are Johnny and Betty who guess what
items their mother brings back from the counter in her basket. Each child
must preface their 'list' by saying 'I guess that my mother had in her
basket . . .' adding one item to the list supplied by previous children.

Have the class give the opposite of the following words. If necessary explain opposite and give examples. Preface each question by saying, 'Give me the opposite of . . .'

| | | | |
|---|---|---|---|
| 1 | empty | 11 | large |
| 2 | heavy | 12 | always |
| 3 | crowded | 13 | sometimes |
| 4 | sweet | 14 | front |
| 5 | push | 15 | help |
| 6 | fast | 16 | young |
| 7 | long | 17 | high |
| 8 | moving | 18 | light |
| 9 | hungry | 19 | busy |
| 10 | brother | 20 | noisy |

# Daily lesson 6

**Materials**
1 Picture cards—cat, dog, hamster, mouse, goldfish, tortoise
2 Clothing cards—shorts, skirt, dress, frock, blouse, jersey, trousers, shoes, socks
3 Puppet
4 Rhymes—*Six little mice sat down to spin, Jack and Jill, Rock a bye baby, Diddle diddle dumpling*
5 Family relationship cards
6 Tape recorder

**Procedure**
This is largely a revision lesson to allow the children to hear again, and recite if they can, the rhymes that they have heard over the week; to bring together some of the topics mentioned such as their pets, their brothers and sisters, the clothes they wear, the names given to the parts of their body.

*Self expression* Puppet introduces the lesson. 'Well, children, I've learned a lot about your pets, your brothers and sisters, and the clothes you wear. Let's see how much I can remember.'

Display animal pictures all at once. Quickly, by question-response procedure, establish name of each animal and the distinguishing features of each.

Puppet intervenes, 'Good, I can remember you told me a lot about your own pets and animals at home, didn't you? They've got eyes and ears and legs and bodies, like us, haven't they? Let's have a look at Jack and Jill again.'

Produce the two manikins and establish names given to each part of the body.

'Now we'll have to put clothes on, won't we? Otherwise they'll feel the cold. Which clothes shall we put on?' Display picture cards of clothes and invite children to place appropriate items of clothing on the manikins.

Puppet intervenes. 'Gosh, Jack and Jill look like they could be your brothers and sisters, don't they?' Puppet will refer to the list made out in previous lesson and mention some of the brothers and sisters listed against the children's names.

Display family relationship cards. 'Here are some more of your relations.' Establish names given and relationship to one another.

*On tape* Conclude this daily lesson by having the children recite along with the tape the rhymes from the weeks work. Remind them to act out *Jack and Jill* and clap or tap to the rhythm of *Diddle diddle dumpling*.

# Daily lesson 7

**Materials**
Picture cards—tiger, lion, giraffe, monkey, elephant, camel, walrus

*Vocabulary*   Display cards one at a time as usual. Ask the children to name them and supply the names where not known. Elicit by question-response procedure what the children know of each. Extend their knowledge and vocabulary by telling a short story about each, emphasizing and explaining 'wild', 'zoo animals', 'not found in our country', 'found in hot countries'. Emphasize the distinguishing features of each—striped and fierce, mane and fierce, long neck and legs, quick moving and with long tail, large with trunk, like a horse with a hump, good swimmer and lives in the sea.

*Sounds*   Ask the children what sounds or noises these animals make. Get them to imitate the actual sound made and teach them the name of the sound. 'Who can make the same noise as a lion? Good, what name do we give the sound he makes? Yes, we say a lion roars.' And repeat the sound.

*Nonsense*   Introduce puppet. Let puppet ask the children individually questions to reinforce their knowledge of the animals listed above. Have puppet pose questions like 'Joe, does a monkey have a hump?' and ask as many children as time and interest allow. Insist that the responses are structured—'No, a monkey does not have a hump.'

# Daily lesson 8

**Materials**

1 Picture cards—group one: horse, cow, pig, sheep, sheepdog, goose, ducks, tractor, chicken; group two: cat, dog, mouse, hamster, rabbit; group three: tiger, lion, walrus, monkey, camel
2 Tape and nursery rhymes—*Baa baa black sheep; Little Boy Blue*
3 Puppet

*Vocabulary* Display animal cards of group one, one at a time as usual. Supply where necessary the name of the animal and its distinguishing features. Enumerate or elicit also the uses of each animal: horse for working (explain how the work of the horse is largely taken over by the tractor and show picture of a tractor briefly); cow for milk and meat; pig for bacon or ham; sheep for wool and meat; sheepdog for helping to control the sheep; goose for meat and eggs; ducks for eggs and meat. Teach or get the children to name the sounds made by each animal, and get the children to imitate the sounds.

*Nursery rhymes* Play *Baa baa black sheep*. Play it twice. Split the class into three groups. Have each group recite one line of the rhyme, coming together on the last line. Play *Little Boy Blue*. Explain the meaning of the rhyme. Play the rhyme again.

*Classification* Explain or elicit that animals in group one are called farm animals. Then display group two seen earlier in the programme and explain or elicit that they are called house, domestic or pet animals. Display group three seen earlier in the programme and explain that they are called zoo or wild animals. Display all the animals in each group together. Introduce the puppet who will select a picture. Get an individual to name the animal and say which group it belongs to.

# Daily lesson 9

**Materials**

1 Occupation cards—group one: butcher, baker, milkman, barber, janitor, grocer, coalman, lollipop man
2 Food cards—group two: meat, sausages, bread, milk, general provisions, coal
3 Shop cards—group three: shops or institutions as in group one
4 Puppet
5 Nursery rhymes and tape—*Rub a dub dub; Pat a cake, pat a cake*

*Vocabulary*  Introduce puppet. 'We are going to have a guessing game. I'm going to show you a picture of someone and see if you can guess what his job is, and how he helps us. I shall give you clues to help you.' Display the occupation cards. Elicit or explain the name given to each. Having established each name, display his particular shop or institution, eliciting or explaining the name given to each shop or institution. Display picture of food cards appropriately.

*Classification*  Display cards in groups one, two and three randomly on the chalk ledge or easel. Introduce puppet. Have him ask an individual child to identify a picture. Ask another child to select appropriate shop. Ask another to select appropriate article sold. Have the three children stand together displaying their cards and structure the cards verbally for the class. 'This is the butcher, and he works in a butcher's shop, and he sells us meat'.

*Nursery rhymes*  Play *Pat a cake, pat a cake, baker's man* twice. Have the children clap in time to a third recital. Play *Rub a dub dub, three men in a tub*.

# Daily lesson 10

**Materials**
Tape recorder

**Procedure**
Explain to the class that you are going to read them a story, called *The station*, and that you want them to listen very carefully because you will ask them questions about it afterwards.

### The station

Jane and Peter had never been in such a big, noisy, bustling place before. They were down at the station with their parents to meet their grandfather who was due to arrive at twelve o'clock.

There was so much to see at the station. There were a great many people around, mostly grown ups. Some stood beside their cases, looking occasionally at their watches or at the big clock in the station. Others sat reading newspapers or magazines. Some were queuing at the ticket office for tickets; some queued at a small newspaper shop that sold sweets, cigarettes, books and papers. Jane and Peter had bought some sweets from that shop earlier.

Some of the grown ups wore different kinds of uniforms—there were luggage porters, ticket collectors, engine drivers waiting for their own particular train and drivers of little cars that hauled trolleys piled with luggage along the platforms.

There was a great deal of noise in the station: engines starting up with a roar; carriages banging together; trolleys clanging their way along the platform; whistles blowing. In the background Jane and Peter could hear a voice speaking very loudly, through loudspeakers. They couldn't make out what the voice was saying but their father explained that the announcer was telling the times of the trains arriving and departing.

There was the noise of the taxis at the main entrance to the station, bringing travellers to and from the trains. There was the noise of heavy iron gates banging and sliding together.

There was so much to see and hear that Jane and Peter were not at all fed up waiting for grandfather. And there he was! Walking slowly towards them. What a surprise! His train was early!

They all greeted him and led him to a taxi outside the station. Having been in the noise and bustle of the station for so long, everything seemed quiet and peaceful once they got home.

Ask the class if they enjoyed the story. Then ask the following questions:
1 What was the name of the story?
2 What were the names of the boy and girl in the story?
3 Who were they with?
4 What sort of things did the grown ups do as they waited at the station?
5 What did the grown ups in uniform do at the station?
6 What had Jane and Peter bought?
7 What different noises did they hear at the station?
8 Who had they come to meet, and why were they surprised to see him?

9 How did they leave the station?

10 Why did everything seem quiet and peaceful once they got home?

Ask the class the opposite of the following words. Explain 'opposite' and give examples. Preface each question by saying 'Give me the opposite of ...'

| | | | |
|---|---|---|---|
| 1 | never | 11 | earlier |
| 2 | noisy | 12 | different |
| 3 | before | 13 | haul |
| 4 | arrive | 14 | noise |
| 5 | many | 15 | starting |
| 6 | stood | 16 | loudly |
| 7 | beside | 17 | couldn't |
| 8 | occasionally | 18 | departing |
| 9 | big | 19 | heavy |
| 10 | sold | 20 | early |

*On tape*   Make a tape recording of the class telling of their own experiences at a station. Play back a selection.

# Daily lesson 11

**Materials**
1. Tools and utensils cards—bottle, knife, fork, spoon, kettle, frying pan, saucepan, cup, saucer, dinner plate, soup plate, teapot
2. Nursery rhymes—*Hey diddle diddle, the cat and the fiddle, Polly put the kettle on, Ladybird, ladybird*
3. Puppet

*Vocabulary* Display cards individually as usual. Elicit or explain by question-response procedure the name and distinguishing features of each utensil. Obtain the objects from the school kitchen or home and display in turn. Elicit and explain what each item is used for and what it is made of. Tap each item to let the children hear the different noises each makes. Display in three categories (knife, fork, spoon; kettle, teapot, frying pan, saucepan; cup, saucer, dinner plate, soup plate) and elicit or explain concepts of 'eat with', 'cook in', 'eat and drink from'.

*Nonsense* Have puppet ask the children to confirm or correct true or false statements e.g. 'I cook my eggs on a fork.' Invite some members of the class to make up true and false statements and have others confirm or correct. Emphasize structured responses to each true or false statement e.g. 'No, you don't cook your eggs on a fork; you can cook eggs in a saucepan or frying pan.'

*Nursery rhymes* Let the children hear the above nursery rhymes or a selection of them as often as they want.

# Daily lesson 12

**Materials**
1. Farm animals—cow, pig, sheep, chickens, ducks, geese
2. Occupation cards—farmer, butcher, milkman, baker, grocer
3. Utensil cards—cup, saucer, plates, knife, fork, spoon, bottle
4. Food cards—meat, sausages, eggs, bread, general provisions
5. Shop cards—as in occupation cards
6. Nursery rhymes—selections from previous lessons

*Vocabulary and classification* This is largely a revisionary lesson. The class teacher should go over each animal display card, emphasizing the points mentioned in previous lessons and giving special attention to any matters raised then. Having revised the animal cards as a group, select one and link it with appropriate occupation card, shop card, utensil card and food card. Repeat for each animal card. Repeat this classification task by having one child select an animal, then invite others to link up with this animal using cards from the rest of the groups.

*Nursery rhymes* Have puppet invite the children to request whatever rhymes they prefer from those played in previous lessons.

# Daily lesson 13

**Materials**

Furniture—table, chair, stool, highchair, armchair, sofa (settee), bed, dressing table, wardrobe, tallboy, carpet, sideboard, cooker, washing machine, refrigerator, television, radio, radiogram, bookcase, linoleum

*Vocabulary and mime*  Explain to the class that you are going to ask them to guess what pieces of furniture you are using. Mime sitting down on an imaginary chair, and pull an imaginary table toward you. When the children have guessed, show the table and chair cards. Then display each card in turn establishing name, distinguishing features and room in which it would be found. Ask the children individually to mime the use of one item and have the rest of the class guess what it is. The child who guesses correctly must then verbalize the actions mimed. Structure and modify the responses as necessary.

*Classification*  Ask the children to select items of furniture that belong in the following rooms: kitchen, sitting room, bedroom. Once all the items have been properly classified run over them again, 'Yes, you find all these pieces of furniture in the kitchen/sitting room/bedroom.' Finally emphasize/elicit/explain what most of these items have in common, or how they are the same, how they are alike—emphasize wood, made of wood.

# Daily lesson 14

**Materials**

'How to do' cards—mother hanging out clothes; mother cooking; father washing a car; boy/girl washing in the morning
Tape, nursery rhyme—*Here we go round the mulberry bush, Sing a song of sixpence*

*Description*  Display picture of mother cooking a meal. By question-response procedure have the children analyze what is depicted in the picture in detail. Work from the general scene of 'mother cooking a meal' to 'What utensils is she using?' 'What food is she using?' 'Is she frying or boiling food?' Pick out the details in the background like cooker, cupboards and shelves, curtains, scenes from the kitchen window. In short, bring the picture to life. Have the children analyze in a similar way each of the other pictures. Remember, begin with the general description and add details and background. Structure the responses of the children and sum up each picture simply but lucidly.

*Nursery rhymes*  Have the children listen to the rhymes, twice each. Act out each rhyme.

# Daily lesson 15

**Materials**
Tape recorder

**Procedure**
Explain to the class that you are going to read them a story called *Snow* and that you want them to listen very carefully because you will ask them questions about it afterwards.

## Snow

Everything in the street was covered with snow. The road was covered, the pavement was covered, the gardens, the doorsteps, the paths, the trees and the roof and chimney tops were all covered with snow. The cars which had been left out overnight were also covered in snow.

Simon and his friends were out playing. Before they had started to play there wasn't a footprint, a tyre mark or any sign in the snow that a bird or a dog or a car had moved that morning. The snow had lain flat and smooth and white and untouched.

Now there were footprints and tyre marks and piles of snow here and there where people had cleared paths. What fun they were having. They threw snowballs; they made snowmen; they rolled tiny balls of snow into bigger and bigger balls until the huge ball they ended up with was too heavy and too awkward to move any further. They cleared paths. They watched and waited for huge piles of snow to fall off the roofs and trees. They made slides.

It had been quite cold when they first started to play. They wore heavy overcoats, scarves, hats, gloves and wellington boots. But with all their work and running around most of them felt very hot. Their faces were bright red with the wind and their hands were red, too, from shovelling and making snowballs.

What fun they were having! The only thing that made them all feel a little bit sorry was that they knew that there wouldn't always be snow. It would lie for only a short time before it melted. Or else it would be swept up by snowploughs and shovels. Or else it would get too hard to play with. What a pity. Never mind, they were determined to make the most of it while they could.

Ask the class if they enjoyed the story. Then ask the following questions:
1 What was the name of the story?
2 What was the name of the boy mentioned in the story?
3 Who did he play with?
4 Name all the different things that were covered with snow in the street.
5 What had the snow looked like before they began to play?
6 How did they play in the snow?
7 How were they dressed?
8 Why were they feeling so hot?
9 Why were their hands and faces so red?
10 Why did they feel sad?
11 Why would the snow not be around for long?

Ask the class the opposite of the following words. Explain 'opposite' and give examples. Preface each question with 'Give me the opposite of . . .'

| | | | |
|---|---|---|---|
| 1 | everything | 11 | tiny |
| 2 | out | 12 | bigger |
| 3 | overnight | 13 | heavy |
| 4 | started | 14 | off |
| 5 | wasn't | 15 | cold |
| 6 | morning | 16 | sorry |
| 7 | smooth | 17 | short |
| 8 | white | 18 | up |
| 9 | here | 19 | hard |
| 10 | threw | 20 | clean |

*On tape*   Tape record the class talking about snow. Play back a selection.

# Daily lesson 16

**Materials**

1 Wild, zoo and pet animal cards; farm animal cards; furniture cards
2 Bird cards—thrush, crow, blackbird, sparrow, owl, seagull, starling, parrot, budgerigar, pigeon, robin
3 Fish cards—shark, whale, salmon, goldfish
4 Rhymes—*Mary had a pretty bird, Sing a song of sixpence, The robin*

*Vocabulary*    Display each bird card individually, establishing name of the bird shown and distinguishing features—size, colour or distinctive appearance. Give a brief story on the robin, the owl, seagull and parrot. Emphasize that these pictures are all birds. Say, 'We walk, don't we? What do birds do?' Establish 'fly in the sky'. Display each fish, establishing name and distinguishing features. Give a short story on each. Emphasize that they are all fish. Say, 'We walk, don't we? What do fish do?' Establish 'swim in the water'.

*Nursery rhymes*    Play all or a selection of the above rhymes.

*Classification*    Display a selection of wild animal cards and say, 'These are all animals, aren't they? They are all wild animals.' Then display pet animal cards and ask what kind of animals they are. Do the same with zoo animals and farm animals. Get the children to classify furniture according to room placement. Finish by asking what class the pictures of the thrush, crow etc belong to, also the shark, whale etc. Summarize slowly each class discovered.

# Daily lesson 17

**Materials**

1 Manikin
2 Clothing cards—shoes, slippers, sandals, boots, stockings, trousers, skirts, jersey, blouse, coat, jacket, gloves, hats

*Vocabulary and instruction*    Have the children stand by their desks. Explain that you want them to do as you do, and listen to your instructions. Then face the wall so that your back is towards the children. Raise your right arm and say, 'I'm raising my right arm.' Ask the children to copy what you do, looking over your shoulder to observe the children's responses. Correct those who do not respond appropriately. Emphasize that they should copy what you do (the response to verbal instruction will develop later). Repeat several times. Do in turn right arm, left arm, right leg, left leg. Quickly assemble manikin, eliciting the names of each part of the body. Display cards individually establishing names and distinguishing features. Establish which articles we wear on our feet, hands, legs, trunk. Establish indoor and outdoor wear.

# Daily lesson 18

**Materials**
1 Pictures as listed below
2 Puppet
3 Tape of previous week's rhymes

*Relationships*   Say, 'Mary is a girl; Tony is a . . . ?' Either elicit or explain 'boy'. Emphasize difference between them and then run through the following list asking for differences in terms of physical features, size, habits, use or origin.

1 elephant, mouse (big, small)
2 blackbird, seagull (black, white)
3 baby, grandfather (young, old)
4 fish, bird (swims, flies)
5 ball, brick (round, square)
6 radio, television (listen, look)
7 chair, bed (sit, sleep/lie)
8 cup, knife (drink, cut) etc

Use as many pictures as you can while the children remain interested in this activity.

*Introduce puppet*   Have him ask the children questions like 'Do elephants fly?' and 'Are cups for drinking from?' Have the children respond. If a negative response, let the children correct the sentence. 'No, elephants walk' or 'No, it's birds that fly' and if a positive response, let them give another example, 'Yes, and we can drink out of a glass too.'

*Nursery rhymes*   Let the children select rhymes from previous week's work.

# Daily lesson 19

## Materials
Distribute five blank, unlined sheets of paper to each child and give each child a red and a green crayon. The children work at their desks.

## Aim
The aim of this lesson is to draw a simple man, to help the children appreciate the parts of the body and their spatial relationships.

## Procedure
1 Draw a large circle on the board with green chalk. Draw it slowly in an anticlockwise direction and as you draw comment: 'I start up here and then I come down and down, round and round, then up and round until I meet with where I started from.' Speak and draw, slowly emphasizing 'up', 'here', 'down', 'round', 'up and round' and 'meet'. Repeat the exercise, then invite the children to draw a similar large circle with their green crayon. As the children draw, quickly look over their work. You will probably find children who will not readily draw a rounded enclosed circle. Help them by taking their hand in yours and draw with them (slowly and commenting) as many circles as time permits before moving on to the next part of the exercise.
2 Say, 'Now we are going to draw a square.' Using red chalk, demonstrate how to draw a square. Begin at the top of the left upright and come down, then draw bottom horizontal, then right upright (from the bottom) and join up the top horizontal from right to left. Do it slowly and comment. Ask the children to draw a square on a new sheet of paper and observe the results, helping out those children by the method suggested previously. Generally children have greater difficulty with a square.
3 Say, 'Now we're going to draw this shape.' Draw a rectangle whose vertical lines are about three times as long as the horizontal. 'We call this shape a rectangle.' Establish the name with the children and ask them to draw on a new sheet of paper. Then proceed as before.
4 'Now we are ready to draw a man. First we'll draw his head.' Draw a circle and invite children to copy your effort on a new sheet of paper. Emphasize that the circle should be placed well up the page. Observe and help out those children in difficulty. 'Now we'll draw his body.' Draw a square under and attached to the head and invite children to do the same. Emphasize 'under' and 'just touching'. 'Now his arms.' Draw the rectangles, joining the 'body' at the shoulders and projecting at 45° angles. Invite the children to draw. Emphasize 'joining' and 'sticking out'. 'Now his legs.' Draw rectangles, joining the body at right angles. Emphasize 'joining the body' and 'straight down'. Add his hands, feet and simple facial features (hair, eyes, nose, mouth and ears) and invite the children to do the same.
5 Ask the children to take a fresh piece of paper and invite them to draw another man—'As good a man as you can.'

# Daily lesson 20

**Materials**
Tape recorder

**Procedure**
Explain to the class that you are going to read them a story called *Puddles* and that you want them to listen very carefully because you will ask them questions about it afterwards.

## Puddles

It had been raining cats and dogs all night. And even when David got up in the morning it was still raining hard. The sky was dark, the clouds were grey and a strong wind lashed the rain against the windows of the house.

On his way to school David, wearing his wellington boots, had fun splashing in the puddles on the pavement and watching the water flow over his boots when he stuck them in the drain running alongside the kerb. He would have liked to have played longer but he didn't want to be late for school.

When he reached the playground he saw that most of the children had on their coats and wellington boots too. There were puddles all over the ground, where the rain had filled in the small holes. Some were small puddles, and others were large and deep, so deep that you couldn't wade too far into them. The children imagined that the biggest puddles were seas. They watched the waves that their feet made and some even pretended to sail boats made of sticks and pencils on their own little seas.

They heard the school bell ringing and they were soon all in their classes. Even there, there was a puddle. Rain had leaked in through a tiny crack in the roof and ceiling. It was quickly cleared up and a bucket placed under the crack to catch the drips of water that fell. The children had fun watching the bucket gradually fill up. They listened as the drips made a noise—first a tinny noise as the bucket was empty, and then a noise like *plop, plop, plop* as the water level rose in the bucket.

They wondered how long it would take for the bucket to get filled right up to the top. But what a pity. Half way through the morning the rain stopped, and soon after the drips stopped falling. And the bucket wasn't nearly full. What a pity.

Ask the class if they enjoyed the story, then ask the following questions:
1 What was the name of the story?
2 What was the name of the boy in the story?
3 What was the weather like during the night?
4 What was the colour of the sky?
5 What caused the rain to lash against the window?
6 How was David dressed on his way to school?
7 What did he do on his way to school?
8 Why did he stop playing?
9 What was happening in the playground when he arrived?
10 Why was there a puddle even inside the school?
11 What did they do to stop puddles forming on the floor?
12 What noises did the drips make and when?

13 Why was the class sorry that the rain stopped?

Ask the class the opposite of the following words. Explain 'opposite' and give examples. Preface each question with 'Give me the opposite of . . .'

| | | | |
|---|---|---|---|
| 1 | night | 11 | biggest |
| 2 | rain | 12 | little |
| 3 | dark | 13 | soon |
| 4 | to | 14 | tiny |
| 5 | longer | 15 | ceiling |
| 6 | late | 16 | quickly |
| 7 | arrive | 17 | under |
| 8 | most | 18 | fill |
| 9 | small | 19 | rose |
| 10 | deep | 20 | top |

*On tape*   Ask the class to tell the tape recorder about rainy days—what to wear, the colour of the sky, the noises made inside and outside, the puddles they play in, what they improvise, how they like or dislike rain and so on. Play back a selection.

# Daily lesson 21

**Materials**

Collect and distribute a sufficient number of miscellaneous articles to supply one to each child. Choose objects that are readily available at home or in the classroom and which the children can reasonably be expected to be familiar with. Keep three objects for yourself, for instance a ball, a piece of chalk and a bottle.

**Procedure**

Hold up the ball and invite the children to describe it in detail. Emphasize colour, shape, texture, function, size and weight, and distinguishing features. You will probably have to prompt responses by asking specific questions, e.g. 'What do we use this for?' Structure each response and summarize after responses are finished. Repeat with piece of chalk and a bottle. Then distribute one object to each child and explain that each of them will be given one minute to describe it. If a child gets stuck invite others to comment on the object, but only after direct questioning and prompting from you has failed; structure and summarize the responses after each object is described by the child.

# Daily lesson 22

**Materials**

1 Colour cubes—blue, yellow, green, black
2 Picture cards (as below)
3 Tape and nursery rhymes—*Daffy down dilly, Baa baa black sheep, Little Betty Blue*

**Procedure**

1 Distribute four colour cubes (as above) to each child. Display a picture of a girl with a blue dress, blue hat, blue shoes and blue umbrella. Describe the picture emphasizing 'She's got on a blue dress and a blue hat.' Invite the class to pick out from their own selection the cube of the same colour as the girl's clothes. Emphasize the name 'blue'.
2 Repeat, displaying in turn pictures of yellow bird, green trees and black kittens. Emphasize the *name* of each colour.
3 Then ask the children to select from their four cubes according to a visual stimulus cube shown by you.
4 Then have the children select from their four cubes according to verbal instructions: 'Pick up the black cube.' Repeat as often as is necessary, and as often as interest and enthusiasm will allow.

*Nursery rhymes* Play the nursery rhymes on the tape, inviting the children to lift the colour cube mentioned in the rhymes.

# Daily lesson 23

**Materials**

1 Picture showing exterior view of house, garden and garage. Pictures showing interior views of kitchen, lounge or living room, bedroom, bathroom
2 Rhymes—*How do you like to go up in a swing? There was an old woman who lived in a shoe*
3 Puppet

*Vocabulary* Display the picture illustrating the house. By question-response procedure, emphasize the salient features e.g. windows, door, chimney, roof, walls, garage, garden, path. Emphasize also the shape of the walls and windows (square or rectangular). Pick out background features of the house and garden, e.g. flower beds, swing or sandpit. Before displaying any of the room pictures, say 'I have a picture of a room in this house. And in this picture there are some taps.' Get the children to guess which picture you are holding on the basis of the clues you give them. After each clue, ensure that the meaning of the clue given is known. Ask 'What is a tap?' 'What is a cooker?' or 'What is a bed?' Remember and structure the children's responses.

*Nursery rhymes* Play the rhymes on the tape. Get the children to imagine they are on the swing and have them recite the poem as far as they can in time to a swing's movement.

*Imagination* What sort of houses do the following people and animals live in?

1 Indians
2 queen
3 bird
4 dog
5 pig
6 cows
7 horse
8 pet fish
9 bee
10 wasp
11 Eskimos

# Daily lesson 24

**Materials**
1 Tape recorder
2 Nursery rhyme—*Boys and girls come out to play*

**Procedure**
Explain to the class that you are going to read them a story called *Out to play*
and that you want them to listen carefully to the story because you will ask
them questions about it afterwards.

## Out to play

It was getting much lighter at nights now. After tea it was light enough to
go out and play for a short time before going to bed. The street in which
Mary and Jonathan lived was usually quite busy with children.

Some had bicycles. Others had roller skates, skipping ropes or balls to
play with. Usually Mary and Jonathan would both end up playing with
someone else's toy and they would exchange their toys. You could see little
boys and girls playing with bicycles belonging to older, bigger boys and
girls. And the bigger boys and girls would play with the toys of the younger,
smaller children.

Occasionally there would be arguments and squabbles but usually
everyone played together very well.

There was very little traffic about after teatime, so the streets were quite
safe. There was one van that the children hoped would appear, and it
usually did—the ice cream man's van.

They would hear the bells and chimes of the van long before they saw it.
This was the signal to stop whatever they were doing and rush into their
homes to ask mummy for some money for an ice cream or an ice lolly.
There was such a choice of things to buy that it was difficult to choose.

Then everyone would rush out again to be first in the queue. Sometimes
Jonathan thought it was just as well to be last in the queue because by the
time he got served, the rest had almost finished their ice creams.

They would stand around lick, lick, licking, the toys and bicycles and
ropes forgotten for the time being.

By the time everyone had finished it was usually time to go in. All that
there was time for was to clear up the toys and say, 'See you tomorrow.'
Then off to bed.

Ask the class if they enjoyed the story. Then ask the following questions:
1 What was the name of the story?
2 What were the names of the boy and girl in the story?
3 What did they do after tea?
4 What toys did the boys and girls play with?
5 Did they play with their own toys only?
6 Did they play well together all the time?
7 How much traffic was there?
8 What did they all look forward to?
9 What did they do when they heard the bells and chimes?
10 Why did Jonathan think it was as well to be last as first in the queue?
11 What did they do after the ice cream man had gone?

Ask the opposite of the following words:

| | | | |
|---|---|---|---|
| 1 | lighter | 11 | stop |
| 2 | now | 12 | difficult |
| 3 | out | 13 | first |
| 4 | short | 14 | stand |
| 5 | busy | 15 | forget |
| 6 | end up | 16 | asleep |
| 7 | bigger | 17 | goodbye |
| 8 | older | 18 | night |
| 9 | very little | 19 | late |
| 10 | safe | | |

*Nursery rhyme* Ask the class to recite, for the tape recorder, *Girls and boys come out to play.*

# Daily lesson 25

## Materials
1 Blank sheets of paper—a sufficient number so that each child can draw on three or four
2 Cardboard cut outs of rectangle and square shapes for those children who are not yet competent to copy these shapes
3 Picture of a house

## Aim
The aim of this lesson is to teach the class how to draw a simple house and to begin to appreciate the spatial relationships of walls, windows and door. The class should be seated at their desks. Teacher should demonstrate by drawing on the board and thereafter help out individuals in difficulty.

## Procedure
1 Draw a large rectangle on the board. Draw it slowly in a clockwise direction and as you draw comment on what you are doing, emphasizing starting and stopping points, straightness of lines, right angles, parallel lines and words such as 'along', 'to', 'here', 'down', 'up'. Ask the children to copy this shape encouraging those who cannot to use the cut out shape.
2 Proceed by drawing a square window well to the left of the rectangle and invite children to copy.
3 Draw another window well to the right of the rectangle and emphasize symmetry of placement.
4 Draw a door in the centre, emphasizing centre placement.
5 Add roof and chimney.
6 Invite the children to look at their drawings commenting on the relationships therein and ask them to repeat as often as enthusiasm remains good. While observing and helping the individual child, name the parts, 'wall, window, door, roof, chimney', pointing to each and asking the child to repeat.

# Daily lesson 26

**Materials**
Narrative poster of boys and girls arriving at school and map of school catchment area

*Conversation*   Discuss with the class what the poster depicts. How many children? How many mothers? Why do they accompany their children to school? How are the people dressed? What can we infer therefore about the weather? What other features are there in the picture?

Ask each child to say their name and address and place a pin appropriately on the map of the catchment area. As you pin each address mention the names of the streets taking the child from home to school.

*Following instructions*   Stand with your back to the children and ask them to copy your actions. Raise your right hand and repeat with left hand, then both hands. Repeat the series, left, right, right and both, but this time instruct verbally along with physical movement, thus: 'Raise your left hand'; 'raise your right hand'; 'raise both your arms'. Repeat this series frequently, gradually reducing the number of physical movements so that the children come to rely on verbal instructions. Make a game of it, speeding up the instructions so that the children gradually 'fall out' leaving an eventual winner.

# Daily lesson 27

**Materials**

1 Nursery rhymes—*The house that Jack built, Humpty Dumpty*
2 Paper and crayons
3 Pictures depicting persons and animals in the rhyme

**Procedure**

1 Explain to the children that you are going to read a nursery rhyme called *The house that Jack built* and that you want them to listen carefully because you will ask them questions about it afterwards.
2 Read the rhyme slowly and clearly, emphasizing main characters and language structure.
3 Ask individuals in the class to tell you about the poem, taking note of those children who were not listening and who cannot answer your simple questions.
4 Reread the poem, introducing pictures depicting persons and animals.
5 Instruct the children who appear to have listened and understood most of the poem to draw or paint or model with plasticine any of the characters of the poem.
6 Take the remainder aside and explain that you are going to read another poem called *Humpty Dumpty* and you want them to listen very carefully. As you read or recite the poem keep the children's attention, or make them aware constantly that you want them to listen actively to what you are saying, fixing each child with your eyes as you read. Question each child about the poem, taking note again of those who do not appear to have learned how to listen. Finally ask the children to draw Humpty Dumpty.

# Daily lesson 28

**Materials**

1 Colour cubes—blue, black, green, red, white (distributed so that each child has all five colours)
2 Puppet
3 Nursery rhymes—*Lavender's blue, Baa baa black sheep, Roses are red, Mary had a little lamb*

**Procedure**

1 Hold up the blue cube and invite the class to match yours. Take note of any child who cannot. Repeat with the remaining four colours.
2 Verbally (i.e. without holding up appropriate colour) instruct the class to hold up blue, taking note of those who do not respond correctly. Display blue and ask these children to correct themselves and tell you what the name of the colour is. Repeat for the remaining four colour cubes.
3 Introduce puppet who will summarize what has gone before i.e. five different colours, each with a different name. Have the puppet pick up each colour as he names it.
4 Ask the children to listen to the rhymes which contain a colour. Ask them to hold up the colour mentioned. Take care that children do not select their own cube to match the colour selected by, say, a brighter child, but that they can or cannot respond to verbal stimulus in the rhyme. Repeat with each rhyme warning the children that in two of the rhymes there are two colours named.

# Daily lesson 29

**Materials**
None

**Procedure**
Explain that you are going to read a story called *The milkman* and that you want the class to listen very carefully because you will ask them questions about it afterwards.

### The milkman

Roger stood on a chair looking out of the window of his bedroom. It was very cold and frosty and he had to keep on clearing the window as his breath steamed it up.

He saw the milkman busy at work unloading heavy crates filled with bottles of milk. He saw him look at a book and then walk up the path to each house leaving two bottles here and three bottles there. He walked slowly and quietly and was careful not to clink the bottles as he placed them on the doorstep of each house.

It was early in the morning and Roger saw the milkman's breath make small clouds in the frosty air. No one else was awake, not even the birds—just Roger and the milkman.

The milkman returned to his cart, placing some empty bottles in a crate. He looked at his book again, then off he went with some more full bottles. He walked up the path to Roger's house. He placed one, two, three, four bottles on the doormat without a sound. He must have sensed that someone was looking for he looked up and saw Roger. He stood for a minute and waved. Roger smiled and waved back. And the milkman strode away, whistling.

Roger watched him go for a minute and then crawled back into his warm bed. He dreamed of Santa Claus.

Ask the class if they enjoyed the story. Then ask the following questions:
 1  What was the name of the story?
 2  What was the name of the boy in the story?
 3  What was he doing at the beginning of the story?
 4  What did he see?
 5  What was the weather like? And how does the story tell us what the weather was like?
 6  Describe how the milkman went about his work.
 7  Why was he so quiet about his work?
 8  Do you think Roger had a big family?
 9  Why did the milkman look up at Roger?
10  Was Roger pleased?
11  What did Roger do after the milkman went away?
12  Why do you think he dreamed of Santa Claus?

Ask the class to give the opposites of the following. Explain to those who are still confused about the word 'opposite' what we mean by it and give examples. Always preface the question by: 'Give me the opposite of . . .'

| | |
|---|---|
| 1 early | 11 quiet |
| 2 bright | 12 quickly |
| 3 empty | 13 many |
| 4 asleep | 14 morning |
| 5 warm | 15 sun |
| 6 soft | 16 little |
| 7 sunny | 17 out |
| 8 happy | 18 up |
| 9 friendly | 19 white |
| 10 quietly | 20 go |

# Daily lesson 30

**Materials**

Occupation cards—milkman, butcher, baker, janitor, grocer, dentist, doctor, nurse, policeman

**Procedure**

Display first five cards, reminding the children that they have seen these men before. Elicit their names and what they sell before displaying the pictures of the new occupations.

*Dentist*  Elicit name and emphasize his concern with the teeth and gums. Ask the children to make a noise with their teeth. Ask them how many they think they have. What are teeth for? How would we manage without them? How do we care for our teeth? Teach the words—'clean', 'brush' and 'toothpaste'. Have the children recite—'This is the way we brush our teeth', with their teeth clenched, and also wide open. Teach the words 'up', 'down', 'along' and 'sideways'.

*Doctor*  Adopt similar lines of questioning for this occupation, emphasizing health and cleanliness; have the children listen to their own heartbeats and that of their neighbour. How many children have visited a doctor recently? What for? Have them recite—'This is the way we wash our hands' and 'This is the way we breathe in air.'

*Nurse*  Emphasize that generally girls do this kind of work. Teach the words 'kind', 'gentle', 'knowledge'.

*Policeman*  Emphasize that generally men do this work; describe uniform and those aspects of police work that the children are most closely concerned with e.g. road safety. Have them recite 'This is the way we cross the road.'

Finally, have the children guess at the names of the following occupations —bus driver, bus conductor, builder, shoemaker, fishmonger, fisherman, engine driver, teacher, gardener and tailor—elicit responses by statements such as 'This man drives us to school each day.'

# Daily lesson 31

**Materials**
Picture cards—telephone, letter, hammer, nail, saw, axe, spade, rake, wheelbarrow, lawnmower

**Procedure**
Display each card in turn, eliciting and/or teaching its name, function, where it would be found, and what it is made of. Have individual children mime the use of each item and ask the rest of the class to guess at it. Ask the children to guess at the item described as follows: 'We use this to call our friends' (telephone); 'This item has one wheel and we push it in the garden' (wheelbarrow) and so on.

# Daily lesson 32

**Materials**
None

**Procedure**
Have the children complete the following sentences:
1 Early in the morning I get out of my_____(bed)
2 To keep my feet warm I put on my _____(slippers)
3 I turn the tap on in the bathroom to fill the basin with_____(water)
4 I wash my hands, face and neck and ears with water and_____(soap)
5 Then I get dressed and go through to the kitchen to eat_____ (breakfast)

Continue in this vein, encouraging free responses, until the child is ready to leave home to go to school. Reverse the procedure by asking the children to say in their own words the meanings of the following words—bed, slippers, tap, water, soap, stairs, kitchen, breakfast. Allow free responses but repeat the child's response in a well structured sentence, asking another to repeat this well structured definition.

*Mime* Demonstrate miming to the class and invite them to guess at some activity in preparation for leaving home in the morning. Ask individuals to mime an activity and invite the others to guess. Keep the activities simple but encourage the children to pay attention to detail and exaggerate actions.

# Daily lesson 33

**Materials**

1 Colour cubes—blue, black, green, red, white, yellow, brown, orange
2 Number cards depicting objects in groups of one, two, three and four
3 Nursery rhymes—*One, two, buckle my shoe, Lavender's blue, Baa baa black sheep, Mary had a little lamb*

**Procedure**

Revise colours taught in lesson 28, first by calling upon the class to match your colour cube and then to select according to verbal instruction. Extend by adding the new colours—yellow, brown and orange.

*Nursery rhyme*   Introduce the rhyme *One, two, buckle my shoe*. On second rendition have the children mime the actions. On the third, encourage them to recite the rhyme along with the actions. Emphasize the numbers in the rhyme.

Display picture of the concept *one*, repeating 'one' in as many ways as you can. Ask the class to respond to the question 'How many then?' 'One!' Display other pictures illustrating concept one. Ask the children to hold up one finger, one arm, one leg. Proceed as above with concepts *two, three* and *four*. Emphasize the number, have the class respond to 'How many then?' and illustrate to you using their fingers the concept taught. End by reciting along with the class *One, two, buckle my shoe*.

# Daily lesson 34

**Materials**
Tape recorder

**Procedure**
Explain to the class that you are going to read a story called *Sunday*, and that you want them to listen carefully to the story because you will ask them questions about it afterwards.

Sunday

Lucy and Terry liked Sundays and always hoped that the weather would be kind. For on Sundays they didn't go to school and Daddy didn't have to go to work. So the whole family was free to do as they liked together. And there was always plenty to do.

Sometimes they would do the garden. Daddy would begin to mow the grass but sooner or later his friend next door would come out and they would stand chatting. Terry always waited for this because he could then take over the mower. He loved to cut grass. And he did a good job too.

Lucy would generally play with her friend, either with dolls, or skipping ropes or balls. They would pop in and out of the house sometimes squabbling but usually laughing and fooling around together.

Mother always had something to do in the house but occasionally she would come out to do a spot of work in the garden. She would chat with her next door neighbour and pop back into the house to do some chore. Always busy doing something.

So they would spend Sunday morning, not doing very much that was important, just enjoying each other's company. By eleven o'clock or so, one of them usually had an idea for the afternoon. A visit to the grandparents, a trip to the zoo or maybe a gentle stroll down to feed the ducks. Then they would rush about tidying up all the tools and toys that had been strewn across the grass. Mother would hurry to make a quick lunch. They'd all get changed and off they would go. Not doing very much. Just enjoying themselves.

Ask the class if they enjoyed the story, and then ask the following questions:
1  What was the name of the story?
2  What were the names of the brother and sister in the story?
3  Why did they look forward to Sundays?
4  What did Daddy usually begin to do each Sunday?
5  What was it that Terry usually had to take over?
6  What did Lucy do on Sundays?
7  What did mother do?
8  What did the family do in the afternoons?
9  Why did they usually have to rush?

*On tape*  Ask individuals in the class to tell the tape recorder what they do on Sunday mornings. Insist on simple, well structured but 'natural' language. Encourage the use of words like 'sometimes', 'usually', 'perhaps', 'not always'. Play back the better stories.

Ask the class to give the opposite of the following words. Explain 'opposite' if necessary. Preface each question by 'Give me the opposite of . . .'

 1 like
 2 short
 3 stand
 4 damp
 5 good
 6 friend
 7 together
 8 happy
 9 indoors
10 something
11 important
12 afternoon
13 gentle
14 quick
15 go
16 very much
17 laughing
18 playing
19 early
20 brother
21 mother

# Daily lesson 35

**Materials**
1 Manikin
2 Sufficient sheets of paper for each child
3 Crayons

**Procedure**
Revise drawing a man. Explain that now you are going to concentrate on the face.

Draw a large face on the board. Make the drawing as realistic as possible and explain that although you have drawn previous heads as circles, they are not really circles. Draw in turn face, mouth, nose, eyes, ears and hair. Stop after demonstrating each stage and ask the children to copy. Have them point to their own face, mouth etc and those of their neighbours. Teach or elicit also what each item on the face is used for.

Take particular note of children in difficulty. Most probably children will have difficulty in placing accurately each item and some will tend to draw simple lines for nose and mouth rather than draw two dimensional figures. Ask the class if they can spot two things that have been missed out— eyebrows and eyelashes. Draw them in and have the children copy.

Leave your drawing on the board and ask the children to draw the face again on a fresh sheet. As you observe individually, comment on what each child is drawing. Mention facial items either from the top or bottom of the face. Ensure that each child knows the names and functions of each.

# Daily lesson 36

**Materials**

Plastic fruit—apple, orange, banana, pineapple, grapefruit, plums, peach, coconut and lemon

**Procedure**

Have the class pass the items among themselves. Retrieve and display on the table. Teach and/or elicit the names of each, bringing out the characteristic features.

*Apple*—round, green or red, like a ball, hard, small dark pips, juicy, smooth skin, nice to eat, it's a fruit, white inside.

*Orange*—round, orange coloured, like a ball, soft but firm, large white pips, very juicy, segmented, rough skin, pleasant to eat, it's a fruit too, orange inside.

Proceed similarly with each fruit. Select pairs from the group of fruits and elicit differences between each in terms of shape, size, colour or texture. Select pairs from the group of fruits and elicit similarities (how are they alike? how are they the same?) between each in terms of shape, size, edibility, grow on trees, have pips etc.

# Daily lesson 37

**Materials**
1 Narrative picture—supermarket scene
2 Tape recorder

**Procedure**
Display the poster. Explain to the class that you will be asking them to describe what is in the picture. Explain that you want them to follow your finger as you 'describe' the picture without words. Then without speaking bring the children's eyes to focus on the main features of the picture—the racks of various foods, baskets and trolleys, cash registers, butcher's counter etc.

*On tape* Invite each child to the tape recorder and ask them to describe in no more than two sentences what they have seen. Insist on them prefacing their remarks by saying 'In this picture of a supermarket I noticed . . .' Play the tape back to the children at intervals of six or seven children.

*Following instructions* Have the children stand by their desks, with one child standing with his back to the class. His job will be to issue instructions, 'Do as I do', and he will in turn lift his left hand, right hand, left leg, right leg. Replace by another child who is sure of left and right. His job will be to issue verbal instructions without visual clue. Repeat with several children. Pick some who may not be sure of left and right so that they learn that there is an actual immediate need for them to learn quickly. Take care however that those who are confused do not get embarrassed.

# Daily lesson 38

**Materials**
1 Tool and utensil cards—watch, clock, alarm clock
2 Pen, pencil, Biro, typewriter, crayon, paper, book
3 Nursery rhyme—*Hickory dickory dock*

**Procedure**
Display each card individually. Elicit and/or teach the name, function, characteristic features of each. Emphasize similarities and differences between the three groups above.

*Nursery rhyme* Recite the nursery rhyme. Emphasize that the clock mentioned is a grandfather clock and describe one. Have the children recite it along with you, crouching down and jumping up at the appropriate time.

*Rhythm* Have the children stand and explain that you are going to clap your hands in a certain rhythm and would like them to try and copy. Inevitably mistakes will be made and the class will tend to explode in laughter. This is not to be discouraged but insist after each explosion on absolute quiet and concentration. Encourage them to focus all their attention on listening to you, rather than looking at your hands. Encourage them to listen self critically to their own rhythms. Are they right or wrong? Work with the class, groups and individuals. Make a game of it. Follow the following rhythms:
1 clap, pause, clap
2 clap, clap, clap
3 clap, clap, clap, pause, clap
4 Clap, clap, pause, clap, clap, clap
5 clap, clap, clap, pause, clap, clap.
Repeat, revise and vary at your discretion.

# Daily lesson 39

**Materials**
Tape recorder

**Procedure**
Explain to the class that you are going to read a story called *The pond in the park*, and that you want them to listen carefully to the story because you will ask them questions about it afterwards.

### The pond in the park

The pond in the park was huge. Or so it seemed to Will and Angela. They had been coming to the park for a long time now and they always made a point of going to the pond.

Sometimes when there was a breeze, model sailing boats would sail back and forth across the pond. Will and Angela would just stand and stare, sometimes wishing they had a little boat to sail. Sometimes they would run round the pond following a boat as it was pushed by the breeze up against the edge of the pond.

Once they tried to catch fish in the pond. They had seen other boys and girls with a piece of stick and string fishing; but they had never caught anything and they didn't really think there were any fish in the pond, but they enjoyed pretending to be real fishermen.

Sometimes they would toss pebbles or stones into the water and watch the ripples and bubbles as the stones sank to the bottom. The water wasn't very deep and they could see the stones disappear into the mud and leaves at the bottom.

There weren't any ducks in the pond. Will thought this must be because there were always too many people around. They would be frightened.

There were some swings and a slide and a merry-go-round beside the pond and usually Will and Angela would wander over and play there. But that's another story.

Ask the class if they enjoyed the story. Then ask the following questions:
1 What was the name of the story?
2 What were the names of the boy and girl in the story?
3 What was sometimes on the pond when they visited?
4 How did Will and Angela play with the boats?
5 What made the sailing boats move?
6 What did they try to do at the pond? What tackle did they use?
7 What else did they do at the pond?
8 Where did the leaves at the bottom of the pond come from?
9 Why weren't there any ducks at this pond?
10 What was situated beside the pond?

Ask the class to give you the opposite of the following words. Explain 'opposite' and give examples. Preface each question with 'Give me the opposite of . . .'

| | |
|---|---|
| 1 in | 10 many |
| 2 huge | 11 different |
| 3 boy | 12 follow |

| | |
|---|---|
| 4 coming | 13 fast |
| 5 to | 14 wide |
| 6 sometimes | 15 shallow |
| 7 pushed | 16 soft |
| 8 real | 17 high |
| 9 bottom | |

*On tape*  Ask the class to tell the tape recorder about visits they make to ponds. Insist on short, simple, well structured sentences. Encourage by question-response procedure practice in the use of the words utilized in the story.

# Daily lesson 40

**Materials**

Animal pictures—gorilla, monkey, woodpecker, albatross, worm, cobra, python, hare, deer, selection of insects, centipede, caterpillar

**Procedure**

Teach and/or elicit the name of each animal, bird, snake or insect. Emphasize the characteristics of each—size, length, colours, habitat, number of legs. Emphasize that they belong to the same group—living things. Then ask individuals in the class in what way any pair of living things are alike and different. Try and bring out differences and similarities in terms of loco-motion, and number of legs.

*Analogies*   Ask individuals in the class to finish the following sentences:
1  A gorilla is big but a monkey is _____ (small)
2  A bird has two legs and a deer has _____ (four legs)
3  A caterpillar's legs are short and a monkey's legs are _____ (long)
4  A cat's ears are short, a rabbit's ears are _____ (long)
5  Suzanne is a girl; Tony is a _____ (boy)
6  Girls grow up to be women and boys to be _____ (men)
7  On our hands we wear gloves; on our feet we wear _____ (shoes)
8  Boys wear trousers; girls wear _____ (dresses)
9  A caterpillar moves slowly; a monkey moves _____ (quickly)
10  A gorilla walks on the ground; an albatross flies _____ (in the sky)

# Daily lesson 41

**Materials**
Colour cubes—blue, black, green, red, white, yellow, brown, orange

**Procedure**
Distribute a set of eight colours to each child. Call upon the class to match the colour held by you and repeat for all the eight colours. Then call upon the class to select on the basis of verbal instructions. Take note of those children who are unable to do this or who appear to be selecting on the basis of a neighbour's choice and not on their understanding of a verbal clue. After each selection has been made, get the class individually and as a whole to say the name of the colour cube they are holding. Insist on sentences—'I am holding a blue cube' or 'The colour of the cube I am holding is blue.' Continue as long as the class is enthusiastic but be wary of boring those children who are confused.

Next ask the children to select three cubes—black, white and red. Explain that you are going to ask them to join them together in a certain order. Insist that they work from left to right and ensure that they know what this means. Instruct them to make a chain of black and white. Confirm by matching that they follow what is required. Proceed as follows:
black, white, red
red, white, black
white, red, black
red, black, white
white, red, black
Continue with other variations. In correcting children emphasize the words 'first', 'then' and 'last'.

# Daily lesson 42

**Materials**
Nursery rhyme—*Monday's child*

**Procedure**
Ask the children what day it is. Ask several children to repeat the name of the day. Explain that there are seven days in the week and repeat the names slowly. Pick out some special feature or activity associated with each day (We all go swimming on a Thursday, don't we?) and then repeat the days again.

*Nursery rhyme*  Play the nursery rhyme on the tape, encouraging the children to say the name of the day at the proper time.

Give each child the name of a day and invite them to perform simple tasks e.g. 'I want all the Mondays to put their hands on their heads.' Award cubes to each 'day' to see which is the best day. Repeat the rhyme. End by asking the children what day it is today.

*Comprehension*  Ask individuals the following questions. Encourage additional elaborations from other children, and ask others to confirm or correct the decisions made.
1  What would you do if you broke a cup at home?
2  What would you do if you came across a little boy/girl crying?
3  Why do we have houses?
4  What would you do if you found a little kitten?
5  What would you do if you went home and found you were locked out?
6  What should you do if you spill ink or milk at school?
7  What should you do if you bump into someone?
8  What should you do if someone bumps into you?

# Daily lesson 43

**Materials**
Shop cards—fishmonger, butcher, baker, furniture shop, newsagent, shoe shop, toy shop, fruiterer, greengrocer

**Procedure**
Display a picture of each shop. Describe and/or elicit the different sorts of goods sold by each—emphasize the functions of the goods sold. Then play a variation of the game 'I went to market and I bought . . .' Ask the first child to say 'I went to the greengrocer and I bought some potatoes.' The next child repeats and adds on one item and so on. Encourage the children to associate each previous person with the goods that they bought. Encourage them to be quick and think before it is their turn to say what they might buy. Encourage them to think of more than one thing but make sure they are listening to what goes on. Keep the game moving fast so that the children remain on their toes.

*Rhyming*   Ask individuals in the class to give you words to rhyme with the following. Work at speed and cover all the class. It will probably be necessary to point out that it is the end of the word that matters and this will have to be repeated throughout.

| | | |
|---|---|---|
| 1 tall | 11 south | 21 door |
| 2 me | 12 nose | 22 kite |
| 3 hat | 13 hair | 23 out |
| 4 will | 14 eye | 24 free |
| 5 cot | 15 pick | 25 ten |
| 6 sit | 16 strong | 26 late |
| 7 ring | 17 hole | 27 none |
| 8 wall | 18 but | 28 treat |
| 9 hand | 19 tack | 29 blow |
| 10 ear | 20 fight | 30 fun |

# Daily lesson 44

**Materials**
None

**Procedure**
Explain to the class that you are going to read them a story called *The swings* and that you want them to listen carefully because you will ask them questions about it afterwards.

### The swings

Mark and Susie loved going to the swings in the park. Sometimes they would go by themselves, but often their parents would come too.

Actually there were more things to play on than just the swings themselves. There was a slide or chute to slide down. There was a merry-go-round to spin round on, and there was a big red horse that several children at a time could rock back and forth on.

Mark and Susie usually started off on the swings. Swinging back and forth they'd go, higher and higher—but not too high because their mother had warned them it was dangerous.

If the slide wasn't too busy they'd have a go on it too. Half the fun was climbing up the stairs and counting them as they climbed. There were twenty steps in the staircase. Then down they'd slide, faster and faster. Sometimes the slide was rather sticky if it had been raining, and it wasn't much fun. But if the slide was dry they'd play on it for ages—climbing up the stairs, sliding down with a *woosh* and running back to climb again.

Mark and Susie were not very fond of going on the merry-go-round. It sometimes made them feel sick and dizzy. But if they were alone there, they could spin round gently and this was just as good fun as going fast.

They didn't often go on the big red rocking horse, although they used to when they were younger. They were too big for it now. But they would stand watching smaller boys and girls enjoying it, helping the very small ones on and off and watching that they didn't fall off by mistake.

They did enjoy going to the swings in the park. There was so much to do.

Ask the class if they enjoyed the story. Then ask the following questions:
1 What was the name of the story?
2 What were the names of the boy and girl in the story?
3 Where were the swings?
4 What three other things were there to play on beside the swings?
5 What was dangerous about the swings?
6 Why was the slide so much fun?
7 How many steps did it have?
8 Why did the slide sometimes get sticky?
9 Why didn't they like going on the merry-go-round?
10 Why didn't they go on the rocking horse too often?
11 What did they do at the rocking horse?

*Nursery rhyme*   Have the class recite *How do you like to go up in a swing?* Emphasize the movement and rhythm written into the rhyme.

Ask the class the opposite of the following words. Explain 'opposite' if necessary. Give examples. Preface by saying 'Give me the opposite of . . .'

| | | | |
|---|---|---|---|
| 1 | loved | 11 | on |
| 2 | alone | 12 | enjoy |
| 3 | down | 13 | much |
| 4 | big | 14 | hard |
| 5 | started | 15 | low |
| 6 | higher | 16 | many |
| 7 | faster | 17 | gentle |
| 8 | young | 18 | laughing |
| 9 | bigger | 19 | quickly |
| 10 | help | 20 | short |

# Daily lesson 45

**Materials**
1 Public institution cards—library, zoo, circus, park, museums, hotel, garage, church, hospital, fire brigade, town house, theatre and cinema
2 Tape recorder

**Procedure**
Teach or elicit the names of each institution and elicit the kinds of activity going on in each, what sort of people work there, and what kind of work they do, and what we go there for. Encourage the children to tell the tape recorder of the time they visited any of the institutions.

Ask individuals to give the opposite of the words below. It will probably be necessary to demonstrate the meaning of opposite before some of the children catch on. Although the teacher should try to maintain the pace of this lesson, always say, 'What is the opposite of . . . ?' when questioning the class. The object of this lesson is not only to elicit the opposite of certain words but to teach the meaning of the word 'opposite' itself.

| | | | |
|---|---|---|---|
| 1 | black | 13 | dark |
| 2 | open | 14 | cold |
| 3 | tall | 15 | dog |
| 4 | wide | 16 | thin |
| 5 | up | 17 | blunt |
| 6 | left | 18 | brother |
| 7 | clean | 19 | boy |
| 8 | tidy | 20 | man |
| 9 | asleep | 21 | deep |
| 10 | morning | 22 | great |
| 11 | sun | 23 | light (heavy) |
| 12 | earth | 24 | light (dark) |

# Daily lesson 46

**Materials**

1 Means of transport cards—legs, horse, car, lorry, train, plane, ship, bus, bicycle, sailing boat
2 Tape recorder

**Procedure**

Display each card in turn. Elicit and/or teach the name given to each. Bring the class's attention to the characteristic features of each emphasizing the difference between them e.g. we walk on two legs; a horse walks on four legs. A car carries a small number of people, generally a family or friends and they don't pay a fare, whilst a bus carries a lot of people, the public, who do have to pay a fare. A train runs on rails, a lorry on the road. A plane goes in the sky, a ship on the sea. Continue along these lines.

Having established the differences among the items ask 'And how are they the same?' The kind of responses you wish to encourage will be those which say 'they both go', 'they both travel', 'they both have engines' i.e. general responses. Although particular responses such as 'they are both the same colour' are not wrong, they are not really acceptable and should be gently discouraged.

Finally revise the names given to each of the items displayed and emphasize again that 'they all go, don't they?' Have the class repeat this in unison.

*Mime*  Have individuals mime driving, or being transported by the above items. The remainder will guess which item is being used.

*On tape*  Have those children who have not had an opportunity to mime go to the tape recorder and let them describe the occasions they have travelled on any of the above vehicles or seen or been close to any of them.

# Daily lesson 47

## Materials

1 Occupation cards—milkman, butcher, baker, janitor, grocer, bus driver, engine driver, nurse, fishmonger
2 Tool cards—spoon, knife, fork, cup, hammer, nail, spade, saw, axe, watch, book, newspaper
3 Nursery rhymes—*Rub a dub dub; This is the way we* (eat our food etc)

## Procedure

Display all the cards of group one. Invite the class to select a card on the basis of their responses to questions such as 'Show me the one who delivers milk to our homes.' Once a card has been selected ask the child concerned to describe the name given and what he does; 'This man is called a milkman. He delivers milk to our homes.' Insist on two sentences and good language structure. Once all the cards have been selected have the children recite *Rub a dub dub, three men in a tub*. Now display all the cards in group two. As above ask the children to select the appropriate card. Have the child then say what his card is and define what it is used for. Some children may try to define their object by describing its physical features. Although this is acceptable, encourage more definitions in terms of function.

*Nursery rhyme* Finish by having the class recite appropriate verses of *This is the way we* (dig the garden etc).

# Daily lesson 48

**Materials**

Nursery rhymes—*Mary had a pretty bird, Baa baa black sheep, Humpty Dumpty, Hey diddle diddle, One, two, buckle my shoe, Six little mice sat down to spin*

**Procedure**

These are all nursery rhymes that have been used in previous class lessons. The aim in this lesson is to question the children closely about the meanings of certain words in the rhymes, and their interpretation of what is going on in the rhymes. The following list of questions should not be regarded as complete. The atmosphere of the 'interrogation' should remain casual but the questioning should be precise. Recite each poem, question (and dramatize each poem if time permits) before moving on to the next.

1. What was the name of the girl in the rhyme?
2. What did she have?
3. What was the colour of the bird's legs?
4. What did the bird do?

1. What did we ask the sheep?
2. What colour was the sheep?
3. How many bags full did the sheep have?
4. Who received the bags?
5. Where did the little boy live?

1. Where was Humpty Dumpty sitting?
2. What happened to him?
3. Who tried to repair him?
4. Did they succeed?

1. What was the cat playing with?
2. What did the cow do?
3. How do we know that the little dog enjoyed this?
4. What did the dish do?

1. What comes after 'one, two'?
2. What comes after 'three, four'?
3. What comes after 'five, six'?
4. What comes after 'seven, eight'?
5. What does 'lay them straight' mean?

1. How many mice sat down to spin?
2. Who passed by?
3. What did she do and what did she say?
4. What did the mice reply?
5. What does 'weaving coats' mean?
6. What did the pussy cat offer to do?
7. What did the mice reply?
8. Do you think the pussy cat really wanted to help?
9. Did the mice know that pussy did not really want to help?

# Daily lesson 49

**Materials**
Tape recorder

**Procedure**
Explain to the class that you are going to read them a story called *Going home after school* and that you want them to listen carefully to the story, because you will be asking them questions about it afterwards.

### Going home after school

It was time to go home. Doug had had a good day today. He had read a little. He had written a story and drawn a good picture about the story. He had watched a programme on television about fish. He'd enjoyed his lunch, which he always had at school. He'd played games in the playground at playtime. And in the afternoon he'd been busy sewing a puppet together.

Now he rushed to get his coat and outdoor shoes on. He didn't live far from the school at all and there were no busy roads to cross. So he was home very quickly.

Mummy was home waiting for him. He told her quickly what he'd been doing and switched on the television set. He wanted to see a zoo programme that he'd seen advertised. He was just in time. His mother brought him a glass of milk and a biscuit and he thanked her.

She asked him what he had been doing today but he didn't answer her very well. He was too busy watching and listening to his programme. His mother understood though, and watched quietly with him. She was interested in animals too.

The programme was so entertaining that time just flew by and before they realized it they heard Daddy opening the front door. 'Hello,' he shouted. 'Hello, daddy,' they shouted back. They both got up, Mummy from an armchair and Doug from the floor where he had been sprawled out, and went to greet him. The programme was finished. So they all trooped through to the kitchen to prepare tea.

Doug had enjoyed school today. But it was nice to be at home too.

Ask the class if they enjoyed the story, then ask the following questions:
1 What was the name of the story?
2 What was the name of the boy in the story?
3 What had he done at school today?
4 What did he put on before leaving for home?
5 Why was he able to be home so quickly?
6 Who was at home to welcome him?
7 What did he do almost as soon as he was home, and why?
8 What did his mother bring him?
9 What was the programme on television about?
10 How does the story tell us his mother became interested too?
11 What does it mean by 'the time just flew by'?
12 Who came home next?
13 What happened then?

Ask the class to give the opposite of the following words:

| | | | |
|---|---|---|---|
| 1 | after | 11 | quickly |
| 2 | good | 12 | on |
| 3 | day | 13 | in time |
| 4 | a little | 14 | quietly |
| 5 | always | 15 | interested |
| 6 | afternoon | 16 | front |
| 7 | together | 17 | hello |
| 8 | outdoor | 18 | shouted |
| 9 | far | 19 | got up |
| 10 | busy | 20 | finished |

*On tape*   Ask the class to tell the tape recorder what they do first when they get home. Play back a selection.

# Daily lesson 50

**Materials**
Plastic fruit and vegetables—potato, tomato, onion, cauliflower, leek, cabbage, lettuce, turnip, carrots, apple, orange, banana, pineapple, grapefruit, plum, peach, coconut, lemon (or pictures of fruit and vegetables if plastic models are not available)

**Procedure**
Display all the plastic vegetables, or pictures of vegetables, simultaneously. Elicit and/or teach that these are all vegetables. Elicit and/or teach the names of each individual vegetable. Question by asking 'What name do we give to this vegetable? Describe it for us.' Encourage descriptions in terms of size, shape, colour. Emphasize likeness and differences in physical characteristics, how they grow, how they are cooked etc. Display the cards illustrating fruits, or plastic models. Remind the class of the names of each and remind them that these are fruits.

Invite one of the class to the front. Whisper the name of a fruit or vegetable to him and ask him to describe this to the rest of the class. Tell him to start by saying, 'The object I'm thinking of is a fruit/vegetable.' Encourage others to deduce what he is thinking about by asking relevant questions—what shape, what colour, what kind of skin, does it have pips? etc. Invite other children to act as quiz master for other items in these two classes. Close by questioning the class very quickly on these two classes of objects.

# Daily lesson 51

**Materials**
1 Insect pictures—ladybird, daddy long legs, spider, cockroach, centipede, grasshopper, moth, butterfly, housefly, bumble bee, wasp, caterpillar
2 Nursery rhymes—*Ladybird, ladybird fly away home, Little Miss Muffet, Fiddle dee dee, fiddle dee dee, the fly shall marry the bumble bee*
3 Paper and coloured crayons

**Procedure**
Display each card in turn, eliciting or teaching the name of each insect. Emphasize colours, number of legs, antennae, habitat and relative size and shape. Introduce the next picture by saying 'Now here is another insect' and repeat the procedure.

*Nursery rhyme*   After ladybird, spider, fly and bumble bee, introduce the appropriate nursery rhyme.

Finally return the class to their desks, distribute paper and crayons. Display the ladybird, wasp or bee, and butterfly. Elicit the colours of these insects. Ask the class to match these colours with their crayons, to choose one of the insects and draw it.

# Daily lesson 52

**Materials**

Animal pictures—cat, dog, mouse, cow, lamb, sheep, rabbit, pony, tiger, lion, kitten, puppy, calf. *It will be necessary to have two pictures of each animal.*

**Procedure**

Establish again the name of each animal. Bring a handful of children individually to each card and have them repeat 'This animal is a cat' or 'Here is a cat' etc. Clear the display area of all cards then show two pictures of the same animal. Then say, showing first one alone and then two together, 'Here is one cat, and here are two cats.' Emphasize 'are' and the final 's' at the end of 'cats'. Have individual children repeat this exercise with the rest of the animals. It will be necessary probably to keep on emphasizing 'are' and the final 's', and in addition it will be necessary to teach 'mice', 'sheep' and 'calves'.

Collect all illustrations and set them up quickly again, scattered around the room but within sight of the class. Have them scattered on top of desks, on ledges, under tables, leaning against walls etc. Ask the children where various animals or groups are scattered. Insist on answers being structured correctly, paying particular attention to the use of 'are', the plural structure and words indicating position such as 'on top of', 'on', 'under', 'against', 'beside'. Restructure and repeat children's responses where necessary and ask the class or individuals to chant the more difficult responses: 'Where are the two mice?' 'The two mice are sitting under a desk.'

# Daily lesson 53

**Materials**

1  Narrative poster depicting autumn scene
2  Collection of leaves, nuts and berries of autumn
3  Nursery rhyme—*One misty moisty morning*

**Procedure**

Discuss the weather today and of previous days. Elicit or teach the words colder, damp, foggy, cloudy, snowing, misty, daylight, darker etc. Display the picture and have the children describe in detail what is depicted. Ensure that all parts of the picture are covered, not just the main features. Emphasize the colours in the picture, the half-covered trees, leaves and brushwood on the ground, the weather, the clothes worn by people etc. Display and bring the class's attention to your collection of leaves, nuts and berries.

*Nursery rhyme*   Finish by introducing *One misty moisty morning.*

# Daily lesson 54

**Materials**
Colour cubes—black, white, green, red, blue, orange, brown and yellow

**Procedure**
Distribute eight colour cubes to each child. Say 'I'm looking at the curtains and I'm holding a cube in my hand which is the same colour. What colour is my cube?' Elicit from individuals the name of each cube in turn. (Be careful to select matching colours around the room and dresses or shirts worn which are either one colour or predominantly of one colour. A child who is still in the process of learning colour names will only be further confused if an article of mixed colours is selected.) After the cubes have been matched up say 'Yes, this is a (pause) blue cube' and so on through the colours. Take a note of those children who are still unsure; they will probably require remedial practice in naming colour and it may be further necessary to check for colour blindness.

Explain to the class that you are going to ask them to make a chain with their cubes. Insist that the chain goes from left to right and demonstrate (with your back to the class) which is left and right. Give visual instructions initially i.e. make a chain of from two to four cubes, display to the class for seven seconds, then conceal from view and ask them to copy it. Do not allow them to start reproducing your chain until the seven seconds is up. Once the class have mastered this, repeat the procedure giving verbal instructions only.

# Daily lesson 55

**Materials**
Tape recorder

**Procedure**
Explain to the class that you are going to read them a story called *The road-workers* and that you want them to listen carefully to the story because you will ask them questions about it afterwards.

### The roadworkers
What excitement! There, in front of their very own school, the road-workers were repairing the road. Most of the class had noticed that there had been many quite large holes appearing in the road. And now they were going to be filled in! What a pity—the holes in the road made such smashing puddles when it rained.

Never mind, it would be exciting to watch the roadworkers repairing them. At playtime they rushed to the wall around the playground and stared at what was going on.

One man had a large bucket of black sticky tar in his hand. He shovelled some of this into one hole while another man pressed it down hard. Then a small steamroller came clanking, clanking towards the hole and rolled back and forth across the repaired hole until it was absolutely smooth and flat. Then they moved on to repair another hole.

There was a lovely smell around where the work was going on. The smell reminded some of the children of burning coal or smouldering wood or burning leaves. The children closed their eyes and breathed in deeply. Ummm!

All the time the work was going on there was a great deal of noise. Buckets banging together, spades and picks banging away at the road, and the biggest noise of all was of course caused by the steamroller.

The noise was so deafening that the children didn't hear the school bell ringing to tell them that playtime was over. So out came teacher, a little angry until she saw what had kept them. So she stayed with the class and watched for a few minutes. Then they all trooped off back to their classroom.

Ask the class if they enjoyed the story. Then ask them the following questions:
1  What was the name of the story?
2  What was happening in front of the school?
3  Why were the class disappointed at the road being repaired?
4  When did they go out to watch the road being repaired?
5  What did one workman have in a bucket?
6  How was each hole repaired?
7  What did the tar smell like?
8  What noises did the children hear?
9  What noise didn't the children hear?
10  Was the teacher very angry?
11  What did she do?

Ask the class the opposite of the following words. Explain 'opposite'.
Preface each question with 'Give me the opposite of . . .'

| | | | |
|---|---|---|---|
| 1 | front | 11 | pleasant |
| 2 | most | 12 | didn't |
| 3 | many | 13 | over |
| 4 | filled in | 14 | out |
| 5 | exciting | 15 | came |
| 6 | black | 16 | angry |
| 7 | into | 17 | stayed |
| 8 | towards | 18 | few |
| 9 | back | 19 | kind |
| 10 | smooth | 20 | smiling |

*On tape*   Have the class describe the times they have seen work being done on pavements or roads. Play back a selection.

# Daily lesson 56

**Materials**

1 How to do cards—mother dressmaking, father at woodwork
2 Colour cubes—black, white, red, green

**Procedure**

Display picture of mother dressmaking. By question and response procedure have the children analyze what is depicted in the picture. What is mother doing? What tools and objects does she use? Detail each object. What is she making? Who for? Why? Detail foreground and background of the picture. Sum up the picture simply but lucidly. Repeat the same procedure with picture of father at woodwork.

*Instruction time*  Distribute the four colour cubes. Explain to the children that you are going to ask them to follow your instructions. Repeat instructions slowly at first, and then increase the pace of the game. Ensure that all of the class are attending to your instructions and not merely copying the actions of their neighbours.

1 Put white cube in your right hand (return to desk)
2 Put white cube on your right knee (return to desk)
3 Put black cube on your right knee (return to desk)
4 Put black and red cubes by (beside) your left foot (return to desk)
5 Put green cube on your left knee (return to desk)
6 Put red cube by your right foot.
7 Put green cube on your left knee and red cube on your right knee.

Carry on in this way, mixing up colour and positions of cubes. Probably it will be necessary to quieten down the class and remind them that they have to listen to and remember all the instructions very carefully. Insist that the class wait till the end of the instructions.

# Daily lesson 57

## Materials
Animal cards—group in threes: whale, shark, salmon, goldfish, fly, wasp, bee, caterpillar, python, worm, cobra, parrot, owl, seagull, camel, tiger, lion.

## Procedure
Explain that you are going to display three pictures, then ask the class to close their eyes and cover them with their hands. While they are doing this, take one picture away and then ask which one is missing. Preface each trial by saying 'no peeping now'. Ensure that the three cards displayed have a 'representative' from different groups. According to the response say 'Yes, it was a fish, but what kind of fish?' Or, 'Yes, it was a salmon, and what family does the salmon belong to?'

Some children will rely on the images they see, remembering the pictures of three animals rather than verbalizing to themselves the names of the pictures. Encourage them not just to look passively at the pictures, but to code the pictures by using words as an aid. Insist that they say the words in their heads—no whispering! Continue to remind the class how much easier it is if they use words to remember things by.

Display three cards ensuring that there is a clear difference in size among the three animals. Ask 'Which is the smallest?' 'Which is the biggest?' Repeat with various selections of two or three cards, getting the children to respond to the questions
1  Which is the smaller?
2  Which is the bigger?
3  Which is the smallest?
4  Which is the biggest?
5  This one is big, but this one is even _____ (bigger)
6  Here is a big one (small one) but here is the _____ (biggest, smallest)

# Daily lesson 58

## Materials
1 Picture cards—teapot, hammer, scissors, telephone, spade, shovel, newspaper, guitar, piano, iron, pencil sharpener
2 Nursery rhyme—*This is the way we . . .*

## Procedure
Do not display cards. Whisper to individuals to mime what they would do with one of the above objects. Ensure that the children use both hands, or hands and feet, and position their body correctly when miming. E.g. to mime using the telephone, the instrument should be placed to the ear while the other hand dials. With the guitar, one hand should strum the strings while the other not only holds the guitar but fingers the strings.

If the class cannot guess the first mime, invite another child to mime until the object is guessed. Do not yet display card. Ask the class to describe the object emphasizing size, shape, function and the material it is made of. Only after these two stages should the picture of the object be displayed. Describe (in simple structured language) the object again.

*Nursery rhyme*   After each object is mimed and described, repeat an appropriate verse of 'This is the way . . .' to the tune of *Here we go round the mulberry bush.*

# Daily lesson 59

## Materials
Bottle, paper bag, cardboard container, tin can, glass jar, polythene bag

## Procedure
Starting at one end of a row of six children ask each to name an object made out of one of the materials listed below. Each child has to repeat those names previously given and add his own. After the sixth, ask the rest of the class, 'In what way are these objects the same?' and elicit 'They are all made of . . .' Continue with the remainder of the list.
*Materials*—glass, wood, metal, cloth, paper, plastic

Display the containers listed under materials and ask the class what different items are usually packaged in these particular containers. Proceed as in activity one so that each child remembers what has previously been mentioned and adds one of his own. Ask the class for other containers and the objects they contain.

# Daily lesson 60

**Materials**
Tape recorder

**Procedure**
Explain to the class that you are going to read to them a story called *The pet shop* and that you want them to listen carefully to the story because you will ask them questions about it afterwards.

### The pet shop

The pet shop was in the centre of the town, up a narrow road off the main street. Kenneth and Julia had come across the shop just by chance, and what a lucky find it was.

They peered through the front window at first. There they could see dog and cat baskets, goldfish bowls and tanks, hamster and rabbit cages and little bags of different food for different animals. At the back of the window they could see dog collars and leads hanging from hooks on the wall, beside fishnets and birdcages.

They popped inside the shop. It was rather dark and there was a very pleasant fresh sort of smell — probably the pet food. All round the walls of the shop they could see every kind of small pet you could think of — birds, rabbits, hamsters, white mice, brown mice, goldfish and other tropical fish, tortoises, cats, dogs, even a monkey and a parrot!

And what a chattering noise there was. The birds whistled and screeched and pecked at the bars of their cage. The cats miaowed and clawed to get out of their baskets. The dogs and puppies barked and yelped, tugging at their leads. The monkey and the parrot made most noise of all! But the rabbits and hamsters and mice chewed quietly away. The goldfish swam sleepily around their bowl and the tortoise didn't make a move or sound.

The pet shop was very busy with girls and boys buying things for their pets. But not everyone was in the shop to buy. Some, like Kenneth and Julia, had just popped in to have a look at the animals. They didn't have a pet of their own at home. But they both decided to ask mum and dad if they could have one after seeing all these. The only difficulty was deciding which one to have!

Ask the class if they enjoyed the story. Then ask the following questions:
1. What was the name of the story?
2. What were the names of the boy and girl in the story?
3. Where in the town was the pet shop to be found?
4. What did Kenneth and Julia see in the window of the shop?
5. What was hanging at the back of the window?
6. What was the shop like inside?
7. What kinds of pet did they see inside the shop?
8. What noises did they hear?
9. What animals didn't make any noise?
10. What were some boys and girls doing in the shop?
11. What were other boys and girls doing in the shop?
12. What idea had the pet shop given Kenneth and Julia?
13. What was going to be difficult?

Ask the class to give the opposite of the following words. Explain 'opposite' and give examples. Preface each question with—'Give me the opposite of . . .'

| | | | |
|---|---|---|---|
| 1 | centre | 11 | fresh |
| 2 | narrow | 12 | every |
| 3 | by chance | 13 | small |
| 4 | lucky | 14 | out |
| 5 | front | 15 | quietly |
| 6 | first | 16 | busy |
| 7 | beside | 17 | didn't |
| 8 | inside | 18 | difficult |
| 9 | dark | 19 | gentle |
| 10 | pleasant | 20 | warm |

*On tape*  Get the class to describe any pet shop they have visited, or any pet they have. Play back a selection.

# Daily lesson 61

## Materials

1 Animal cards—cat, dog, hamster, rabbit, puppy
2 Tape recorder
3 Miscellaneous objects—blackboard duster, chalk and other items which can be seen in the classroom

## Procedure

Distribute the animal cards and miscellaneous objects to individuals in the class. Explain that you want them to tell the tape recorder about them. Ask more than mere description of the brighter children. Make a note of the position on the tape of no more than six of the best attempts and play these back to the class. It will be necessary to prompt the children as they talk but explain beforehand that you don't really want to do this.

Redistribute the cards and objects so that each child has a different item from the above activity. Draw four circles of different coloured chalk on the floor (two feet by two feet) so that all the children can easily see them. Explain the following game to them. 'When I say "I'm thinking of an animal", those children with animals in their hands stand up. Then I might say "this animal lives in a cage", and those whose animals don't live in a cage sit down. Then I might say "those whose animal has long ears come and put it in the blue circle", and someone has to guess who I mean.' This is a guessing game; the children have to guess which object or animal you are thinking of.

# Daily lesson 62

**Materials**

1 Furniture and house pictures—kitchen, lounge or living room, bedroom, bathroom
2 Furniture pictures—table, chair, armchair, stool, highchair, carpet, bed, dressing table, wardrobe, tallboy, cooker, washing machine, refrigerator, sofa, television, radio, radiogram, bookcase, heater, sideboard

**Procedure**

Display group two pictures individually. Have the children recall their names and in which room they would find each item. Having run through these quickly, display the four rooms in group one. Select a card from group two and invite a child to point to the item as displayed in one of the room pictures. Have the child structure his response verbally: 'Yes, this is a refrigerator, and here it is in the kitchen.' Discuss with the class the use made of each room.

*Nursery rhyme*  Finish by singing four verses of 'This is the way . . .' to the tune of *Here we go round the mulberry bush*.
*This is the way we waken up.*
*This is the way we wash our face.*
*This is the way we eat our food.*
*This is the way we read our books.*

# Daily lesson 63

**Materials**
1  Narrative picture—family in living room
2  Tape recorder
3  Paper and crayons

**Procedure**
Display narrative picture and elicit from the class the general theme of the picture, moving on to details after that. What are the individuals in the picture doing? What are the relationships of the people in the picture? How is the room furnished? From this base, get the children to draw and describe their living rooms. Emphasize that it is their own living rooms you are interested in. Get them especially to use the correct colours for floor covering, walls, curtains and furniture.

# Daily lesson 64

**Materials**
Articles of clothing cards

**Procedure**
Ask one of the class to approach your desk. While the rest of the class close their eyes, show him or her an article of clothing and ask him to mime putting it on. The rest of the class have to guess what it is. Remind the person who is 'it' to pay attention to details e.g. zippers, buttons, hoods, laces, buckles, glove fingers, cuff buttons, toggles etc. After each mime, question the answerer on why he thought of that article. Structure the differentiating features of each article verbally. Ask the class what different articles go on the head, on the feet, on the top of the body, on the legs, which are worn in cold weather and which in warm weather.

Play an odd one out game with the cards. Display three cards, one of which is 'odd'. Use the following features as a basis for odd one out:
1  indoor/outdoor wear
2  parts of the body
3  presence or absence of fasteners
4  sex differences

# Daily lesson 65

**Materials**
Tape recorder

**Procedure**
Explain to the class that you are going to read them a story called *A visit to grandma's* and that you want them to listen carefully to the story because you will ask them questions about it afterwards.

### A visit to grandma's

Paula's parents would often take her to visit her grandma's house. She liked this very much. Grandma's house was different from her own and Paula liked to explore in all the corners of the house.

She liked the front room best. There was an old record player there that never seemed to be used except when Paula took it out. She would have to turn a handle to wind it up before it would play. The one at home was an electric record player that you just plugged in. Grandma's records were fairly old too and Paula wasn't really fond of them. She didn't like the music and she couldn't make out the words. But it was fun playing the record player all the same.

There was also a big glass cabinet in the front room in which grandma kept all her best dishes and glasses. Paula liked opening and closing the doors of the cabinet and would pretend to have tea parties. She would arrange all the cups and saucers and plates carefully and lay out the very odd shaped spoons and knives that grandma kept in a drawer.

Most of all Paula liked grandma's big settee. This settee was so big that it seemed to take up all the space on the carpet. She had never seen a settee of such a size anywhere else. It was very old. Paula would stand on the arm of the settee and jump whoops! down onto the seat, bouncing up and down before rolling gently onto the floor.

Paula's parents liked to see her having fun but they didn't really like her playing with the record player, or the glass cabinet or on the settee. They were frightened she might damage them. But grandma said she didn't mind as long as Paula was happy and was careful not to hurt herself. So Paula was careful not to hurt herself, and careful not to damage grandma's record player, glass cabinet or settee. She knew she would never be allowed to play at home like this.

And that was really, I suppose, why Paula liked coming to grandma's house. She could do things there that she couldn't at home, as long as she was careful.

Ask the class if they enjoyed the story. Then ask the following questions:
1 What was the name of the story?
2 What was the name of the little girl in the story?
3 Which room did Paula like most in grandma's house?
4 What three things did Paula play with in this room?
5 What did she have to do to the record player before it played?
6 How was it different from the one she had at home?
7 What did the glass cabinet hold?
8 What did Paula pretend to have?

100

9  What was kept in the drawer of the glass cabinet?
10  What did Paula like best in the room?
11  What did she do on the settee?
12  Did Paula's parents mind what she did? Why?
13  Did grandma mind?
14  Why did Paula really like coming to grandma's house?

Ask the class to give the opposite of the following words. Explain 'opposite' and give examples. Preface each question with: 'Give the opposite of . . .'

| | | | |
|---|---|---|---|
| 1 | liked | 11 | stand |
| 2 | different | 12 | down |
| 3 | front | 13 | gently |
| 4 | best | 14 | break |
| 5 | old | 15 | didn't |
| 6 | never | 16 | happy |
| 7 | out | 17 | careful |
| 8 | opening | 18 | couldn't |
| 9 | carefully | 19 | kind |
| 10 | anywhere | 20 | spoiled |

*On tape*  Ask the class to describe what they like most about visiting grandma's house, or any other relative's house.

# Daily lesson 66

**Materials**
None

**Procedure**
Say 'What do we do with our eyes?' Confirm reponses such as 'close them', 'blink them', 'cry' and 'wink' but emphasize especially 'we see with our eyes'. Repeat for ears, nose, mouth and hands, confirming any feasible response but emphasizing 'we hear with our eyes', 'we smell with our nose', 'we taste with our mouth' and 'we feel and touch with our hands'. How would we test the sense of the following?

| | |
|---|---|
| 1 salt is sweet | 9 buses are big |
| 2 syrup is sticky | 10 tables are hard |
| 3 dogs bark | 11 the sky is green |
| 4 snow is hot | 12 the moon is square |
| 5 dogs' fur is soft | 13 dogs bark quietly |
| 6 food smells nice | 14 flowers are colourful |
| 7 brick is hard | 15 plasticine is soft |
| 8 car horns are loud | |

Have the children mime in an exaggerated way the five senses of looking, hearing, smelling, tasting and touching. Have them:
1 look far out to sea; peer at small print
2 cup their hand to their ear as if deaf, cover their ears as if deafened by a loud noise
3 sniff at a pleasant smell and at an unpleasant smell
4 taste something pleasant and something unpleasant
5 touch something soft and hard, hot and cold

Say the following and invite replies:
1 We look with our eyes and hear with our _____.
2 We feel with our hands and see with our _____.
3 We smell with our noses and taste with our _____.
4 We listen with our ears and sniff with our _____.
5 A cat has kittens and a dog has _____.
6 Brick is hard and plasticine is _____.
7 Dogs bark and lions _____.
8 Syrup is sweet and salt is _____.
9 The moon is round and a desk top is _____.
10 Ice cream is cold and soup is _____.

# Daily lesson 67

**Materials**
Tape recorder

**Procedure**
Read the following story to the class slowly. Tell them that they must listen very carefully because you will be asking them questions about it afterwards.

Once upon a time there was a little black poodle named Peppy. One sunny day he was sitting on the pavement outside his house. Suddenly he noticed a large juicy bone on the other side of the street. Without thinking or looking he jumped to his feet and ran straight across the road to fetch the bone. Just as he did so a car came along the road, and the driver just managed to brake and stop before he hit Peppy. Peppy got such a scare that he stood shaking and crying in the middle of the road. The driver picked him up and brought him home. As he carried him Peppy heard him say, 'What a silly poodle to run across the road without looking first to see if there were any cars coming. You're lucky not to have been hurt, little poodle. So remember—next time look and listen before you run.' And Peppy promised himself that he would remember everything the driver said.

Question the class on specific points raised in the story. Question also on the wisdom of the poodle, the actions of the driver and the general 'moral' of the story.

*On tape* Using the tape recorder, ask the children to narrate a story, real or imagined, but preferably real, about any accident or near accident they have witnessed or any lucky escape they have had.

# Daily lesson 68

**Materials**

How to do cards—cleaning shoes, washing clothes, setting a table

**Procedure**

Display one picture. Elicit or teach what is going on in the picture. Take account of the background, middle ground and foreground. Itemize the articles required for cleaning one's shoes and use the differences of colour, style and type between the picture and the class as focus of interest. Elicit or explain why we clean our shoes (for smartness and protection) and what shoes can be made of. Display the other pictures individually and proceed as above. Finish this section by having the class recite with actions 'This is the way we . . .' (to the tune *Here we go round the mulberry bush*).

*Following instructions*    Have the class stand by their desks and follow simple instructions, using their left hand, right hand, left foot, right foot etc. Proceed in three stages as in previous lessons.

Stage 1   Stand with your back to the class and have them copy, without verbal instructions, what you do.

Stage 2   Still standing with your back to the class, have them copy your actions, giving verbal instructions also.

Stage 3   Have them follow instructions given verbally only.

# Daily lesson 69

**Materials**

Tool cards (or collection of objects from the classroom)—glue, iron, clothes pegs, needle, thread, soap, towel, pen, pencil, tin opener, straw, hat, ball, book, house, pliers

**Procedure**

Before displaying any cards, ask the class individually the meanings of the above words. Phrase the question 'What do we mean by . . . ?' or 'What is the meaning of . . . ?' Children will tend to respond with one word, or at best a response describing some physical feature of shape or colour. Try to encourage higher level responses, especially in terms of function, and always repeat the child's response in a simple well structured sentence. Have other children repeat your well structured response. It may be necessary to use prompting questions such as 'Yes, but what do we use it for?' But try to get the class to respond with higher level responses without having to keep on prompting. After each word has been defined, display the picture and move on to the next. Then ask the following questions, eliciting agreement or disagreement, with confirming or correcting explanations:

Do we wash our hands with a needle?

Do we read a ball?

Do we write with a towel?

Do we suck things through a tin opener?

Do we live in a house?

Proceed with similar questions.

# Daily lesson 70

**Materials**
Tape recorder

**Procedure**
Explain to the class that you are going to read them a story called *Ships in the harbour* and that you want them to listen carefully to the story because you will ask them questions about it afterwards.

### Ships in the harbour

Julie and Scott loved to go down to see the ships in the harbour. During the week the harbour was very busy and quite dangerous too, but on Sundays when they visited there was no work being done. So Julie and Scott and their father could walk round slowly, stopping and looking at anything that caught their interest.

The harbour was always packed with boats and ships on Sundays. There were big and little ships, and some ships that were so huge that Julie and Scott couldn't see how long, or how tall, they were! Julie thought that most of the little ships looked very dirty and rusty and they always seemed to be cluttered up with long thick rope, bits of iron and funny looking bits of machinery.

The big ships looked very clean and smart by comparison. They were often painted white and had only small patches of rust on them. Julie and Scott could just about see through some of the windows in the sides of the big boats. These were called portholes, so daddy said.

Although there were so many boats and ships in the harbour, it was usually very quiet on Sundays. You could hear seagulls squawk, squawk, squawking away and the sound of the water lapping the walls of the harbour, but very little else.

Stacked beside the ships on the quayside were such a lot of different things—enormous stacks of wood; huge heaps of black shiny coal; crates the size of a room. Julie and Scott often wondered what was in these crates. They would love to have played inside them.

Soon it was time to go home for lunch and they all piled into the car. It was a lovely way to spend Sunday mornings. They hoped they would come back again next Sunday.

Ask the class if they enjoyed the story. Then ask the following questions:
1 What was the name of the story?
2 What were the names of the boy and girl in the story?
3 Why did they visit the harbour only on Sundays?
4 What did Julie think of the little ships?
5 What did the children think of the big ships?
6 What sounds did they hear at the harbour?
7 What sort of things were stacked on the quayside?
8 How had Julie, Scott and their father travelled to the harbour?

Ask the class to give the opposite of the following words. Explain 'opposite' and give examples. Preface each question with 'Give me the opposite of . . .'

| | |
|---|---|
| 1 loved | 11 enormous |
| 2 dangerous | 12 shiny |
| 3 slowly | 13 inside |
| 4 long | 14 go |
| 5 tall | 15 lovely |
| 6 dirty | 16 would |
| 7 cluttered | 17 far |
| 8 thick | 18 deep |
| 9 white | 19 hungry |
| 10 quiet | 20 happy |

*On tape*  Get the class to describe their visits to a harbour or canal and play back a selection.

# Daily lesson 71

**Materials**
Animal cards—a selection of any used in previous lessons

**Procedure**
Distribute an animal card to each member of the class. Ask each child to name his animal. Arrange the class in couples. Using one couple to demonstrate have the class repeat: 'This (animal) is mine, that (animal) is yours.' Have each member of the pair say this phrase. Let the class say it in unison and select children who are having difficulty to say it alone. Then repeat to the class, 'Yes, this (animal) is mine—it belongs to me, and these animals are yours—they belong to you.'

Rearrange the class into groups of four (two boys and two girls). Following a similar procedure as above, teach the relationships as follows, 'This (animal) is mine; that (animal) is yours. That (animal) is hers, and that (animal) is his.' Have the appropriate members of each foursome repeat in unison with others from similar foursomes. Have individuals repeat alone. Emphasize that children preface animals not belonging to them with 'that' and preface the animal they hold with 'this'. Emphasize 'mine, yours, his and hers', and the 'and' before the last member's item. Finally select one foursome and say, 'Yes, this animal is mine—it belongs to me; that animal is hers—it belongs to her; that animal is his—it belongs to him; that animal is hers—it belongs to her, and that animal is his—it belongs to him.'

Redistribute the cards. Have the children stand in a U shape. Say to one member of the class, 'I see your (animal) has four legs. Pick someone else in the class who has an animal with four legs.' After the selection has been made invite this new child to select another animal which is like his. After each selection the previous child sits down. Ask the children to explain their selection of 'like'. Continue until all the class are sitting. Redistribute the cards and repeat for as long as time and enthusiasm permit.

# Daily lesson 72

**Materials**
Nursery rhyme—*Monday's child*

**Procedure**
Say, 'Who can tell me what day we call today?' Having established the day, have the rest of the class repeat the name in unison. 'Yes, it's——today.' Then play the nursery rhyme. Ask what days were mentioned in the poem. Elicit or teach the days mentioned. Select seven children from the class and name them Monday to Sunday. Have the class chant their names two or three times. Repeat the name given to each of the seven in front of the class and then ask each of these seven to give their names in order. Return the children to their places.

Get the children to carry out the following instructions.
1 Clap your hands twice, that is two times.
2 Clap your hands once, that is only one time.
3 Clap your hands thrice, that is three times.
Repeat these three instructions at random, two or three times. Then add additional instructions like:
1 Clap your hands once, and after that put your hands on your head.
2 Clap your hands twice, and after that put your hands on your toes.
Continue in this way. Ask members of the class to give similar instructions. Insist on their using 'once', 'twice' and 'thrice' and on their adding 'and after that' before issuing additional instructions.

# Daily lesson 73

**Materials**
1 Colour cubes—red, green, brown, orange, blue, black, white and yellow
2 Narrative picture—zoo scene

**Procedure**
Distribute the colour cubes so that each child has a set of eight. Have the class match your colour cube first without verbal instructions, then along with verbal instructions, and finally with verbal instructions only. Take a note of those children who cannot yet follow stage three.

Have the class make the following 'chains' on the basis of verbal instructions only. Insist that the class work from left to right.

| | | | |
|---|---|---|---|
| 1 | black, white, red | 10 | brown, white, green |
| 2 | black, white, green | 11 | brown, white, blue |
| 3 | black, white, blue | 12 | brown, white, yellow |
| 4 | red, green, yellow | 13 | blue, red, green |
| 5 | green, red, yellow | 14 | blue, black, brown |
| 6 | yellow, red, green | 15 | black, blue, brown |
| 7 | orange, yellow, red | 16 | orange, green, red |
| 8 | orange, yellow, black | 17 | white, brown, red |
| 9 | orange, yellow, white | 18 | white, green, blue |

Display narrative picture—zoo scene. Have the class analyze the picture—what animals are pictured, how many of each type, how are they housed, what colour are they, what is the weather like? What are the relationships of the people visiting the zoo?

# Daily lesson 74

**Materials**
1 Narrative poster—zoo scene
2 Tape recorder

**Procedure**
Remind the class of yesterday's lesson and display poster. Have the class individually tell the tape recorder of a visit they have made to the zoo or of a zoo they have seen on television or of zoo animals they have seen at a circus. Have the children emphasize the noises each animal makes, and ask them to imitate the characteristic movements of some of the more bizarre animals (seals, elephants, monkeys etc).

# Daily lesson 75

**Materials**
Tape recorder

**Procedure**
Explain to the class that you are going to read them a story called *A new pair of shoes* and that you want them to listen carefully to the story because you will ask them questions about it afterwards.

### A new pair of shoes

Sheila and Neil were out shopping with their mother. Out shopping for a pair of shoes for each of them. Both of them had been in shoe shops before, but it was always exciting and fun to go again and choose a new pair. Neither of them knew exactly what sort of shoes they would like.

The shop was a very modern one in the main street. There were several large glass windows at the front of the shop, displaying all sorts of shoes. Most of them were ladies' shoes, some very expensive and some not quite so dear. There were evening shoes, walking shoes, shoes with high heels and shoes with just a little heel. There were black shoes, red shoes, white shoes, shoes of every colour in the rainbow. Some were plain, others had buttons or bows or buckles or very fancy stitching.

There were some men's shoes in the window—mostly black or brown, some with buckles, but mostly with laces. There weren't many children's shoes on display, but mummy knew that there would be plenty to choose from inside.

In they went, all excited. The shop was very large inside, with a high ceiling. It was brightly lit and carpeted from wall to wall. Along one side of the shop were shelves, completely filled with shoe boxes. They sat down and a shop assistant, smartly dressed in black, walked up to them. 'Can I help you?' she asked politely. Mother explained that they had come to buy shoes for Sheila and Neil. Could they see some from which to choose? The shop assistant was soon back with several pairs—different colours, different styles and different sizes. Sheila and Neil tried on this pair and that pair, walking up and down the carpet to see if they were comfortable and fitted well. The shop assistant helped them in and out of each pair with a shoe horn.

'Well, what do you think Neil, and you Sheila?' asked mummy. 'I like this pair I have on mummy,' said Sheila. They were a pair of navy blue simply styled shoes with a small gold buckle on each. Neil preferred the first pair he had tried on—a pair of brown shoes with laces.

Their new shoes were parcelled up and they put on the ones they came in. They felt strange and looked very old and shabby compared to the shiny new ones they had just been trying on. But no doubt their new ones would soon look the same way.

Ask the class if they enjoyed the story. Then ask the following questions:
1 What was the name of the story?
2 What were the names of the boy and girl in the story?
3 Where was the shoe shop and what was it like on the outside?
4 What kind of ladies' shoes were displayed?

5 What colours were they?
6 How were they decorated?
7 What colour were the men's shoes mostly?
8 What did the shop look like inside?
9 Who came to serve them?
10 How did she help Neil and Sheila?
11 What sort did Sheila choose?
12 What sort did Neil choose?
13 How did they feel about their old shoes?

Ask the class the meaning of the following words:

| | | | |
|---|---|---|---|
| 1 | shoes | 6 | shoe horn |
| 2 | shop | 7 | seat |
| 3 | window | 8 | shop assistant |
| 4 | carpet | 9 | door |
| 5 | shelf | 10 | box |

Ask the class to give the opposite of the following words:

| | | | |
|---|---|---|---|
| 1 | new | 11 | different |
| 2 | like | 12 | comfortable |
| 3 | modern | 13 | simple |
| 4 | ladies | 14 | first |
| 5 | expensive | 15 | strange |
| 6 | plain | 16 | shabby |
| 7 | high | 17 | quiet |
| 8 | brightly | 18 | quickly |
| 9 | smart | 19 | pleased |
| 10 | buy | 20 | busy |

*On tape*   Ask the class to describe any visits they have made to shoe shops.
Replay a selection.

# Daily lesson 76

**Materials**
Tape recorder

**Procedure**
Read the following story. Read it very slowly, hanging onto almost every word, while at the same time maintaining the natural flow and structure of the language. Remind the class to listen very carefully because you will ask them questions about it later.

One day, a little girl called Angela went to visit her cousins. They were called Rona and Diane. Angela was only a little girl aged three but because she was almost always happy and laughing, her cousins, who were older than she was, always looked forward to seeing her.

This day they took her to see some ponies who lived in a field quite near their daddy's house. The ponies ran to the fence to welcome the three girls. And the girls ran about feeding the ponies with bunches of grass. One pony especially, named Biscuit, seemed very hungry and by mistake he nipped little Angela's fingers as he took some grass from her hand. Angela burst out crying and Rona and Diane were a little upset. 'Naughty pony, naughty pony,' said Angela, and had she been taller she would have smacked the pony for biting her. Rona and Diane tried to explain to her that the pony hadn't really meant to bite her; it was a mistake. But little Angela was too young to understand. But funnily enough Rona and Diane thought that the pony, Biscuit, had heard them and understood because they noticed that he was extra careful from then on to take the grass from Angela's hand very carefully and gently.

Soon it was time to go home and the girls said goodbye to Biscuit and the other ponies. And, just as they left, Angela shouted back to Biscuit, 'Bye bye Biscuit, I'm sorry I said you were naughty. I know now you only made a mistake. Bye bye Biscuit.' Rona and Diane looked at each other and smiled. Biscuit looked up and seemed to smile too. Then he went on munching.

Ask the class if they enjoyed the story. Then question them about it. Ask factual questions mostly, but also ask the class to exercise their judgment on Biscuit's actions, Angela's reaction and whether they both understood later that they had made a mistake.

*On tape*   From this, move on to get the class as individuals to talk about occasions when they've been misunderstood, or feel they've been mistreated. Ask questions about what happened, how they felt and how the other parties concerned felt. Where necessary verbalize the children's feelings and those of the others concerned. Ask questions such as 'Do you think that was a fair (right, correct, kind, honest) thing to do?' 'How would you have felt if that had happened to you?'

# Daily lesson 77

**Materials**
1 Toy telephone
2 Shop pictures
3 Nursery rhymes—*Pat a cake, pat a cake, Simple Simon*

**Procedure**
Display all the shop pictures at once. Revise quickly the name given to each shop and the kind of goods sold in each. Invite two children to converse over the telephone, one pretending to be the shopkeeper and one a customer ordering goods. Limit the kind of goods ordered to two or three. Encourage correct use of quantity or container (a *tin* of peas, one *pound* of steak, a *packet* of tea). Have the shopkeeper repeat the order.

Although it may be difficult to teach young children, it seems worthwhile to encourage correct telephone technique:
1 Shopkeeper identifies himself appropriately and says, 'May I help you?'
2 Customer identifies himself/herself.
3 Each order prefaced by saying something like 'I wonder if you could deliver the following to my house?'
4 Make sure the order is clear.
5 Shopkeeper repeats order and thanks the customer.
6 Customer thanks shopkeeper and says 'Goodbye'.

*Nursery rhymes*   Finish by repeating each nursery rhyme, if possible to music.

# Daily lesson 78

**Materials**
1 Narrative poster—bonfire night
2 Paints and paper

**Procedure**
Display narrative poster and have the children analyze the action, colours, people, weather etc. Discuss particularly the sounds and smells they will have experienced on such an occasion, also the dangers. Remember to insist on well structured sentences in response to your questions and also to repeat the response in confirming and correcting well structured sentences.

Have the class sit at their desks with their heads leaning on their arms, and eyes closed. Ask for absolute silence so that all that can be heard is the wind outside. Speak in a very soft voice so as not to disturb the silence. The children should be 'listening to the silence'. Then ask them to guess at three sounds in succession:
1 a drawer opening
2 a ball bouncing once
3 a piece of chalk falling
Return to silence and repeat with the following sounds:
1 chalk drawn across the board
2 a door handle being turned
3 a pencil being sharpened
Return to silence and repeat:
1 a bottle of water being emptied (try to reduce the sound of water falling into the basin)
2 a tap running
3 a key being turned
Elicit the objects being used and get the class to describe in well structured language the sounds being made.

Get the class to paint a bonfire, using as many colours as they can, but especially yellows, oranges and reds. Use black paper if possible. Ensure that the children know the names of the colours they are using.

# Daily lesson 79

## Materials
Animal cards—cuckoo, worm, adder, turtle, snail, tortoise, hedgehog, octopus, porpoise, crab, swordfish, penguin

## Procedure
Elicit or teach the names given to the above creatures. Emphasize similarities and differences in terms of physical characteristics or habitat. Tell a little story about the more bizarre features of some of the creatures e.g. the snail, turtle and tortoise who carry their 'houses' with them.

*Rhyming game* Ask the class to give you words which *end* in the same sound as the words you give. On occasion limit the responses to animals, colours or flowers.

| | | | |
|---|---|---|---|
| 1 | bat | 13 | toy |
| 2 | house | 14 | pant |
| 3 | log | 15 | to |
| 4 | big | 16 | fill |
| 5 | laugh | 17 | blue |
| 6 | tree | 18 | bed |
| 7 | feel | 19 | mellow |
| 8 | flush | 20 | remember |
| 9 | carrot | 21 | soon |
| 10 | hole | 22 | door |
| 11 | tale | 23 | tear |
| 12 | fear | 24 | moss |

Ask the class to give you words which *begin* with the same sound as the word you give. Use the same list as above.

# Daily lesson 80

**Materials**
1 Tape recorder
2 Nursery rhyme—*Pat a cake, pat a cake*

**Procedure**
Explain to the class that you are going to read them a story called *The baker's shop* and that you want them to listen carefully to the story because you will ask them questions about it afterwards.

## The baker's shop

Winifred and Tom were out shopping with their mother. They had done a lot of shopping already and now they were going to the baker.

They stopped outside the baker's shop and looked at what was displayed in the window. They could see freshly baked bread, cream cakes, biscuits, sponge cakes, and right in the middle of the window was an iced birthday cake for some lucky boy or girl. It made their mouths water just looking at it.

In they went to the shop and stood waiting in the queue to be served. The shop assistants behind the counter looked very clean and smart, dressed in white overalls. Winifred noticed how clean and tidy the rest of the shop was too. Everything was arranged neatly in rows. There was white bread, and brown bread, some wrapped in white tissue paper, some not wrapped at all. There were dozens of tins of biscuits lining shelf upon shelf at the back of the shop. And finally, there was a large glass display case bursting with very fancy looking cakes—chocolate cakes, meringues, cream buns and doughnuts.

At last it was their turn to be served. Tom was buying the bread today. 'Could I have one sliced loaf of white bread, please and two packets of biscuits,' he asked the shop assistant politely. The shop assistant got his order quickly and handed them over the counter. Tom in turn placed them in the basket that Winifred held and then he handed over the money for the bread and biscuits. He got some change back and gave it to his mother.

Winifred and Tom liked to go shopping with their mother, especially when they got the chance to actually ask for things and hand over the money. It made them feel so grown up, even although they knew they were still very young.

Ask the class if they enjoyed the story. Then ask the following questions:
1 What was the name of the story?
2 What were the names of the boy and girl in the sotry?
3 Did they often go shopping with their mother?
4 What did they see displayed in the baker's shop window?
5 Describe the shop assistants.
6 Was the shop busy?
7 Was the shop clean and tidy?
8 What sort of bread was there?
9 What was there at the back of the shop?
10 What did Winifred notice in the glass display case?
11 What did Tom buy?

12  Who held the basket?
13  What did Winifred and Tom like best about shopping?

Ask the class the opposite of the following words. Explain 'opposite' and give examples. Preface each question by saying 'Give me the opposite of . . .'

1  out
2  stopped
3  fresh
4  lucky
5  boy
6  clean
7  smart
8  wrapped
9  back
10  finally
11  quickly
12  liked
13  grown up

*Nursery rhyme*   Have the class listen to *Pat a cake, pat a cake* and then recite it for the tape recorder.

# Daily lesson 81

**Materials**

1 Tool cards—group one: knife, fork, spoon; group two: kettle, saucepan, toaster; group three: hammer, nail, pliers; group four: mirror, towel, soap
2 Means of transport cards—group one: legs, horse, mule; group two: camel, car, lorry; group three: van, train, plane; group four: boat, ship, bus
3 Animal cards—group one: cat, dog, hamster; group two: mouse, puppy, kitten; group three: horse, cow, pig; group four: sheep, goat, calf

**Procedure**

Select from your collection the three cards in group one of each category—giving nine cards in all. Display these out of sight of the class. Explain to the class that you are going to play a memory game, called Kim's game. You will let them see these pictures for just thirty seconds and ask them to recall the items they have seen. Let the class see the display of nine cards for thirty seconds. Insist on quietness—no whispering to distract others. Then hide the cards and ask the class to recall the items. Only a few should recall all the items. Next elicit from the class what aids they used or neglected to use in memorizing the cards. Did they count the nine cards? Did they see that there were three easily identifiable groups of three cards each? If not, encourage them to use these two simple techniques to aid their memory.

Display groups two, three and four in turn. Take a note of the number of successes as the trials progress to see if a temporary improvement is achieved. Always encourage the children to verbalize to themselves the names of each item, count how many items there are (if they can) and classify into the most obvious groups.

# Daily lesson 82

**Materials**

1 Occupation cards—hairdresser, barber, car mechanic, actor, artist, glazier, tailor, pilot, soldier, lollipop man, bricklayer, shop assistant, dentist, coalman, milkman, butcher, baker
2 Colour cubes—eight basic colours as in lesson 54

**Procedure**

Ask the following questions and elicit more information about the work a person does from the child who answers.

1  Who sets hair?
2  Who cuts hair?
3  Who would mend a car?
4  Who plays a part in the theatre or television?
5  Who paints pictures?
6  Who mends broken windows?
7  Who makes clothes?
8  Who flies aeroplanes?
9  Who fights in an army?
10  Who helps us cross the road at school?
11  Who builds houses?
12  Who serves customers in shops?
13  Who attends to our teeth?
14  Who delivers fuel for our fires?
15  Who delivers milk?
16  Who runs a shop that sells meat?
17  Who runs a shop that sells bread?

Distribute colour cubes. Repeat the exercises as suggested in previous lessons. Then let the class make colour chains. Give different but challenging chains for the class to attempt.

# Daily lesson 83

## Materials

1 Family relationship cards—mother, father, grandmother (2), grandfather (2), uncle, aunt, sister, brother, cousin, niece, nephew, boy, girl, baby, friend, neighbour, colleague
2 Tape recorder

## Procedure

Revise family relationships taught previously. Then arrange cards on the board in a family tree working down from grandparents, so that the class can follow the links from grandparents, to parents and to themselves. Explain especially the relationship of their parents to their grandparents.

Similarly arrange cards to illustrate the relationships of their uncle and aunt to their parents and to themselves. Repeat for cousin, niece and nephew.

*On tape*   Ask several of the class to give their full name and their address. Explain that full name means their first name and their last name. Explain that by 'address' you mean where they live, or where their house is i.e. name of street, road, avenue, terrace, lane etc and the number of the house. Make them repeat their name and address in a well structured sentence: 'My name is John Smith and my address is 12 High Street, Townsville.' Let some of the class record these details on tape and play back. Invite comments about clarity of speech and ease of understanding. Encourage the children to speak slowly.

Invite the class to complete the following sentences:

1 My mother is a woman; my father is a _____ .
2 Boys grow up to be men and girls to be _____ .
3 Mother is to father as grandmother is to _____ .
4 My mother's mother is a grandmother; my mother's father is a _____ .
5 My mother's sister is an aunt; my mother's brother is an _____ .
6 Henry is my brother; Linda is my _____ .

# Daily lesson 84

**Materials**

1 Shape cards—i.e. cards with drawings of the following shapes on them: horizontal line, vertical line, diagonal line, cross (St Andrew), cross (St George), circle, square, ellipse
2 Picture of the sea to illustrate horizontal; picture of a tree or flagpole or chimney stack for vertical
3 Coloured crayons and paper

**Procedure**

The purpose of this lesson is not so much to teach children to draw shapes as to let them hear words associated with shapes: straight, up, down, along, across, cross, narrow, round, point, angle, top and bottom, start and finish, here and there, above and below, round, square etc. Most children in the infant stage will be competent enough to draw acceptable reproductions of all the above shapes. They may have some difficulty with the square. The procedure to follow is simply to draw each shape slowly on the board, commenting as you go and then inviting the class to copy. Correct only gross errors e.g. lines crossing too far off the mid points in the crosses or squares too much like rectangles. Remember, the emphasis is on the words associated with shapes. Comment as you draw on the board and invite the class to comment. When teaching individuals comment also on what you are doing and invite the pupil to repeat what you say.

# Daily lesson 85

**Materials**
Tape recorder

**Procedure**
Explain to the class that you are going to read them a story called *Favourite toys* and that you want them to listen carefully to the story because you will ask them questions about it afterwards.

## Favourite toys

Douglas and Wendy had quite a lot of toys. They had got them as presents mostly—for birthdays, on holiday, at Christmas time, and surprise presents from mummy and daddy or grandma and grandpa. Like most other girls and boys they had favourite toys.

Douglas had two favourite toys. One was a set of coloured bricks. There were red bricks, blue bricks, yellow bricks and white bricks and more—bricks of every colour in the rainbow. Sometimes he built a tower with the bricks. Higher and higher he would build them until crash! down they fell with a clatter. Sometimes he built bridges or tunnels. Sometimes he used them for fences if he was playing at zoos or farms. Sometimes he built houses with them.

His other favourite toy was a top which he had learned to spin round and round, faster and faster, so that it could stay up for ages and ages. Sometimes he spun the top on the floor and it would gradually move across the floor, wobbling more and more until it struck a piece of furniture and would lie motionless on its side. Sometimes he would spin it on a table top and he would blow it nearer and nearer to the edge of the table until wheeeeee! down it would fall.

Wendy loved a small brown furry teddy bear which she called Cocoa most of all. She had had this teddy bear for ages, ever since she was a little girl, and she always took it to bed with her. It was quite old now, almost as old as she was. She would lie awake at night sometimes, speaking to Cocoa, tucking the blankets round him to make sure he wasn't cold and sometimes scolding him too if he wouldn't go to sleep. She couldn't imagine ever being without Cocoa; he was just like one of the family.

Both Douglas and Wendy played a lot with the rest of their toys and with the toys that their friends had. And they would share their toys with their friends too. But somehow Douglas never felt happy to share his bricks or his top with anyone else, and Wendy usually clung firmly to Cocoa. These toys were special toys, their very own favourites.

Ask the class if they enjoyed the story. Then ask the following questions:
1 What was the name of the story?
2 What were the names of the boy and girl in the story?
3 Where had they got most of their toys from?
4 What were Douglas's favourite toys?
5 What did he build with his bricks?
6 Where did he play with his top?
7 What was Wendy's favourite toy?
8 What was its name?

9 How long had Wendy had Cocoa?
10 What did she do with Cocoa at night time?
11 Did Douglas and Wendy share their toys with friends?
12 Why didn't they share their favourite toys?

Ask the class to give the opposite of the following words. Explain 'opposite' and give examples. Preface each question with: 'Give me the opposite of ...'

| | | | |
|---|---|---|---|
| 1 | more | 11 | nearer |
| 2 | sometimes | 12 | loved |
| 3 | higher | 13 | always |
| 4 | down | 14 | old |
| 5 | round | 15 | awake |
| 6 | faster | 16 | cold |
| 7 | up | 17 | without |
| 8 | move | 18 | like |
| 9 | motionless | 19 | friends |
| 10 | top | 20 | happy |

*On tape* Get the class to talk about their favourite toys. Play back a selection.

# Daily lesson 86

**Materials**
How to do cards—hammering a nail, sawing a piece of wood, moulding with plasticine, tightening screws, answering the telephone, closing and locking a door

**Procedure**
Display one picture at a time. Elicit and/or teach the names of the objects used in each activity. Teach especially around the words used to describe each activity and insist on individuals in the class using as many of these words as they can.
1 hammer, nail, into, plank of wood, through, on top of, bent, bang, split, join, together
2 saw, through, edge, teeth, plank of wood, hold, lean, back and forth, across, cut, piece, large, small, smooth
3 hard, soft, knead, lump, soft, hard, long, slim, large, small, model, rub
4 screw, slot, into, through, lean, screwdriver, sharp, handle, turn, round, press
5 receiver, listen, speak, remember, lift, replace, number
6 key, lock, handle, turn, gentle, gently, round, latch

*Miming*   Invite individuals to mime the following activities and let the rest of the class guess what they are doing. Insist on a structured sentence in every response.
1 hopping across the floor
2 running round in circles
3 marching
4 drying dishes
5 washing dishes
6 turning on a tap
7 locking a door
8 hammering a nail
9 throwing a ball
10 waving goodbye
11 sawing wood
12 bouncing a ball
13 catching a ball
14 cleaning windows
15 making a bed
16 pushing a pram
17 riding a bike

Where appropriate, invite the class to discuss the tools, objects and items used in each activity and get them to elaborate on the actions e.g. 'He's drying dishes. He would need a dishcloth and the dishes. He'd rub the dishes with the cloth until they were dry then place them in a pile and put them in the cupboard. He'd have to be careful and not let them fall.'

# Daily lesson 87

**Materials**
Narrative picture—flooding in a town, countryside or farm

**Procedure**
Have the class analyze the picture. Have them try and explain what has happened. What will the damage be? What are the dangers? What would you do if it happened? What would you save first if it happened? What would float and why? What would sink and why? How could the mess be cleared up? How could the flood be prevented? How would the area immediately surrounding the school be affected (the houses, the shops etc)?

Divide the class into five groups. Invite each group in turn to name as many members of the following classes as possible in half a minute. Keep a tally of members mentioned. Make sure that each child in every group takes a turn. Do not allow a bright child to dominate his group.
1  animals (excluding birds and fish)
2  furniture
3  clothing
4  tools
5  occupations
6  miscellaneous objects in the classroom
7  colours or shapes
8  seasons of the year, months of the year, days of the week
9  foodstuffs
10  birds and fish

# Daily lesson 88

**Materials**

None

**Procedure**

Read the following story. Read it slowly, hanging on almost every word and/or phrase.

### The birthday party

It was Saturday at last. Thelma had looked forward so much to this day because it was her birthday. Today she was five years old. Mummy had helped her prepare a party. She had invited six of her friends. Three of them lived in the same street as she did. Three of them she had met at school.

They played all sorts of games at the party. And they had lots of things to eat. They all had fun setting the table with paper cups and plates and straws and spoons. They had sandwiches, jelly, ice cream, lemonade and so many other things that they couldn't remember them all.

Thelma's friends had been very kind to her. They gave her some very exciting presents—a jigsaw, different coloured crayons, a book of stories and a book of nursery rhymes. How she would remember this birthday.

When the party was over Thelma and her friends said goodbye to one another. Thelma thanked them for coming to the party and for their lovely presents. They thanked Thelma for inviting them to the party. How nice it is to have friends. How nice it is to have birthdays.

Ask the class if they enjoyed the story. Then ask the following questions:
1  What was the name of the story?
2  What was the little girl's name?
3  How old was she?
4  How many friends did she invite to the party?
5  How had she met them?
6  What two things did they do at the party?
7  What sort of games do you think they played? (Point out that no mention is made of the games in the story: 'We have to imagine the kind of games they played.')
8  What did they have to eat?
9  What did they set on the table?
10  What did Thelma's friends give her?

Ask the class to tell you the opposite of the following words. Preface each question with: 'What is the opposite of . . . ?' Give an example to illustrate. Ask the class to give examples, once the opposite is established.

| | | | |
|---|---|---|---|
| 1 | hot | 10 | quiet |
| 2 | soft | 11 | day |
| 3 | happy | 12 | sunny |
| 4 | many | 13 | old |
| 5 | glad | 14 | kind |
| 6 | start | 15 | sweet |
| 7 | lovely | 16 | high |
| 8 | hallo | 17 | under |
| 9 | near | 18 | quickly |

# Daily lesson 89

**Materials**
1 Animal, transport, tool and utensil cards mentioned in the nursery rhyme *The owl and the pussy cat*
2 Tape recorder

**Aim**

The primary aim is to let the class simply enjoy listening to, acting out, and chanting the nursery rhyme. However children will often miss a great deal of enjoyment in such a song or rhyme because although they are familiar with the sequence of sounds that make up words, they may not have given thought to the meaning, or ever appreciated or been taught that there is a meaning and a narrative in most rhymes. A secondary but important aim of this lesson therefore is to help the class appreciate that the sounds and words have meaning.

*On tape*  Play the nursery rhyme on tape. Question the class very quickly about the characters in the rhyme and the outline of the narrative. Display the pictures of each item as they are mentioned and explain simply words or phrases that may confuse the class e.g. pea green. Play the nursery rhyme again. As it is playing, act out the actions and introduce the pictures of the characters and items. Exaggerate your actions and facial expressions. Play the rhyme a third time if time and class interest permit.

# Daily lesson 90

**Materials**
Tape recorder

**Procedure**
Explain to the class that you are going to read them a story called *Ill in bed* and that you want them to listen carefully because you will ask them questions about it afterwards.

### Ill in bed

Clive and Shirley had been in bed ill for a few days now. They no longer felt very ill, but mummy and the doctor said they both must stay in bed until tomorrow. They had the measles.

They could remember only a few days ago how ill they had felt—hot and sore all over and oh so tired. They couldn't be bothered doing anything. All they wanted to do was sit in front of the fire. They didn't even want to watch television. Shirley had felt peculiar first of all on Tuesday morning and by the evening Clive felt the same way. So they were put to bed and the doctor was called next day.

He was a nice man. He came up to see them, tucked in their beds. Shirley and Clive shared the same bedroom. He had looked down their throats, asked them to say 'Ah!', looked into their ears and eyes and then sounded their chests with his stethoscope. This was a little tickly. He'd looked at their backs and tummies and, sure enough, there were the spots. It was measles. They had never had measles before although they'd heard other boys and girls talking about it.

The doctor told their mother to keep them warmly tucked in bed and to give them some medicine. They wouldn't feel like eating much food, so she had to give them plenty of hot and cold drinks. Clive and Shirley felt a lot better when they heard this.

So for a few days they stayed in bed. They listened to the radio. They played ludo. They drew. They wrote stories. They read. And mummy kept popping upstairs to see how they were. Yes, they felt they were getting better. She gave them hot milk and hot and cold blackcurrant and orange drinks. They didn't feel at all like food, but they did enjoy these drinks.

But they were getting a bit bored and fed up and wanted to go back to school. The doctor called a few days later and said yes, they could go back, but not till after the weekend. Could they get up? Yes, he thought they could, but they had to be careful and not catch cold. Good. They could go back to school. They had missed their friends so much, and their teacher too!

Ask the class if they enjoyed the story. Then ask the following questions:
1 What was the name of the story?
2 What were the names of the boy and girl in the story?
3 How had they felt when they first became ill?
4 Did they feel like doing anything?
5 Who came to see them?
6 What did he do?
7 What did he think was wrong with them and why?

8 What did he suggest to help them feel better?
9 How did Clive and Shirley spend their time?
10 What did they eat? What did they drink?
11 Did they want to go back to school? Why?

Ask the class the meaning of the following words:

| | |
|---|---|
| 1 bed | 6 book |
| 2 fire | 7 game |
| 3 television | 8 milk |
| 4 ear | 9 school |
| 5 eye | 10 teacher |

Ask the class the opposite of the following words:

| | |
|---|---|
| 1 ill | 6 up |
| 2 hot | 7 yes |
| 3 in front of | 8 upstairs |
| 4 nice | 9 better |
| 5 morning | 10 later |

*On tape* Ask the class to describe how they felt and what they did when they were ill in bed.

# Daily lesson 91

**Materials**
1 Colour cubes—all eight basic colours
2 Animal cards—cat, dog, mouse, hamster, horse, rabbit, tiger, seal, monkey, sparrow, eagle, wasp, bee

**Procedure**
Distribute colour cubes. Revise the names of the colours, by means of matching, without and with verbal instructions, and then with verbal instructions only. Ask the children to form chains (of no more than four colours) on the basis of verbal instructions only: 'Make a chain of the following colours. Remember to work from the left hand side.' (Confirm that the children know left and right and correct those who are still confused.) 'The colours are black, white, red and green.' Continue with various selections of colour cubes and at a speed which extends the class but which is not too challenging. The class teacher may feel it worthwhile to introduce an element of competition by devising simple team games— points being awarded to the teams according to the correct number of chains within a given time.

Display the individual animal cards. Revise the name given to each. Discuss where each animal lives—what kind of home it has as a pet, in a zoo or in the wild. Once the name of each animal has been established have the class name other animals which have similar homes. Make comparisons within each home style e.g. both a sparrow and an eagle have nests but the latter would obviously need a bigger one.

# Daily lesson 92

**Materials**

1 Two colour cubes (of any colour) for each child
2 Occupation cards—coalman, milkman, policeman, plumber, joiner, glazier and others with whom the class are familiar

**Procedure**

Get the class to stand by their desks. Have them place their two colour cubes on the top of the desk at the start and then carry out the following instructions:

1 Touch your toes then put your cubes on the floor.
2 Pick up the cubes, put one in your left hand, and one in your right hand, and lean on your knees.
3 Place the cubes on your desk, touch the floor with your hands, then stand on one foot.

Repeat similar instructions. Try and involve the class in placing the cubes in various situations so as to teach the following words: 'on top of', 'alongside', 'behind', 'under', 'together' and 'separately'.

Display the occupation cards individually. Invite individuals in the class to name the man's occupation and elicit or teach the actual work he does: What materials does he use? When is he called upon? Is the job a skilled one? Does he require tools? How does he carry them? Does he travel around? If so, how? What hours does he work? What would we do without him?

# Daily lesson 93

**Materials**
Tool cards—random selection

**Procedure**
Ask the class as individuals and then collectively what they would do in
the following situations. Elicit how they would feel (happy, sad, uneasy,
frightened, helpless etc). Would they ask for help? Teach, if necessary,
what they should do.
1  They break a bottle or container and spill some milk.
2  They lose a pencil belonging to someone else.
3  They knock a younger, smaller child over by mistake.
4  They forget to bring something to school.
5  They are locked out of the house by mistake.
6  They get lost in a large supermarket.
7  They go to the grocers for mother and the shopkeeper says he doesn't
   have what they ask for.
8  Mother feels unwell.
9  They find what they think is a stray cat.
10 They see an old lady struggling with heavy shopping, trying to get onto
   a bus.

Display tool cards individually. Ask individuals in the class to mime the use
made of each. Insist where necessary that both hands, or hands and feet,
are used. Encourage them to mime secondary actions or facial gestures.
E.g. the child would be encouraged to breathe heavily and grimace slightly
with the effort of using a spade. Use as many tool cards as enthusiasm and
time permit.

**Materials**
Tape recorder

**Procedure**
Explain to the class that you are going to tell them a story called *A friend comes to supper*, and that you want them to listen carefully to the story because you will ask them questions about it afterwards.

A friend comes to supper

Mummy put down the phone. 'Sarah!' she cried, 'Sarah!'

'Yes, mummy,' replied Sarah.

'That was Philippa's mummy on the phone. She has to go out and wondered if Philippa could have supper with us. Won't that be nice?'

'Super,' said Sarah. 'Can I help you make it?'

They both trooped through to the kitchen to prepare for Philippa.

'If you set your table, I'll make the tea, Sarah. All right?' said mummy.

'Yes,' said Sarah, and she pulled the little table she sometimes used away from the wall and placed two small chairs against it.

'What will we have?' asked Sarah.

'What would you like?'

'Well, could we have sausages?'

'Yes.'

'And peas?'

'Yes.'

'And chips?'

'Yes, that will do nicely. Would you like some jelly afterwards?'

'Oh, yes please, mummy,' said Sarah, licking her lips.

So Sarah went about setting the table, while mummy prepared the tea.

Sarah cleaned the table with a cloth and placed a knife, a fork and a small teaspoon for each of them. What else?

'Could we have orange with a straw, mummy?' asked Sarah.

'Yes,' said mummy, 'you'll find the plastic cups in the cupboard, and there's a packet of straws beside them.'

So Sarah went to the cupboard and took out two plastic cups, a blue one and a yellow one. She stuck two straws in each and carried them over to the table.

While Sarah had been busy setting the table, mummy had been frying the chips and sausages and heating the peas on the cooker. She'd already boiled a kettle of water for the jelly and was waiting for it to cool and set. She'd been very quick because she expected Philippa to arrive any minute. And there she was! She heard the door bell ring.

Sarah ran to the door and welcomed Philippa and her mother, 'Come on in Philippa. Supper's just about ready; I set the table,' said Sarah. 'Come on in and we'll get started.'

Wasn't it good fun having someone to eat with.

Ask the class if they enjoyed the story, then ask the following questions:

1  What was the name of the story?
2  What was the name of the girl in the story?

3 What was her friend's name?
4 Why was she coming to supper?
5 What did Sarah ask to have for supper?
6 What did Sarah do while her mother cooked the supper?
7 What did she use to set the table?
8 What were they going to drink out of?
9 How did Sarah's mother cook the supper?
10 Did Sarah have to wait long for Philippa to arrive?

Ask the class the meaning of the following words:

| | |
|---|---|
| 1 telephone | 6 cup |
| 2 table | 7 straw |
| 3 chairs | 8 kettle |
| 4 food | 9 bell |
| 5 knife | 10 door |

Ask the class the opposite of the following words:

| | |
|---|---|
| 1 put down | 6 cleaned |
| 2 go out | 7 took out |
| 3 pulled | 8 heat |
| 4 small | 9 quick |
| 5 afterwards | 10 ready |

*On tape*  Ask the class to talk about anytime they have prepared a mea
for a friend. Play back a selection.

'Super', said Sarah. 'Can I help you make it?'
They both trooped through to the kitchen to prepare for Philippa.

# Daily lesson 95

**Materials**
Articles of clothing cards—shoes, boots, slippers, sandals; socks, stockings, tights; skirt, dress, trousers; jacket, coat, anorak; blouse, jersey, cardigan; assorted headgear; gloves, mittens

**Procedure**
Display each picture individually and elicit its name, the part of the body on which it is worn and by which sex. Then select two cards, each from different groups, and elicit the differences in where the items are worn, and the material they are made of, if necessary. Insist on structured responses, e.g. 'You wear shoes on your feet and gloves on your hands.' Select two cards from the same group and elicit similarities and differences. 'You wear both on your feet but wear the boots outside, and the slippers inside.' Finally elicit or teach that all the above articles are the same, or alike, because they are all clothes or they are all worn.

Ask the class to answer the following questions:
1 Why do we have houses?
2 Why do we have windows in our houses?
3 Why do we have beds?
4 Why do we wash?
5 Why do we wear clothes?
6 Why do we eat and drink?
7 Why do we sleep?
8 Why do we have books?
9 Why do we watch television?
10 Why do we come to school?

# Daily lesson 96

**Materials**

1 Animal cards—dog, cat, mouse, puppy, kitten, horse, cow, calf, pig, piglets, tiger, lion, giraffe, elephant, cheetah, seagull, snake, tortoise, rabbit, goldfish, bee, spider, snail, monkey

2 Nursery rhymes—*Hey diddle diddle, Hickory dickory dock, Three little kittens, Six little mice, This little pig, Little Miss Muffet*

**Procedure**

Display all the above cards. Give one of the clues numbered below and ask the class to select the animal you are thinking of, after each selection ask the class if they know a nursery rhyme about the animal and if so have them recite it. Also, after a child has chosen a card have him verbalize why he selected that particular card; 'I chose this card because . . .'

1  This animal has four legs and a very long neck and sometimes can be seen in zoos. (giraffe)
2  This animal swims in water and can be kept as a pet. (goldfish)
3  This animal makes honey and lives in a hive. (bee)
4  This animal lives in a sty. (pig)
5  This animal has four legs and we can sometimes ride on it. (horse)
6  This animal's mother is called a cat. (kitten)
7  This animal is the fastest animal in the world. (cheetah)
8  This animal loves to swing in the trees. (monkey)
9  This animal has a trunk. (elephant)
10  This animal spins webs and has eight legs. (spider)
11  This animal can climb up walls and leaves a trail. (snail)
12  This animal's mother is called a dog. (puppy)
13  This animal is a bird that eats fish. (seagull)
14  This animal can sometimes be seen on farms and makes a noise like a sheep. (goat)
15  This animal has a loud roar. (lion)
16  This animal slithers along the ground. (snake)
17  This animal is like a big, striped cat but is very fierce. (tiger)
18  This animal's mother is a pig. (piglet)
19  This animal has four legs, a long tail and whiskers, and is very small. (mouse)
20  This animal gives us milk. (cow or goat)
21  This animal has long ears, and can be kept as a pet. (rabbit)
22  This animal has four legs and carries its house on its back. (tortoise)
23  This animal will grow up to be a cow. (calf)
24  This animal has soft fur and whiskers. (cat)
25  This animal barks. (dog)

Invite class members to imitate the noise each of the animals makes. For animals which don't make a noise, e.g. a spider, have the class imitate what noise they imagine they would make.

Have the class recite together those nursery rhymes previously recited by individual children and add those omitted.

# Daily lesson 97

**Materials**
1  Tool cards (as below)
2  Nursery rhyme—*Monday's child*

**Procedure**
Ask the class what today is called. Ask them to say the names of other days.
Then ask them to chant the names of the days of the week. Repeat as often
as enthusiasm allows. Vary the pace of the chant, and have the class
emphasize the first syllable of each day. Ask several children who are
familiar with the order questions like 'What day comes after Tuesday?' and
'What day comes before Thursday?' Ask those who are still confused to
chant out the days they are familiar with, in order. Finish by having the
class recite *Monday's child*.

Make the children close their eyes as you describe one of the tools. Have
them guess what the object is. Try and avoid mentioning its function in
your description although you may need to say where or in what activity
the object is used. Ask the child who answers to name the function of the
tool. Then display the appropriate picture.

| | | | |
|---|---|---|---|
| 1 | knife | 16 | lawnmower |
| 2 | telephone | 17 | car |
| 3 | spade | 18 | rubber (eraser) |
| 4 | hat | 19 | screwdriver |
| 5 | soap | 20 | needle |
| 6 | light bulb | 21 | thread |
| 7 | pencil | 22 | toaster |
| 8 | bottle | 23 | shoe |
| 9 | tap | 24 | glass |
| 10 | book | 25 | letter |
| 11 | clock | 26 | hammer |
| 12 | scissors | 27 | wheelbarrow |
| 13 | spoon | 28 | hairdryer |
| 14 | straw | 29 | tin opener |
| 15 | bicycle | 30 | pencil sharpener |

Have the class follow simple instructions like 'close your eyes and stand
on one leg'. Vary the length and difficulty of your instructions according
to the level of the class. Repeat as often as the enthusiasm of the class
allows. Increase the pace of the instructions as you go along.

# Daily lesson 98

**Materials**

1 Nursery rhymes—*I love little pussy, Pussy cat, pussy cat, where have you been?, A cat named Fred*
2 Tape recorder

**Procedure**

Explain to the class that you are going to read them a story called *Fred* and that you want them to listen carefully to the story because you will ask them questions about it afterwards.

### Fred

Fred was a pussy cat. What a funny name for a cat, you might think, but he was a very pleasant cat. He didn't belong to Samantha or Samantha's parents, but he spent a lot of his time in their garden or in their house. He was a big, fluffy, ginger cat with a white tip on his tail and white patches on his four paws and tummy. He always moved very slowly with his tail straight up in the air and his nose and whiskers twitching and sniffing.

He wouldn't be seen for days on end. Then, some lunchtime or teatime, Samantha would hear *scrape, scrape, scrape,* at the kitchen door. And sure enough, there was Fred, sitting there patiently, quite sure that someone would eventually open the door. Then taking his time he'd wander in slowly, padding across the floor. He'd rub himself against the doorway, then Samantha's legs, then the legs of the table. Then he'd hurry across to where mummy was standing at the cooker, quite sure that he'd get some titbit. He was always right. Then he'd rub himself against the furniture and your legs a few more times and park himself in the warmest place in the house—almost under the radiator.

He would stay there for hours and hours and hours, dozing away. His eyes would remain tight shut almost all the time. Occasionally he'd half open one of them just to see he wasn't missing something. Then he'd relax again, head on paws and tail circled round. He'd lie like that all afternoon, through teatime and all through the evening. He never ever moved from his position under the radiator and was so quiet that Samantha and her parents would forget completely that he was there until just before bedtime. Gosh, his owners would be worried! So Samantha would go across and pick him up. He was so lazy and sleepy-headed and dozy and warm that it was like picking up a hot water bottle.

Open the door and plonk him out. He'd stand and yawn, flick his tail and not appear to be in any hurry to move off. 'Good night, Fred,' Samantha would say. He wouldn't even bother to turn his head.

Ask the class if they enjoyed the story, then ask the following questions:
1 What was the name of the story?
2 Who was Fred?
3 What was the name of the girl in the story?
4 Who did Fred belong to?
5 What was Fred like?
6 How did he move?
7 How would Samantha know Fred was near?

8　What would he do as he came into the house?
9　What did he do then?
10　How did he doze?
11　Did he stay long?
12　Why did they usually forget about him?
13　How did Samantha get him out of the house?

*Nursery rhyme*　Ask the class to repeat the following verse:
*A cat named Fred,*
*A sleepy head,*
*Would wander into our house.*
*He wasn't mine*
*But wasn't it fine*
*When he wandered*
*Into our house.*

Ask them also to recite the rhymes *I love little pussy,* and *Pussy cat, pussy cat, where have you been?*

*On tape*　Have the class describe to the tape recorder any animal visitors who come to their house—birds, dogs or cats.

# Daily lesson 99

**Materials**
Manikin

**Procedure**
Tap out rhythms on the desk with a pencil or by hand and have the class copy them. Begin with simple short rhythms which become progressively more difficult.

*Rhyming* Ask the class to give you rhyming words. You may have to explain what rhyming means—emphasize that it is a word that sounds like another word, a word that ends in the same sound.

| | | | |
|---|---|---|---|
| 1 | door | 14 | shoulder |
| 2 | wall | 15 | head |
| 3 | table | 16 | hair |
| 4 | chair | 17 | eye |
| 5 | chalk | 18 | nose |
| 6 | board | 19 | leg |
| 7 | rose | 20 | knee |
| 8 | red | 21 | shin |
| 9 | neck | 22 | foot |
| 10 | wrist | 23 | feet |
| 11 | hand | 24 | toe |
| 12 | finger | 25 | arm |
| 13 | bend | 26 | mouth |

Pin the manikin on the board. Point to the several parts and ask individuals to point to their corresponding parts, and elicit the names of each as you go. Invite individuals to describe the function of each part. Insist on structured responses e.g. 'This is my eye and it is for seeing things.'

# Daily lesson 100

**Materials**
1 Miscellaneous objects in the classroom, or a selection of cards
2 Christmas party narrative poster

**Procedure**
Divide the class into four groups. Explain that you will arrange four objects on the floor. The class will have ten seconds to look at these objects and memorize them. They must close their eyes while one object is removed and then guess which object has been removed. Have the groups compete against each other. Increase or reduce the number of objects, or the amount of time given to view the objects, displayed according to the level of the children. Insist on a well structured response: 'It is the pencil sharpener that is missing.' Repeat as often as enthusiasm allows.

Display the narrative poster and have the class analyze the picture. Emphasize the background and middle ground as well as the foreground. Elicit the colours of clothing worn. Have the class verbalize the feelings of the adults and children portrayed in the picture. Summarize the picture quickly and then have a few of the class describe a party they have been to. Insist on simple, short, well structured sentences.

*Game time*   Play a variation of the game 'I went to the supermarket and I bought . . .' Begin by saying 'I went to a party the other day and I saw . . .' Invite the class to add something new to the previous things seen. Insist on as quick a pace as possible.

# Daily lesson 101

**Materials**
1 Tool cards
2 Nursery rhyme—*The bells of London (Oranges and lemons)*

**Procedure**
Ask the class as a whole, or a group, or individuals to repeat exactly what you say, as follows:
 1 one, three, four (at a rate of one per second)
 2 boy, dog, wall (at a rate of one per second)
 3 He went over to the door and closed it. (hang on every word)
 4 one, six, seven, eight
 5 two, five, three, one
 6 red, blue, yellow
 7 The girl wore black shoes and white socks.
 8 She went to the desk, opened the drawer and took out a pencil.
 9 one, nine, six, four
10 three, five, seven, eight
11 blue, yellow, green
12 red, black, green, yellow
13 three, seven, eight, nine
14 The dog chased the cat, until it ran quickly up a tree.
15 Because it was such a warm day, they decided to go swimming.

Place the tool cards in a pile on the desk. Invite a member of the class to pick one at random and ask him or her to describe the item, while the class, competing group against group, have to guess what the item is. Award points for correct guesses, and deduct points for wrong guesses. Repeat as often as enthusiasm allows.

*Nursery rhyme*   Sing the song *Oranges and lemons* and have the class listen. Repeat no more than twice, inviting the class to join in when they can.

# Daily lesson 102

**Materials**
Tool cards—kettle, tap, basin, dishcloth, soap, miscellaneous dishes and utensils, chair, picture of kitchen, picture of mother and daughter

**Procedure**
Explain to the class that you are going to read a story called *Drying dishes* and that you want them to listen carefully to the story because you will ask them questions about it afterwards.

### Drying dishes

Although Kate was only a little girl she was always keen to copy her mummy and help her with jobs around the house. One day just after breakfast she asked her mother if she could help her dry the dishes. Mummy said, 'Of course, Kate, but you will have to be very careful because the dishes will be very slippery with soapy water and they may slip out of your hands.'

Kate said she would be careful and her mother lifted her onto a chair so that she could reach the dishes. She was so small, you see, that she needed a chair to stand on.

So they began to do the dishes, mummy washing them, and Kate drying. Kate was very careful, and mummy kept a gentle eye on her to see how she was doing. And she was doing very well.

However, just as they were almost finished, Kate noticed a blackbird hopping along the top of the fence just outside the kitchen window. Just for a second she forgot what she was doing and, very excited, she pointed to the bird and shouted, 'Look, look, a lovely blackbird on our fence!'

Can you guess what happened? In her excitement, she dropped a saucer and down it went, smash, onto the kitchen floor. Kate looked down and mummy looked down at the saucer, broken into little pieces. Poor Kate was so upset. But before she began to cry her mummy took her into her arms and told her not to worry. 'These things happen, dear,' she said, 'I've broken many a dish in my time, but it's not worth crying about. But I've learned to be very careful.' Kate felt much better when her mother spoke like this, although she was still a little upset, and as she was drying the rest of the dishes she concentrated hard. She was very careful. Occasionally she looked up at her mother who usually smiled down to her. Kate smiled back, holding on very carefully to the dish she had in her hand at the time.

Ask the class if they enjoyed the story. Then ask the following questions:
1  What was the name of the story?
2  What was the name of the little girl?
3  How can we tell that she was a helpful little girl?
4  Why did she have to be careful when drying dishes?
5  Who washed the dishes?
6  What did Kate notice outside the window?
7  What happened then?
8  Was her mother angry?
9  What did her mother say to her?
10  How did Kate feel after this?

Ask the class how to go about washing and drying dishes. Go into detail.

# Daily lesson 103

**Materials**
Tape recorder

**Procedure**
Explain to the class that you are going to tell them a story called *The paddling pool* and that you want them to listen carefully to the story because you will ask them questions about it afterwards.

### The paddling pool

Julie and Andrew had an inflatable paddling pool. It was made of rubber and you blew it up. When it was not blown up Julie could fold it up into a tiny cardboard box and store it in the garage. They only used it in the summertime, when it was warm. They could have used a pump to blow it up but Julie and Andrew managed to blow it up without one. They would kneel on the grass, put their mouths to the hole in the paddling pool and huff and puff and blow till it was firm enough to stand by itself.

The pool didn't look very big and you wouldn't think that it would hold much water. But it took quite a long time to fill up. Julie and Andrew would collect buckets and pans and trip back and forth from the tap in the kitchen to the garden, carrying bucket after bucket of water. It took eight journeys to fill the pool.

Then off with their socks and shoes and in they would jump. When it was very hot weather they would put on their swimming costumes and lie flat out in the water to keep cool. Sometimes they would sail their little boats in the pool, or splash each other with saucepans full of water. Often they would just fill and empty bottles of water, watching the sun glistening on the water as it fell, and watching the bubbles in the pool as the water tumbled into it. It made a lovely rushing noise, too.

There were only two things that troubled Julie and Andrew about the pool. First, if they left it standing too long out in the sun the air would escape, the walls of the pool would begin to sag and the water would begin to seep out into the grass. The second thing that troubled them was that the water in the pool seemed to attract wasps and bees. Wasps and bees like water. Many a time Julie and Andrew had taken the trouble to unpack the pool, blow it up and fill it with water, only to find that they daren't go near it for the amount of bees and wasps buzzing around. What a nuisance.

Ask the class if they enjoyed the story. Then ask the following questions:
1  What was the name of the story?
2  What were the names of the boy and girl in the story?
3  What kind of pool did they have?
4  How did they blow it up?
5  When did they play with it?
6  How did they fill it up with water?
7  Did it hold a lot of water?
8  What did they do in the pool?
9  What happened if they left the pool standing in the sun?
10  What was attracted to the water in the pool?

Ask the class the meaning of the following words:

| | |
|---|---|
| 1 pool | 7 boat |
| 2 summer | 8 bottle |
| 3 winter | 9 puddle |
| 4 bucket | 10 wasp |
| 5 tap | 11 nuisance |
| 6 shoes | |

Ask the class the opposite of the following words:

| | |
|---|---|
| 1 tiny | 6 off |
| 2 summertime | 7 hot |
| 3 warm | 8 fill |
| 4 big | 9 first |
| 5 much | 10 unpack |

*On tape*　Ask the class to describe any paddling pool they are familiar with, and their feelings about wasps and bees.

# Daily lesson 104

**Materials**
1 Miscellaneous objects mentioned below
2 Tape recorder

**Procedure**
Have the class finish the following sentences:
1 Here is a pencil; here are some more _____ . (pencils)
2 Here is a desk; here are some more _____ . (desks)
3 Here is a book; here are some more _____ . (books)
4 This pencil is big; this pencil is even _____ . (bigger)
5 This piece of chalk is small; this piece is even _____ . (smaller)
6 This book is slim; this book is even _____ . (slimmer)
7 Joan is tall; I am even _____ . (taller)
8 John is tall, Peter is even taller and Joan is the _____. (tallest)
9 This book is small, this book is even smaller and this book is the _____ . (smallest)
10 This piece of chalk is short; this pencil is _____ . (long)
11 This book is slim; that book is _____ . (fat)
12 Joan is tall; Mary is _____ . (little)
13 (Tuesday) is today; (Monday) was _____ . (yesterday)
14 (Tuesday) is today; (Wednesday) is _____ . (tomorrow)
15 Today it is cold; yesterday was even _____ . (colder)
16 Here is a mouse; here are two _____ . (mice)
17 Here is a horse; here are two _____ . (horses)
18 Here is a cow; here are two _____ . (cows)
19 Here is one man; here are two _____ . (men)
20 Here is a woman; here are two _____ . (women)

*On tape* Tell the class that they each have one wish granted to them. They will be invited to tell the tape recorder what they would like—a toy, somewhere to go, something to happen. Insist on no conferring among individuals. Play back the tape.

# Daily lesson 105

## Materials
1 A large and wide selection from animal, tool, articles of clothing, occupation, shop, family relations, furniture and house cards
2 Nursery rhyme—*The bells of London (Oranges and lemons)*

## Procedure
Display the cards and invite individuals to select one according to your instructions: e.g. Choose one that is made of metal; choose one that has four legs; choose one that is worn. Keep the instructions fairly general. Invite the responder to name the object and describe it in detail and in functional terms. Let the child keep the card until after the game is over. Allow each child two or three turns.

Tell the class to select one card and return the rest to the desk. Then have them stand and display their card so that each card can be seen by the whole class. Explain that you want them to find their 'families' i.e. all those with animals will join together and so on. Have the class change their cards quickly and when you say 'go', they must find their new family. Repeat often. Do not designate areas of the room as 'tool areas' or 'animal areas' etc. Insist on the class moving around without a whisper, and without running or walking quickly. Allow the class to sort themselves out.

*Nursery rhyme*   Finish by singing *Oranges and lemons*.

# Daily lesson 106

## Materials
1 Narrative poster—children's playground in the city
2 Tape recorder
3 Nursery rhyme—*How do you like to go up in a swing?*

## Procedure
Have the class analyze the picture in detail, emphasizing background and, middle ground as well as foreground. Bring their attention to the apparatus depicted, mentioning their names, what they are for, what they are made of and the dangers of misuse. Point out and explain special features of the pictures. Are there adults around? If so, who might they be? What are they doing? Are there queues anywhere? If so, why? Ask questions about the weather, the clothing, the ages of the children depicted. Summarize the picture quickly.

*On tape*   Have the class tell the tape recorder how they feel about a playground they visit. Try to encourage them to express their feelings about their fears as well as their enjoyment of the apparatus and crowds.

*Nursery rhyme*   Have the class recite *How do you like to go up in a swing?*

# Daily lesson 107

## Materials
Colour cubes

## Procedure
Invite those children with brown shoes to stand together in a group. Repeat for shoe colours until the whole class is grouped. Repeat for articles of clothing above the waist, and articles of clothing below the waist.

Hold up a colour cube, elicit its name and invite the class to name articles of the same colour which are visible in the room or cubicle. Repeat for all eight basic colours. Invite the class to make chains according to your verbal instructions. Begin with short, simple chains and gradually make the chains more challenging. Encourage speed.

Whisper the following sentences to one member of the class. Have that member of the class whisper it to the next and so on until the last child tells the class what she has heard. Compare the original sentence with the final effort.
1 Tracy raced under the bridge and across the river.
2 The wild wind swept the trees bare of leaves.
3 Johnny joined his jolly group of friends and was offered a sweet.

# Daily lesson 108

**Materials**
1 Tape recorder
2 Nursery rhymes—*How do you like to go up in a swing? When I climbed up the apple tree*

**Procedure**
Explain to the class that you are going to read a story called *The apple tree* and that you want them to listen carefully because you will ask them questions about it afterwards.

## The apple tree

The apple tree stood in a corner of the garden, close by a wooden fence that ran right round the garden border. In the wintertime it didn't have any leaves or apples on it. Its branches were quite bare and cold looking. Now however in the summertime, its branches were covered in leaves and there were hundreds of apples weighing down the branches. The apples weren't ready yet. They were mostly small and light green in colour, although some of them showed signs of turning red.

Cats were very fond of this apple tree. Alice and Robert didn't have a cat of their own, but there were several cats in the street where they lived. Often they would wander through their garden. They would scramble and scrape up the trunk of the tree, along its branches, and then hop onto the fence and down the other side to another garden. Or they would lie quietly waiting in the branches of the tree, hidden in the thickly growing leaves. They'd wait for birds to come and perch on the branches, or wait for them to fly down onto the grass to eat the breadcrumbs that Alice and Robert sometimes put out for the birds. Weren't the cats naughty?

Alice liked this apple tree just as much as the cats did. That was where she played on her swing in the summertime. Her daddy had screwed in two hooks on the strongest branch of the tree and the swing hung from there. Alice loved swinging and she used her swing almost every day. The grass under the swing was almost completely bare and worn away with her feet scraping back and forth. Swinging in the apple tree in the summertime was even more fun because as she swung faster and faster, the branches above in the tree would also begin swinging. Then down the apples would fall, *thud, thud, thud,* onto the ground below, sometimes falling on Alice's head as they came. The first time this had happened she got an awful scare and cried. But now she expected it to happen. Half the fun was dodging the apples.

Ask the class if they enjoyed the story. Then ask the following questions:
1 What was the name of the story?
2 What were the names of the boy and girl in the story?
3 What did the apple tree look like in wintertime?
4 What was the apple tree like in summertime?
5 Did the cats like this tree? Why?
6 Did Alice and Robert have a cat?
7 What did the cats wait for?
8 Why did Alice like the apple tree?

9 What was the grass under the swing like?
10 What happened when Alice swung in the summertime?
11 What did Alice do the first time this happened?
12 What was half the fun of swinging now?

Ask the class the opposite of the following words:

1 close by
2 wintertime
3 bare
4 ready
5 fond
6 up
7 quietly
8 thickly
9 strongest
10 often
11 back
12 faster
13 above
14 cried
15 half

Ask the class the meaning of the following words:

1 apple
2 winter
3 summer
4 cat
5 bird
6 swing
7 cup
8 straw
9 knife
10 teeth

*Nursery rhymes*  Recite the two nursery rhymes and have the class recite them.

*On tape*  Have the class describe to the tape recorder any apple tree that they are familiar with, or any cats that prowl around near their home.

# Daily lesson 109

**Materials**
None

**Procedure**
Ask the class to confirm or correct the following sentence, 'The sky is always blue.' Ask those who think this correct and those who think it inaccurate to raise their hands. Explain and teach the differences between 'always', 'sometimes' and 'never', and ask them to respond to the following statements.

1 Dogs never fly.
2 Hammers never speak.
3 Birds always fly.
4 It sometimes rains in summer.
5 The moon never comes out during the day.
6 Grass is always green.
7 Trees sometimes don't have leaves.
8 It's always cold in wintertime.
9 Teacher never makes a mistake.

Ask the class to give you a simple sentence using the following group of words. Give an example of a sentence: 'I'm going to say a sentence with the words *ball* and *bat* in it. Listen: "Johnny hit the ball across the room with the bat".' Ask two or three children to make sentences from the same group of words.

1 dog, cat
2 down, water
3 teeth, mirror
4 cooker, water
5 melt, puddle
6 chalk, covered
7 muddy, trouble
8 join, hammer
9 cream, broken
10 warm, curtain
11 van, ice cream
12 yawn, cat
13 ribbon, eyes
14 dip, open
15 cry, mother

# Daily lesson 110

**Materials**
None

**Procedure**
Take the class for a walk. Bring their attention to the common, everyday sights and sounds that they tend to pass by without a second look or thought. Bring their attention to details using every opportunity to describe interesting things in common settings e.g. flowers and weeds growing out of a crack in the wall, a dog or cat with a bell round its neck, an unpainted gate, an uncut hedge. When you return, have the class verbalize what they saw and draw pictures of it.

# Daily lesson 111

**Materials**
1 Tape recorder
2 Nursery rhymes as selected by the class

**Procedures**
Ask the class to repeat exactly what you say. No omissions or alterations are to be allowed.
1 Anna picked the apple from the bowl and chewed it.
2 Mary pushed her toy pram up the slope.
3 Sid rolled his marbles into the hollow.
4 Christine opened the tin of peas very carefully.
5 Frankie sat quietly at the breakfast table.
6 Jane placed the cauliflower in her shopping bag.
7 The bird sat perched on the branch of the bush.
8 The mouse crawled quickly along the garden fence.
9 Hugh played with a sailing boat in his bath.
10 The duck waddled across and pecked at the bread on the grass.

*On tape* Have the class identify themselves to the tape recorder—name, address, age and date of birth. Let them describe themselves briefly and tell the tape recorder something they've done recently. Play back a selection and gently criticize or praise responses.

Have the class give the appropriate plural in the following sentences:
1 one sheep, two _____
2 one mouse, two _____
3 one house, two _____
4 one cat, two _____
5 one cow, two _____
6 one calf, two _____
7 one lion, two _____
8 one goose, two _____
9 one knife, two _____
10 one axe, two _____
11 one man, two _____
12 one watch, two _____
13 one foot, two _____
14 one knee, two _____
15 one toe, two _____

*Nursery rhymes* Play and have the class recite any nursery rhyme or rhymes that they enjoy.

# Daily lesson 112

**Materials**
Tape recorder

**Procedure**
Read the following story called *Feeding the ducks*. Explain that you want them to listen carefully to the story because you will ask them questions about it afterwards.

### Feeding the ducks

Jennie looked forward to every Sunday and she hoped that the weather would be kind. For Sunday was the day she and her daddy went to feed the ducks at the pond. There were lots of ducks at the pond. Big ones, little ones, brown ones, white ones, and some that had many coloured feathers.

Jennie had been going to feed the ducks for such a long time now that she thought they almost knew her. For whenever she came near the pond they would fly or swim in a rush to where she was standing, *quack-quacking* as they came.

Jennie fed them with stale bread and buns that her mother collected for her during the week. She carried the bread and buns in a paper bag. She would lay the bag down beside her as she tore some bread into small pieces and threw it to the ducks. Some very hungry ducks who were not so frightened would come out of the water and almost take bread from her hand. Sometimes they nipped her fingers by mistake but she never cried because it didn't really hurt much. She was always careful to feed those ducks that remained in the water and to share her bread among those who weren't so greedy as the others.

She liked the big white ducks best because they always came last and were slower than the rest. They would stand close to her, not quacking but waiting patiently. And they never fought with the other ducks.

The only thing that troubled Jennie was that she never seemed to have enough bread to feed all the ducks. But fortunately there always seemed to be someone else who came along after her with some more bread for them. So she was able to go home again knowing that she wasn't the only one who cared for them. But she was always glad when Sunday came round again to see that they were all right.

Ask the class if they enjoyed the story, then question them about it. Elicit the facts of the story—what did they think the ducks felt about being fed, how did Jennie feel about the ducks? etc.

*On tape*  Get the class to tell the tape recorder about visiting duck ponds or about feeding pigeons in the park etc.

# Daily lesson 113

**Materials**

1 Cards illustrating objects made of glass, wood, metal, plastic, paper, leather and fibre (as listed below)
2 Nursery rhyme— *What are little boys (girls) made of?*

**Procedure**

Ask the class to give a word that rhymes with the following. Explain 'rhymes with'.

1  you
2  queen
3  he
4  mouse
5  pink
6  town
7  thing
8  on

9  quick
10 corn
11 bare
12 grow
13 wall
14 two
15 head
16 still

17 sea
18 spice
19 bell
20 thread
21 star
22 weather
23 wife
24 pot

Have the class classify the following objects using what they are made of as the criterion. Say 'What is this made of?' and ask for another object made of the same thing. Then classify the group again.

*Glass*
1 bottle
2 window
3 tumbler
4 television screen
5 mirror
6 spectacles

*Wood*
1 table
2 window
3 chair
4 toys
5 floor
6 door

*Metal*
1 car
2 pencil sharpener
3 engine
4 knife
5 plough
6 money

*Plastic*
1 bottle
2 pencil sharpener
3 toys
4 pens
5 straws
6 handles

*Leather*
1 shoes
2 case
3 handbag
4 furniture
5 coats
6 ball

*Fibre*
1 clothes
2 toys
3 carpets
4 towels
5 tablecloths
6 blankets

*Nursery rhyme*   Have the class listen to the nursery rhyme *What are little boys (girls) made of?* Play and replay as often as interest is high and invite the class to join in.

# Daily lesson 114

**Materials**

Nursery rhyme—*See saw Margery Daw*

**Procedure**

Have the class say what you say. Repeat the words or digits at the rate of one per second.

1 seven—two—four
2 three—two—five
3 eight—one—six
4 five—nine—seven
5 four—seven—six
6 three—four—six—five
7 one—nine—five—seven
8 two—five—one—six
9 five—eight—nine—six
10 two—five—three—one
11 door—window—floor
12 light—desk—chalk
13 tree—fence—road
14 pavement—walk—shoes
15 cloud—sun—star
16 yellow—grandma—baby
17 cat—elephant—hat
18 green—round—envelope
19 blue—book—watch—nail

Ask the class to finish the following sentences. (Anything that makes sense is acceptable; encourage one word responses: preferably adverbs.)

1 Peggy walked _____ .
2 The mouse ran _____ .
3 The pussy cat sat _____ .
4 The car drove _____ .
5 The bucket was filled _____ .
6 The ladder leaned _____ .
7 The vase of flowers fell _____ .
8 Paddy sat _____ .
9 The washing hung _____ .
10 They pushed _____ .
11 The sun shone _____ .
12 The top spun _____ .
13 The boys and girls ran _____ .
14 The water flowed _____ .
15 The fish swam _____ .
16 They climbed _____ .
17 They stick stars _____ .
18 The light went _____ .
19 The ball bounced _____ .
20 The painter splashed paint _____ .

Ask the class to point out the absurdity of the following sentences and to complete them correctly.

1 The joiner sawed the piece of wood with his hammer.
2 Mother poured some water into the tap.
3 Michael put his shoes on and went off to bed.
4 He closed the book and began to read.
5 Jean switched off the cooker and began to cook breakfast.
6 Ann said, 'I will do it yesterday.'
7 Pamela put her gloves on her head.
8 The hands of the clock went up and down.
9 The rain fell up in sheets.
10 The cat barked at the mouse.

*Nursery rhyme* Let the class listen to *See saw Margery Daw*. Invite them to join in and rock back and forth to the rhythm of the poem.

156

# Daily lesson 115

**Materials**
1 Pictures as listed below—snow, tree etc. Do not display pictures until after each response.
2 Nursery rhyme—*Boys and girls come out to play*

**Procedure**
Ask the class to give you as many words as they can to describe the following objects. Structure the responses given and ask finally 'What do we do with it?' or 'What is it for?'

| | |
|---|---|
| 1 snow | 11 giraffe |
| 2 tree | 12 cat |
| 3 hair | 13 ball |
| 4 onion | 14 chair |
| 5 glass | 15 knife |
| 6 sky | 16 clock |
| 7 orange | 17 bicycle |
| 8 banana | 18 car |
| 9 violin | 19 bus |
| 10 piano | 20 iron |

Have one individual at a time complete the simple actions mentioned below. The remainder of the class have to describe in simple but detailed language what has happened—i.e. analyze the movement of a general action.

| | |
|---|---|
| 1 open a window | 9 tie shoe laces |
| 2 open a door | 10 bounce a ball across a room |
| 3 lift a desk lid | 11 put on a light switch |
| 4 open a drawer | 12 clean a board |
| 5 pick up a book | 13 pin up a poster |
| 6 lift a crate of milk | 14 prepare to read |
| 7 move a table | 15 switch on television |
| 8 stretch and yawn | |

Ask the class to give a word which means roughly the same as the following. Have the class use the new word in a sentence if possible. If not complete a sentence for them.

| | |
|---|---|
| 1 quick | 9 fix |
| 2 gentle | 10 glad |
| 3 light | 11 big |
| 4 cry | 12 crafty |
| 5 unkind | 13 hard |
| 6 cure | 14 soaking |
| 7 unhappy | 15 small |
| 8 dark | |

*Nursery rhyme*   Teach the nursery rhyme by playing, analyzing the story line casually, replaying and inviting the class to join in.

# Daily lesson 116

**Materials**
1 Colour cubes
2 Narrative picture—a building site

**Procedure**
Ask the class the opposite of the following words. Explain 'opposite' and give examples. Preface each question with 'Give me the opposite of . . .'

| | | | |
|---|---|---|---|
| 1 | rich | 11 | good |
| 2 | dry | 12 | ill |
| 3 | soft | 13 | dark |
| 4 | clean | 14 | early |
| 5 | short | 15 | fast |
| 6 | tall | 16 | pleasant |
| 7 | high | 17 | open |
| 8 | fierce | 18 | noisy |
| 9 | kind | 19 | sunny |
| 10 | difficult | 20 | hot |

Distribute colour cubes. Revise names of the colours. Have the class match colours displayed by you and select colours according to verbal instructions. Then have the class chain colours from left to right according to verbal instructions. Start with easy chains of two or three colours then increase to four.

Display the picture of a building site and analyze with the class the background, middle ground and foreground. Emphasize the main features and details. Structure the picture in language quickly at the end.

# Daily lesson 117

**Materials**
Tape recorder

**Procedure**
Explain to the class that you are going to read them a story called *The toy department*, and that you want them to listen carefully to the story because you will ask them questions about it afterwards.

### The toy department

Rodney and Christine were out shopping with their parents. They were in a huge department store that sold everything under the sun—clothes, furniture, carpets, jewellery, everything you could think of. They weren't shopping for anything in particular, just having a look round. Rodney suggested they might have a look at the toy department. Why not? they thought, so up they went in the lift to the third floor.

Out they stepped into this huge carpeted room. What a lot of toys! Wouldn't it be marvellous to live in a place like this. There were rocking horses, motorcars, scooters, bicycles, prams, pushchairs and tractors. There was a host of soft toys—dolls, teddy bears, golliwogs, pandas, dogs, cats and monkeys. There were smaller toys like skipping ropes, roller skates, building blocks, paint boxes, crayons and colouring books.

Rodney and Christine wandered round, stopping and staring wishfully at this toy or that toy. A lot of the toys they saw displayed they had at home already, and they realized that they hadn't played with some of them for a long time, and had even forgotten about them. They both promised themselves to search them out when they got home.

They looked round for their parents and saw them standing at the counter talking to the shop assistant. Daddy had a small paper bag in his hand. Had he just bought something? What could it be? They ran over and as they were on their way daddy held out two bags—one for Rodney and one for Christine. He smiled broadly at the surprised look on their faces. They tore open their bags impatiently. Balloons! Brightly coloured balloons. 'Oh, aren't they super! Oh thank you, daddy, thank you!' What a surprise. They were tempted to begin blowing them up right now but thought it would be better to wait till they got home. They could hardly wait though. What fun they would have.

Ask the class if they enjoyed the story. Then ask the following questions:
1  What was the name of the story?
2  What were the names of the boy and girl in the story?
3  Where were they shopping today?
4  What sort of things did the department store sell?
5  Were they shopping for anything in particular?
6  Who suggested looking at the toy department?
7  How did they reach it?
8  What sort of large toys did they see?
9  What sort of soft toys did they see?
10  What sort of small toys did they see?
11  What did looking at the toys remind Rodney and Christine about?

12 Where were their parents when they looked for them?
13 What had their parents bought for them?
14 Were they in a hurry to get home?

Ask the class the meaning of the following words:

| | |
|---|---|
| 1 department store | 6 pram |
| 2 clothes | 7 balloon |
| 3 lift | 8 carpet |
| 4 book | 9 cat |
| 5 bicycle | 10 car |

Ask the class the opposite of the following words:

| | |
|---|---|
| 1 went | 9 forgotten |
| 2 huge | 10 lost |
| 3 everything | 11 standing |
| 4 up | 12 small |
| 5 our | 13 bought |
| 6 push | 14 important |
| 7 soft | 15 begin |
| 8 warmer | |

*On tape* Ask the class to describe any visit they have made to a toy department.

# Daily lesson 118

**Materials**
Nursery rhyme—*The owl and the pussy cat*

**Procedure**
Ask the class to finish the following sentences. Invite a variety of responses
to each word. Insist on their repeating your part of the sentence.

1 a pair of _____
2 a book of _____
3 a set of _____
4 a bottle of _____
5 a plate of _____
6 a pint of _____
7 a handful of _____
8 a pocketful of _____
9 a row of _____
10 a box of _____
11 a bag of _____
12 a cup of _____

Split the class into four groups giving each a colour: blue, red, green and
yellow. They are to follow your instructions only if you name their colour.
Now give these directions:

1 Blue—clasp your hands behind your backs
2 Red—put your feet together
3 green—clap your hands three times
4 yellow—stand with your feet apart
5 yellow—sit on the floor
6 blue—hands on head
7 green—touch your toes
8 red—fold your arms
9 yellow—stretch your arms as high as you can
10 blue—clap your hands four times
11 red—stand on one leg
12 green—squat on all fours
13 yellow—clench your fists tightly
14 red—touch your left toe with your right hand
15 blue—sit on the floor

*Nursery rhyme* Sing the song *The owl and the pussy cat*; analyze the story
line quickly and invite the class to join in.

# Daily lesson 119

**Materials**
1 Animal, clothing and tool cards as listed in the riddles
2 Nursery rhymes (the class to choose)

**Procedure**
Ask the class to solve the following riddles. What has
1 two wheels, a handlebar and saddle (bicycle)
2 four legs, whiskers and soft furry coat (cat)
3 big ears and a white tail, and hops (rabbit)
4 four legs, looks like a horse but has stripes (zebra)
5 wings, is black, and has a yellow beak (blackbird)
6 wings, big eyes, and sees at night (owl)
7 four legs, is fat and has a flat nose and curly tail (pig)
8 a handle and spout (kettle)
9 a handle and a head, and is used to knock in nails (hammer)
10 teeth and handle, and goes backwards and forwards across wood (saw)
11 a face and hands, and numbers on it (a clock)
12 sleeves and buttons and keeps out the rain (coat)
13 five fingers and keeps us warm (gloves)
14 a handle and keyhole (door)
15 four legs and a lot of black and white keys on it (piano)
16 one eye and is long and thin (needle)

Ask the class to complete the following sentences:
1 a dog has four legs; a man has _____ .
2 a rabbit has long ears; a cat's ears are _____ .
3 a giraffe's legs are long; a mouse's legs are _____ .
4 pigs have short tails; horse's tails are _____ .
5 a lion is fierce; a dog is _____ .
6 a sheep has four legs; a spider has _____ .
7 a puddle is shallow; an ocean is _____ .
8 sugar is sweet; vinegar is _____ .
9 scissors cut; a needle _____ .
10 a ball is round; an envelope is _____ .

Ask the class to name things that are round. Classify the objects with them according to round like a ball, round like a pencil and round like a penny.

*Nursery rhymes* Ask the class which nursery rhymes they would like to recite or hear read again. Read their selections and invite them to join in.

# Daily lesson 120

**Materials**
1  Tape recorder
2  Nursery rhyme—*The queen of hearts*

**Procedure**
Ask individuals to say exactly what you say. The only acceptable response is one which repeats exactly what you say with no omissions or changes in the order of words or alterations.
1  Joseph placed the apple on the table.
2  Sophie stroked the kitten carefully.
3  Elizabeth looked out of the window at the cars.
4  William sat on the chair drawing.
5  Jane rode her bicycle on the pavement.
6  Kay went dancing on Friday.
7  Scott liked to go fishing.
8  Margaret washed her clothes in the sink.
9  Betty gave Charles one of her sweets.
10  Gordon bounced the ball against the door.
11  Edward helped mummy in the garden.
12  Ann knocked quietly on the door.


Ask the class to imagine that they are in the following situations. Invite a couple to converse appropriately. Prompt beforehand and use the tape recorder.
1  butcher shop (assistant and customer)
2  baker shop (assistant and customer)
3  grocer shop (assistant and customer)
4  friends
5  asking a policeman the way
6  hairdresser or barber (assistant and customer)
7  parent and child
8  brother and sister
9  ice cream man and customer
10  garage attendant and motorist


Play a variation of the game 'We went to market and we bought ...' Ask the class to imagine they were in the following situations and they have to tell what they saw or bought, contributing one item to the list mentioned previously and repeating what has gone before. We went to the ...

| | |
|---|---|
| 1  zoo | 6  supermarket |
| 2  park | 7  baker |
| 3  garage | 8  butcher |
| 4  town | 9  fruit shop |
| 5  farm | 10  chemist |

*Nursery rhyme*   *The queen of hearts.* Teach this nursery rhyme by reciting or playing once or twice. Have the class join in if they can. Explain the simple story line.

# Daily lesson 121

**Materials**
1 Narrative picture—hospital ward
2 Nursery rhyme—*London Bridge is falling down*

**Procedure**
Display the narrative picture and have the class analyze the picture with your help. Emphasize background, middle ground and foreground. Emphasize main features of the picture (beds, patients, nurses) and details (flowers, toys, cabinets, water jugs). Use the picture also as an introduction to having the class talk about any illnesses they have had, or any occasion they or any close friend or relative has been in hospital. Try and get them to verbalize their feelings especially.

Have the class complete the following sentences. Some sentences will allow various responses; more than one word may be used.
1 _____ flew in the sky.
2 He bounced the ball against _____ .
3 Rosie had a little _____ .
4 He cut himself and _____ .
5 She was crying. What a _____ .
6 The cat ____ for its milk.
7 She _____ her sweets.
8 The fish _____ in the sea.
9 Beautiful flowers _____ all over the garden.
10 _____ shone brightly in the sky.
11 He _____ his shoes and _____ his coat.
12 The little girl drew _____ .

*Miming*  Ask individuals in the class to mime the following simple actions. Invite others to guess what the action is. If a mime is inadequate, whisper suggestions for improving it. Insist on structured responses.
1 brushing teeth
2 washing one's face
3 combing one's hair
4 pulling on shoes
5 speaking on the telephone
6 setting a table
7 playing a piano
8 playing a violin
9 pulling off shoes
10 sharpening a pencil

*Nursery rhyme  London Bridge is falling down*—Teach this rhyme by playing and replaying it as often as possible. Explain the story line. Invite the class to join in when they can and to use actions where appropriate.

# Daily lesson 122

**Materials**
None

**Procedure**
Explain to the class that you are going to read them a story called *The dustbin men* and that you want them to listen carefully to the story because you will ask them questions about it afterwards.

### The dustbin men

It was Thursday morning, the day that the dustbin men came to clear the rubbish of the week. Stanley and Maureen passed piles of rubbish outside every home as they went on their way to school. Most of the rubbish had been placed in bins or buckets. Some buckets were very large, others quite small, made of steel, with a big handle sticking up at the top. Occasionally there would be a coloured plastic bin, yellow, red or black. And sometimes small black plastic bags.

Apart from the buckets and bins and bags there were bundles of old newspapers, some tied up neatly and safely with string, other piles not tied up at all, but weighed down by a stone. It was a bit windy that morning and some of the old newspapers had escaped and blew among the gardens. Stanley and Maureen could see sheets of old newspaper clinging onto bushes and trees, very untidily.

As they walked, the children spotted the occasional cat or dog sniffing at the buckets. The animals had managed to open the lid of one bucket. One cat had dragged what looked like a bag of potato peelings onto the street, and another dog nosed around the open bins. Stanley and Maureen felt they should shoo the animals away, but they felt sorry for them, too. No doubt the owner of the bucket would come out of the house and chase them away.

Here came the bucket men, hanging onto their slow moving van. They jumped off as it moved and ran to each bucket, lifting it with one hand, and lifting the old newspapers with the other. Stanley noticed they all wore gloves. They carried the rubbish to the back of the van and tossed it in, banging the buckets noisily as they made sure they were empty. Then on further down the street.

What a dirty, noisy job, thought Stanley and Maureen, and they stopped watching and carried on their way to school. And then they thought, gosh, but what a useful job! What would mummy do with her rubbish without the bucket men?

Ask the class if they enjoyed the story, then ask the following questions:
1  What was the name of the story?
2  What were the names of the boy and girl in the story?
3  What day was it?
4  What sort of buckets did they pass on their way to school?
5  What else apart from bins and buckets and bags were there?
6  How were they tied up?
7  What happened to those which were not tied up?
8  What did the children see moving around the buckets?

9   Why didn't they shoo them away?
10  Why do you think the bucket men wear gloves?
11  Why did they bang the buckets on the van?
12  What is bad about the dustbin men's job? What is good about it? How is it useful?

Ask the class the meaning of the following words:

| | |
|---|---|
| 1 bucket | 6 van |
| 2 newspaper | 7 gloves |
| 3 string | 8 bush |
| 4 potato | 9 dog |
| 5 house | 10 cat |

Ask the class the opposite of the following words:

| | |
|---|---|
| 1 morning | 9 tidy |
| 2 day | 10 open |
| 3 outside | 11 slow |
| 4 in | 12 noisily |
| 5 large | 13 dirty |
| 6 top | 14 useful |
| 7 old | 15 without |
| 8 safe | |

# Daily lesson 123

**Materials**
1 Tool, animal, occupation and clothing cards as listed below
2 Colour cubes
3 Nursery rhyme—*There was an old woman who lived in a shoe*

**Procedure**
Ask the class in what way the following objects and items and persons are different. Insist on a structured sentence for every response.

| | |
|---|---|
| 1 cup, knife | 9 gloves, jersey |
| 2 milkman, coalman | 10 engine driver, bus driver |
| 3 coal, snow | 11 chair, bed |
| 4 bird, dog | 12 cooker, washing machine |
| 5 cat, pig | 13 scissors, hammer |
| 6 horse, mouse | 14 clock, newspaper |
| 7 owl, sheep | 15 tap, kettle |
| 8 shoes, hat | |

Ask the class in what way the following objects, items and persons are the same.

| | |
|---|---|
| 1 newspaper, book | 9 tiger, lion |
| 2 cup, mug | 10 sparrow, blackbird |
| 3 spoon, fork | 11 nurse, dentist |
| 4 scissors, axe | 12 grocer, butcher |
| 5 soap, washing powder | 13 sky, sea |
| 6 milk. water | 14 kitten, puppy |
| 7 tin, drawer | 15 cobra, python |
| 8 cat, mouse | |

Distribute the colour cubes; revise the colour names. Have the class match colours displayed by you, then have them select colours according to your verbal instructions. Then ask them to chain their colour cubes according to your verbal instructions. Chains should start at the left.

| | |
|---|---|
| 1 red, white, blue | 6 brown, red, black |
| 2 red, green, black | 7 yellow, blue, brown |
| 3 yellow, green, orange | 8 green, black, white |
| 4 white, yellow, black | 9 blue, black, yellow |
| 5 black, red, green | 10 white, green, brown |

*Nursery rhyme* Teach the class the rhyme *There was an old woman who lived in a shoe* by playing, singing, reciting the rhyme, analyzing the story line casually and inviting the class to join in for the final recital.

# Daily lesson 124

**Materials**
Tool, clothing and occupation cards as needed for the first activity

**Procedure**
Ask the class to guess what item or person is being thought of. The responder must hold up the appropriate card.
1 This keeps our hands warm.
2 This cuts paper.
3 This tells the time.
4 This cuts the grass.
5 This opens tins.
6 This writes.
7 This cleans the floor.
8 This knocks in nails.
9 This screws in screws.
10 This toasts bread.
11 This holds milk.
12 This chops wood.
13 This saws wood.
14 This man delivers coal.
15 This man sells fish.
16 This man looks after our teeth.
17 This man works with wood.
18 This man flies aircraft.
19 This man looks after us in hospital.
20 This man is our father.
21 This man drives a taxi.
22 This man plays music.
23 This man catches fish.
24 This man makes bread.
25 This man cuts hair.

Ask the class to give a sentence with the following words. Encourage the responder to give an elaborated response. E.g. 'I bounce the ball' is acceptable but 'I bounce the ball against a wall' is better.

| | | | |
|---|---|---|---|
| 1 | ball | 9 | pencil |
| 2 | shoe | 10 | car |
| 3 | hat | 11 | cup |
| 4 | aeroplane | 12 | towel |
| 5 | dog | 13 | sink |
| 6 | bottle | 14 | train |
| 7 | scarf | 15 | horse |
| 8 | chalk | | |

*Rhythm*   Ask the class to copy rhythms clapped or tapped out by you. Begin with very short and simple rhythms and make them increasingly challenging. Insist that the class copy in unison so that you can hear the children who are not picking up the rhythms. Ask individuals as well as groups and the class as a whole to copy your rhythm.

# Daily lesson 125

**Materials**
1 Miscellaneous objects from the classroom
2 Narrative picture—fire scene

**Procedure**
Distribute the objects among the class. Explain that you want them to describe the object in such a way that someone who doesn't know what it is can guess what it is. Give as little prompting as possible but bring out the characteristic features of each object in terms of size, shape, material, texture and function. Structure each response for the class afterwards: 'Yes, it's square shaped, it's small, it's made of hard stuff, may be metal, and we use it to sharpen pencils.'

Display clearly and analyze the picture of the fire scene with the class, emphasizing background, middle ground and foreground. Have the class use their imagination to describe the noises present and how the fire might have started. Quickly structure in language the main points of the picture.

Play a variation of the game 'We went to market and we bought . . .'— 'We went into the centre of the town and we saw . . .' Have individuals in the class contribute one item to a list compiled by previous individuals. Play also 'We went into the countryside and we saw . . .'

# Daily lesson 126

**Materials**
1 Animal cards as below
2 Tool cards
3 Nursery rhyme—*One misty moisty morning*

**Procedure**
Explain to the class that you are going to go round asking them to name anything or say any sensible word that comes into their head. Anyone who cannot contribute drops out. Proper nouns are not acceptable. Start at one end of the class and count how many words are said in three minutes or continue until no one else is left, whichever is the earlier. Repeat this exercise three times, making a note of the number of words spoken.

Tell the class that you are going to test their memory. Display three cards, ask the class to look at them for ten seconds and then to close their eyes. Withdraw one card and ask which is missing. (Withdraw the bracketed card.)
1 cat (mouse) dog
2 sheep horse (tiger)
3 fish (bird) cow
4 pig parrot (leopard)
5 (lamb) kitten pony

At this stage interrupt and explain that the task is made much easier if they name the items quietly to themselves.
6 worm (hedgehog) octopus
7 ladybird (salmon) wasp
8 (fly) crab cobra
9 (ant) penguin otter
10 gorilla (thrush) peacock
11 clock (watch) pen
12 (telephone) letter cup

Ask the class where the following would live or be kept. Insist on a structured response. E.g. cups would be kept in a cupboard; bees would live in a hive.

| | | | |
|---|---|---|---|
| 1 | bird | 9 | cow |
| 2 | dog | 10 | pig |
| 3 | cat | 11 | lion |
| 4 | rabbit | 12 | fish |
| 5 | horse | 13 | eagle |
| 6 | Red Indian | 14 | baby |
| 7 | Eskimo | 15 | bicycle |
| 8 | car | 16 | fork |

*Nursery rhyme*  Play or recite *One misty moisty morning* and have the class listen. Analyze the simple story line of the poem. Play or recite the poem again and have the class try to recite it along with you.

# Daily lesson 127

**Materials**
Tape recorder

**Procedure**
Explain to the class that you are going to read them a story called *Soaked to the skin* and that you want them to listen very carefully to the story because you will ask them questions about it afterwards.

### Soaked to the skin

School was over for the day and the boys and girls rushed to put on their coats and hats and outdoor shoes. Then they wandered towards the door with their friends, looking forward to going home. When they reached the door of the school they looked up at the sky and could see that it had become very dark and grey. It had been quite sunny all day, although a little cold. Now it looked as if it might suddenly begin to rain quite heavily.

Robin and Isabel decided to rush home as quickly as they could before it started to rain. But they were only half way home when down it came. A cloudburst. They had never seen such rain. Huge, heavy drops of water came thudding down onto the street, pavement and gardens. Pools of water quickly formed in the gardens, flowerbeds and grass. The rain bounced off the road and went rushing down the edge of the pavement in torrents, like a river. The noise was almost deafening.

Robin and Isabel looked for shelter but couldn't see any—not a tree, not a shop doorway, nothing. They made a rush for home. The rain beat down on their hats, their hair, their faces and clothes. Their feet squelched into puddles as they ran. They couldn't help giggling and laughing as they ran, even although they were getting soaked.

Eventually they reached home, puffing for breath, and giggling too. Their clothes were dripping water from top to bottom. Their mother, who had been worried about the rain, was glad to see them happy even although they were soaked. She helped them get their wringing wet clothes off. Gosh, the rain had gone right through the front and backs of their coats; even their underclothes were wet! Their shoes and socks of course were sodden.

Their mother piled the clothes in a bundle and gave them each a towel to dry their hair and bodies. They sat in front of the fire while she made hot orange. What fun, they thought. Why couldn't it rain like that more often?

Ask the class if they enjoyed the story. Then ask the following questions:
1  What was the name of the story?
2  What were the names of the boy and girl in the story?
3  What did the sky look like?
4  What had the weather been like all day?
5  What did the children decide to do?
6  What happened then?
7  Describe how the rain fell?
8  Why didn't the children shelter?
9  What did they decide to do?
10  How did they arrive home?

11 What did they look like?
12 What did their mother do?
13 What did Robin and Isabel do?

Ask the class the meaning of the following words:

| | |
|---|---|
| 1 school | 6 hat |
| 2 puddle | 7 shoes |
| 3 garden | 8 towel |
| 4 dark | 9 orange |
| 5 sunny | 10 fine |

Ask the class the opposite of the following words:

| | |
|---|---|
| 1 boys | 11 top |
| 2 outdoor | 12 worried |
| 3 up | 13 glad |
| 4 dark | 14 front |
| 5 sunny | 15 wet |
| 6 cold | 16 sat |
| 7 suddenly | 17 tall |
| 8 quickly | 18 happy |
| 9 heavy | 19 pleased |
| 10 laughing | 20 comfortable |

*On tape*  Ask the class to describe any occasion they have been caught in the rain. Play back a selection.

# Daily lesson 128

**Materials**
1 Tool cards as listed below
2 Nursery rhyme—*Twinkle, twinkle, little star*

**Procedure**
Have the class complete the following:

1 Here is one finger; here are two _____ .
2 Here is one hand; here are two _____ .
3 Here is one boy; here are two _____ .
4 Here is one girl; here are two _____ .
5 Here is one desk; here are two _____ .
6 Here is one chair; here are two _____ .
7 Here is one dress; here are two _____ .
8 Here is a man; here are two _____ .
9 Here is one horse; here are two _____ .
10 Here is a house; here are two _____ .
11 Here is a mouse; here are two _____ .
12 Here is a book; here are two _____ .
13 Here is one tortoise; here are two _____ .
14 Here is one woman; here are two _____ .
15 A mouse is small; an ant is even _____ .
16 A kitten is small; a ladybird is even _____ .
17 A puppy is small; a wasp is even _____ .
18 A lamb is small; a rabbit is even _____ .
19 A bird is small; a butterfly is even _____ .
20 A bush is small; a flower is even _____ .

Ask the class what the following items do or are used for. Use cards where appropriate:

| | |
|---|---|
| 1 legs | 11 tap |
| 2 hammer | 12 straw |
| 3 ball | 13 clock |
| 4 shoes | 14 letter |
| 5 eyes | 15 nail |
| 6 book | 16 rubber (eraser) |
| 7 kettle | 17 mirror |
| 8 cup | 18 axe |
| 9 brush | 19 pencil |
| 10 soap | 20 needle |

*Nursery rhyme* Have the class listen to the nursery rhyme *Twinkle, twinkle, little star* and repeat. Question the meaning of the rhyme. Repeat the rhyme and have the class try to say it along with you.

# Daily lesson 129

## Materials

Nursery rhyme—*I saw a ship come sailing, come sailing on the sea*

## Procedure

Explain to the class that you want them to give you a word that rhymes with the word you say. Explain that two words rhyme if they end in the same sound e.g. *hat* rhymes with *cat*. They have the same sound at the end. Hat rhymes with cat, head rhymes with red. Say 'Give me a word that rhymes with . . .'

| | | | |
|---|---|---|---|
| 1 | log | 11 | hen |
| 2 | house | 12 | pill |
| 3 | fat | 13 | rot |
| 4 | bun | 14 | fun |
| 5 | fin | 15 | mail |
| 6 | met | 16 | mole |
| 7 | mine | 17 | now |
| 8 | pool | 18 | tree |
| 9 | sup | 19 | goat |
| 10 | goose | 20 | feel |

Ask the class what they would do if

1 A ball they were playing with bounced onto the busy road.
2 They lost some money on their way to buy some groceries for mummy.
3 They spilt some milk on the carpet at home.
4 They had two sweets and a friend had none.
5 They were hungry.
6 They were thirsty.
7 They were cold in bed at night.
8 They were too hot in bed at night.
9 They lost their way.
10 They lost a toy belonging to someone else.

*Nursery rhyme*   Repeat the nursery rhyme. Analyze casually, and have the class try to learn it.

# Daily lesson 130

**Materials**
1 Tape recorder
2 Nursery rhyme—*I saw a ship come sailing, come sailing on the sea*

**Procedure**
Explain to the class that you want them all to listen carefully to what you say, and then select a few to repeat what you have said (at the rate of one per second).

1 three—six—eight
2 four—nine—seven—five
3 three—two—eight—four
4 one—seven—six—three
5 two—three—seven—one
6 five—seven—two—three
7 two—eight—ten—four
8 nine—three—two—six
9 seven—four—five—eight
10 two—two—three—nine

11 green—boy—desk—snow
12 white—pig—hello—ball
13 table—house—paper—card
14 finger—eye—nose—knee
15 peg—chalk—leg—shoe
16 yellow—duck—kitten—car
17 house—rose—mat—girl
18 dress—table—light—handle
19 door—glass—curtain—flower

*On tape*  Tell the class that you want them to tell the tape recorder something about themselves—their full name, address, date of birth and age. Many children may not know either address or date of birth. Teach them this by day of the month, name of month and year. Have the class structure their descriptions: 'My name is John Smith, my address is (I live at) 20 Main Street, Fordham, England, and I am six. My date of birth is the third of July 1968.' Encourage the class to criticize their own and other children's efforts.

*Nursery rhyme*  Have the class listen to *I saw a ship come sailing, come sailing on the sea*. Repeat and have the class try to recite it along with the tape or yourself. Analyze the rhyme casually so that most of the meaning is clear to the class and play once again.

# Daily lesson 131

**Materials**
1 Animal cards—bird, dog, tortoise, rabbit, elephant, mouse
2 Clothing cards—hat, coat, gloves, shoes, trousers, stockings
3 Tool cards—knife, cup, hammer, spade, axe, saw

**Procedure**
Ask the class to finish the sentence you say.
1 Coal is black, snow is _____ .
2 The dog has four legs, the bird has _____ legs.
3 A table is hard, a pillow is _____ .
4 Grass is green, the sky is _____ .
5 Boys grow up to be men; girls grow up to be _____ .
6 Mary is a girl, Maurice is a _____ .
7 Coffee is hot, milk is _____ .
8 An elephant is large; a sparrow is _____ .
9 A tiger is fierce; a lamb is _____ .
10 Young boys run fast; old men _____ .
11 In the daytime it is light; at nightime it is _____ .
12 Snow falls in wintertime; the sun shines in _____ .
13 When we're happy we smile; when we're miserable we _____ .
14 When we're hungry we eat; when we're thirsty we _____ .
15 We see with our eyes, we hear with our _____ .

Ask the class to carry out the following instructions:
1 Put your left hand on your head.
2 Put your right hand on your head.
3 Stand on one leg.
4 Stand on the other leg.
5 Look sideways.
6 Stand with feet apart.
7 Close your eyes.
8 Stand at attention.
9 Raise both arms above your head.
10 Raise both arms level with your shoulders.

Ask the class how the following are different. Do not use cards on every occasion.
1 bird, dog
2 tortoise, rabbit
3 elephant, mouse
4 zebra, pony (no card)
5 hat, coat
6 gloves, shoes
7 trousers, stockings
8 skirt, trousers (no card)
9 knife, cup
10 hammer, spade
11 axe, saw
12 hammer, pliers (no card)

# Daily lesson 132

**Materials**

Tape recorder

**Procedure**

Explain to the class that you are going to read them a story called *The furniture van* and that you want them to listen carefully because you will ask them questions about it afterwards.

### The furniture van

There must be new people moving into the street, thought Tim and Gillian. There, just two doors up from their own house, was a huge furniture van. They stood at their gate watching.

The back of the van was down, flat on the ground, and they could see right into the van. What a lot of furniture! They couldn't make much of it out, because it seemed to be either upside down or covered in sheets and sacking. Two furniture men appeared from the house two doors up and marched up to and into the van. They wore white aprons almost touching their feet.

Tim and Gillian saw them untie some rope and take off a large sheet and bundle it into the street. Puffing slightly the two men lifted out a big white refrigerator. Gosh, it looked heavy. The men moved slowly, taking tiny awkward steps, shuffling their feet along the back of the van onto the pavement. They both had worried looks on their faces. They disappeared, shuffling, into the doorway of the house, two doors up.

Tim and Gillian moved nearer. They could make out some chairs stacked on one another. A table lamp. A mattress. A few rolls of carpet. The furniture men reappeared, walking briskly this time.

Again they untied some ropes and bundled a covering sheet onto the street. Then they heaved out a dressing table. At least Gillian thought it was a dressing table—only it didn't have a mirror. Then she saw that the mirror must have been taken off, and she noticed it leaning against one of the sides of the van. Up into the house the men went carrying the dressing table.

This was interesting. Gillian and Tim made up their minds to stand and watch until the van was empty. They couldn't wait to see what came out next. They wondered what the people who would be moving in looked like. Would they be nice? Would they have any children to play with?

Ask the class if they enjoyed the story. Then ask the following questions:
1  What was the name of the story?
2  What were the names of the boy and girl in the story?
3  Why weren't they able to see much of the furniture in the van at first?
4  How many men were there?
5  What were they wearing?
6  What had the men to do before they lifted anything out of the van?
7  Why did they move awkwardly?
8  Why did they look worried?
9  What could Gillian and Tim see in the van?
10  What did they see being taken out of the van?

11 Why did the dressing table look funny?
12 Where was the mirror and why?
13 What did Gillian and Tim wonder about?

Ask the class the meaning of the following words:

| | |
|---|---|
| 1 house | 6 chair |
| 2 van | 7 mattress |
| 3 apron | 8 mirror |
| 4 rope | 9 pavement |
| 5 refrigerator | 10 door |

Ask the class the opposite of the following words:

| | |
|---|---|
| 1 new | 9 heavy |
| 2 into | 10 nearer |
| 3 down | 11 briskly |
| 4 upside down | 12 interesting |
| 5 covered | 13 empty |
| 6 appeared | 14 nice |
| 7 white | 15 child |
| 8 tie | |

*On tape* Ask the class to describe any time they may have seen furniture men working, either moving furniture in or out of a place. Play back a selection. Have some of the class mime the efforts and movements of the furniture men.

# Daily lesson 133

**Materials**
1. Animal cards—cat, dog, cow, pig, eagle, budgerigar
2. Clothing cards—shoes, stockings, coat, gloves, hat, dress
3. Tool cards—knife, spoon, hammer, screwdriver, pencil, pen

**Procedure**
Ask the class 'In what way are these alike?' Show the cards, and name the objects as you ask the question. Note that in some cases no cards are to be shown.

1. cat, dog
2. cow, pig
3. eagle, budgerigar
4. whale, salmon (no cards)
5. shoes, stockings
6. coat, gloves
7. hat, dress
8. jacket, blouse (no cards)
9. knife, spoon
10. hammer, screwdriver
11. pencil, pen
12. towel, soap (no cards)

Ask the class to tell you a word or give a name to describe the following persons or objects.

1. tree
2. pencil
3. sky
4. I deliver milk
5. I drive a bus
6. I direct traffic
7. stones
8. water
9. plasticine
10. boiling water
11. ball
12. grass
13. I grow corn and tend animals
14. I collect fares on a bus
15. I drive a train
16. I lay bricks for a house
17. fire
18. snow
19. wind
20. sea

Select members of the class and whisper instructions to perform simple tasks as follows. The rest of the class have to describe accurately what the child does.

1. put left hand on your head
2. stand on right leg
3. open and close mouth
4. blink
5. raise right hand
6. raise left hand
7. touch left foot with left hand
8. touch right foot with right hand
9. turn head to left, then right
10. walk on tip toe
11. march
12. curl up into a ball

# Daily lesson 134

**Materials**
1 Tape recorder
2 Nursery rhyme—*Wee Willie Winkie*

**Procedure**
Have the class tell the tape recorder their name, address, age and date of birth. In addition have them describe themselves or their clothes to the recorder. Play back a selection.

Ask the class what they would do if
1 The lights went out.
2 Teacher forgot the playtime bell.
3 They found some money in the classroom.
4 They cut themselves.
5 They felt ill.

Tell the class that you are going to say a sentence, and that there is something funny, odd or wrong about what you say. Ask them to point out what is funny, odd or wrong and to correct the sentence.
1 The snow lay thick in summertime.
2 The dog miaowed loudly.
3 He toasted the bread in the kettle.
4 He put his gloves on his feet.
5 Father lit his newspaper and read his pipe.
6 He opened the window and walked in.
7 He ate his milk quickly.
8 He poured water into the fire.
9 The rain poured up from the sky.
10 They walked towards the ceiling.

*Nursery rhyme*　Teach the nursery rhyme *Wee Willie Winkie* by playing, replaying, analyzing casually and replaying. Invite the class to join in.

# Daily lesson 135

**Materials**
1 Tools and animal cards as listed below
2 Nursery rhymes—tape recorder

**Procedure**
Ask the class the difference between the following:
1 scissors and garden shears
2 a potato and a banana
3 a cricket bat and a tennis racquet
4 a fork and a spoon
5 a watch and a clock
6 a pencil and a pen
7 a newspaper and a book
8 a nail and a screw
9 a jug and a bottle
10 a bottle and a saucepan
11 a cat and a dog
12 a mouse and a rat
13 a tiger and a lion
14 a sparrow and an owl
15 a rabbit and a hamster
16 a horse and a zebra
17 an elephant and a giraffe
18 a wasp and a bee
19 an ant and a centipede
20 a ladybird and a butterfly

Ask the class to do the opposite of what you say.
1 sit down
2 look to your left
3 stand up
4 close your mouth
5 open your eyes
6 lie on your backs
7 look in front of you
8 make yourself as small as you can
9 make as much noise as you can
10 stand up straight

Ask individuals to think of an object, or animal, or anything at all. Have each child describe it to the rest of the class who have to guess what it is.

*Nursery rhymes* Ask the class to nominate their favourite rhymes and have them record, individually or in groups, or as a class.

# Daily lesson 136

**Materials**
Nursery rhymes—*Little Miss Muffet, Little Jack Horner*

**Procedure**
Ask the class to give you at least two words to describe each of the following.
Then ask for a sentence which includes these two words and the object.

| | | | |
|---|---|---|---|
| 1 | tree | 11 | donkey |
| 2 | river | 12 | hand |
| 3 | dog | 13 | pig |
| 4 | pencil | 14 | razor blade |
| 5 | sand | 15 | key |
| 6 | table | 16 | radiator |
| 7 | chalk | 17 | needle |
| 8 | car | 18 | scissors |
| 9 | aeroplane | 19 | fire |
| 10 | coat | 20 | snow |

Draw a 'doodle' or 'squiggle' or 'nonsense shape' on the board. Make some shapes open and others closed. Invite the class to explain in words what the shape reminds them of and why. Have them verbalize differences and similarities. Discourage phrases such as 'that bit' and 'over there', and encourage phrases like 'the top corner' or the 'left hand bottom corner'.

Play a variation of the game 'I went to market and I bought . . .' What would we find in a

| | | | |
|---|---|---|---|
| 1 | supermarket | 6 | museum |
| 2 | zoo | 7 | hairdresser |
| 3 | harbour | 8 | toy shop |
| 4 | beach | 9 | garage |
| 5 | house | 10 | chemist |

*Nursery rhymes*   Teach the rhyme *Little Miss Muffet* and have the class verbalize their feelings about spiders and their feelings about Miss Muffet's reaction. Teach *Little Jack Horner* and have the class verbalize their feelings about Jack's reaction to pulling out a plum. What do they like to eat most?

# Daily lesson 137

**Materials**
Tape recorder

**Procedure**
Explain to the class that you are going to read them a story called *The seaside* and that you want them to listen carefully to the story because you will ask them questions about it afterwards.

### The seaside

Rachel and Noel hadn't been to the seaside often because they lived in a town, quite far away from the sea. But during the school holidays their parents had taken them down to the coast for a few days. The weather had been very warm and sunny so they were able to spend most of their time on the beach.

They wore swimming costumes almost all day long. What they liked doing most was building high piles of sand and digging down deep into the sand, making sand castles and tunnels. They used their plastic buckets and wooden spades for this. The sand on top of the beach was fine and dry and they found they couldn't build very high piles. But the sand underneath the beach was moist and wet, rough and gritty, and there were even small sharp stones mixed in with it. It made your hands and feet and knees sore. But they found they could dig deep holes and tunnels, big enough to crawl into and hide. If they dug too deep they found that the walls of the holes would collapse, which was a nuisance.

Nearer the sea the sand was almost like clay. You could make shapes with it and Rachel and Noel spent a lot of time making row upon row of sand pies. They'd watch as the sea came in sometime during the day, gradually washing away what they had built. Then they'd start again.

Farther along the beach from where they sat you could get rides on a donkey. There was always a queue for the donkey because he was popular with all the boys and girls on the beach. It was worth waiting for, even though you could only get a short ride. It was super, feeling his rough, warm, woolly coat against your bare legs and to feel him swaying this way and that as he plodded along the sand, *clippity-clop, clippity-clop*. He was a quiet donkey, and patient too—he never made a noise or a move unless the man who owned him said so. He'd just walk up and down, up and down all day carrying little girls and boys like Rachel and Noel. They wondered what he would be doing just now. Where do donkeys go in the wintertime?

Ask the class if they enjoyed the story, then ask the following questions:
1 What was the name of the story?
2 What were the names of the boy and girl in the story?
3 Where did they live?
4 When did they go to the seaside?
5 What was the weather like?
6 What did they like doing most?
7 What did they use?
8 What was the sand on top of the beach like?

9 What was the sand underneath like?
10 What happened if you dug too deep?
11 What did the children make with the sand nearer the sea?
12 Why was there always a queue for the donkey?
13 What did the children like about him?
14 What did Rachel and Noel wonder?

Ask the class the meaning of the following words:

| | |
|---|---|
| 1 bucket | 7 pool |
| 2 spade | 8 car |
| 3 hands | 9 boat |
| 4 feet | 10 towel |
| 5 donkey | 11 nuisance |
| 6 coat | |

Ask the class the opposite of the following words:

| | |
|---|---|
| 1 often | 11 moist |
| 2 town | 12 rough |
| 3 far away | 13 sharp |
| 4 warm | 14 start |
| 5 sunny | 15 farther |
| 6 build | 16 popular |
| 7 high | 17 bare |
| 8 down | 18 patient |
| 9 deep | 19 wintertime |
| 10 on top | 20 sorry |

*On tape* Ask the class to describe any visit they have made to the seaside. Play back a selection.

# Daily lesson 138

**Materials**
1 Occupation cards as listed
2 Miscellaneous cards as listed
3 Nursery rhymes as selected by class

**Procedure**
Ask the class to identify the following people. Have them select from the displayed cards the appropriate occupation.
1 He fits windows. (glazier)
2 She works on the stage or in films or in television. (actress)
3 He works in an orchestra. (musician)
4 He attends to our teeth. (dentist)
5 He keeps our streets and pavements tidy and clean. (road sweeper)
6 He travels on a ship. (sailor)
7 She types letters. (typist)
8 She works at home, taking care of her husband and family. (housewife)
9 He works underground, digging out coal. (mineworker)
10 He tells us the news on television or radio. (a television or radio announcer)
11 He repairs our roads. (roadworker)
12 He makes pottery. (potter)
13 He tells an orchestra what to do and when. (orchestra conductor)
14 He takes our fare on the bus. (a bus conductor)
15 He fits electric cookers and plugs in a house. (an electrician)

Ask the class the meaning of the following words. Insist on a structured sentence response. Display the card only after a verbal response.

| | |
|---|---|
| 1 shoe | 11 chalk |
| 2 spoon | 12 apple |
| 3 pencil | 13 umbrella |
| 4 flask | 14 cup |
| 5 book | 15 saw |
| 6 ashtray | 16 aeroplane |
| 7 lighter | 17 hat |
| 8 telephone | 18 boot |
| 9 desk | 19 glove |
| 10 bottle | 20 chair |

*Nursery rhymes* Ask the class to name as many nursery rhymes as they can as quickly as they can. Have every child say or attempt to say as much of any rhyme as he knows. Make a note of the rhymes that seem to be misunderstood or only vaguely understood by the class.

# Daily lesson 139

**Materials**
1 Narrative picture—puppet show at the seaside
2 Nursery rhyme—*Punch and Judy*
3 Tape recorder

**Procedure**
Display the narrative picture and analyze with the class the background, middle and foreground. In other words talk with the class generally about the seaside, the Punch and Judy show and the reactions of the children watching. Finally structure the picture in language quickly and simply.

*On tape*   Have the class verbalize their feelings about a Punch and Judy show they have seen—were they frightened, did they think Punch was cruel and unjust, did they think Judy was stupid? etc.

*Nursery rhyme*   Teach the class the short rhyme *Punch and Judy*.

# Daily lesson 140

**Materials**
Occupation cards as listed

**Procedure**
Ask the class where they would expect the following to work, and have them describe what they imagine the working conditions are like.

1 hairdresser
2 dentist
3 newspaper reporter
4 roadsweeper
5 steelworker
6 car mechanic
7 fishmonger
8 tailor
9 orchestra conductor
10 actress
11 painter and decorator
12 glazier
13 potter
14 gardener
15 soldier

Ask the class to give simple sentences using the following words:

1 after
2 before
3 later
4 left
5 right
6 soon
7 join
8 alone
9 quickly
10 try
11 on
12 orange
13 rain
14 letter
15 water
16 pleased
17 hope
18 sorry
19 going
20 ball

Ask the class to name as many words as they can—any words at all will do other than the names of the members of the class. Begin by having the class stand and each child give his/her word as quickly as possible. Allow four seconds for each response; and any child who cannot respond sits down. The winner is the child who is left standing. Count the words given during each period of play and let the class compete against this number each time.

# Daily lesson 141

**Materials**
1 Tape recorder
2 Nursery rhyme—*Old King Cole*

**Procedure**
Ask the class to finish the following sentences.
1 A chair is heavy; a table is even _____ . (heavier)
2 A pencil is light, a feather is even _____ . (lighter)
3 A table is heavy; a piano is even _____ . (heavier)
4 A bottle is light; a penny is even _____ . (lighter)
5 A pavement is wide; a road is even _____ . (wider)
6 A ruler is narrow; a crack in the floor is even _____ . (narrower)
7 A river is wide; the sea is even _____ . (wider)
8 A river is deep; the sea is even _____ . (deeper)
9 A bird flies high; an aeroplane flies even _____ . (higher)
10 A table is broad; a floor is even _____ . (broader)
11 A wall may be high, but a building is usually _____ . (higher)
12 A man can be tall, but a lampost is even _____ . (taller)
13 A dog can be small, but a butterfly is usually _____ . (smaller)

Ask the class to name as many things or say as many words as they can beginning with the following letter or sound. Split the class into groups and have the groups compete against one another. Limit the time on each letter or sound to sixty seconds.
1 *a* for apple
2 *b* for big
3 *c* for cow
4 *d* for dog
5 *f* for frog
6 *g* for goat
7 *h* for hat
8 *j* for jam
9 *l* for leg
10 *m* for man

*On tape*  Ask the class to tell the tape recorder their full names, address, age and date of birth. Have them give a brief description of themselves, and have them tell the recorder their likes.

*Nursery rhyme*  Teach *Old King Cole* by telling, retelling, analyzing casually and inviting the class to join in.

# Daily lesson 142

**Materials**
Tape recorder

**Procedure**
Explain to the class that you are going to read them a story called *Daddy shaving* and that you want them to listen carefully to the story because you will ask them questions about it afterwards.

### Daddy shaving

Tracy and Gerald didn't often see daddy shaving. He went out very early in the morning most days but at the weekend the family usually got up around the same time. So occasionally, at the weekend, Tracy who was six, and Gerald who was a little boy of only three, would go in and watch.

First daddy would collect all the tools he needed to shave—a towel, a razor and a razor blade, soap, a tin of shaving soap and his shaving mirror. Tracy would stand at one side of him and Gerald would kneel on a chair at the other side, watching his every move.

'Why do you do that, daddy?' asked Gerald.

'Do you mean why do I shave, Gerald?'

'Yes.'

'Well, the hair on my face grows overnight, and if I didn't shave it off, it would grow longer and longer and wouldn't look smart,' replied daddy.

'I don't have hair,' said Gerald.

'Nor do I,' said Tracy.

'No, you don't have hair,' said daddy. 'Girls don't have hair on their face, and neither do little boys. But when you are bigger, Gerald, you will have hair and have to shave it off too.'

Daddy began to wash his face with soap and hot water and the other two watched. Having washed his face, he then pressed the tin of shaving soap into his hand and rubbed it onto his face until it was nearly covered.

'Can I have some of that, daddy?' said Gerald.

'Me too,' said Tracy.

'Just a little then, and be careful not to rub it into your eyes or it will sting.'

They both felt very grown up, and pushed him gently out of the way to get a look at themselves in the mirror. Daddy was as patient as he could be. He always liked to shave without being pestered or bothered, but seeing as it was the weekend and there was no real need to hurry he let himself be pestered.

'Right, then,' he said. 'Now I'm going to shave with the razor. Now, it's very sharp and I don't want to cut myself, so no talking, no asking questions, no pushing.' Gerald and Tracey liked their daddy, and they knew that he liked them too. Although he was nearly always kind and gentle with them, they could tell that he meant what he said. So they stood quietly, and motionless, just watching him.

He stood looking into the mirror, scraping the razor across his face, this way and that. Quickly and often he would dip the razor into the basin of hot water to clean off the soap suds and then he'd scrape his face some more. All this time they stood quietly and motionless, just staring.

'Now,' he said, 'that's that.' And he washed the rest of the soap off his face, rubbing himself dry with the towel. Gerald pulled the plug of the basin and watched the soapy water disappear down the plug hole.

'Let's feel your face, daddy,' said Tracy, and he knelt down so that she could reach it. 'Gosh, isn't it smooth. You feel it, Gerald. Isn't it smooth?'

'Yes,' said Gerald, wishing he was old enough to shave just the way daddy did.

Ask the class if they enjoyed the story and then ask the following questions:

1 What was the name of the story?
2 What were the names of the boy and girl in the story?
3 Why didn't they often see daddy shaving?
4 What did he need to shave?
5 Why did Gerald not shave, nor Tracy?
6 What did Gerald and Tracy ask for?
7 What did they do then?
8 What did their daddy say to them then?
9 How did he shave?
10 What did Gerald do after daddy had finished?
11 What did Gerald and Tracy do next?
12 What did Gerald wish?

*On tape* Ask the class to describe any occasion on which they have watched their father shave. Try to get them to express their feelings—did they wonder why they didn't have to shave? Why do some men prefer to grow beards? Does daddy seem to get irritated and angry, and if so, why? What does a face of stubble feel like? Which do the children prefer, a bearded or shaved face?

# Daily lesson 143

**Materials**
Narrative picture—picture of television character with which the class are familiar e.g. Dougal and Dylan of the *Magic Roundabout*

**Procedure**
Ask the class to repeat exactly what you say. Do not accept omissions or alterations.
 1  He filled the kettle with water and plugged it in.
 2  She placed a knife, a fork and two spoons on the table.
 3  It was snowing heavily in the morning when they got up.
 4  I would like to go and ride on a donkey as often as possible.
 5  We go swimming every Saturday morning.
 6  You should always be kind to dogs, cats and hamsters.
 7  They tried to lift the heavy table through the doorway.
 8  We won't be able to see the castle because of the fog.
 9  He sat on the edge of the carpet cutting bits of paper.
10  She shouldn't shout so sharply at her shy sister.

Ask the class to play a variety of the game 'I spy with my little eye . . .' Using the following situations, have every class member say what they see, adding one item to the list previously mentioned.

| | |
|---|---|
| 1  bedroom | 4  classroom |
| 2  kitchen | 5  garage |
| 3  living room | 6  baby's nursery |

Display picture of television character and have the class identify him. Have them describe his character, his antics and general behaviour. Have them verbalize their feelings about their liking, disliking etc.

# Daily lesson 144

**Materials**
Tape recorder

**Procedure**
Ask the class to compile a list of the different sounds they would hear in the following places.
1 garage
2 house
3 classroom

Tap out rhythms with your hands or with a pencil. Begin with simple rhythms and gradually make them increasingly challenging. Ask individuals to take over leadership of the class occasionally and to suggest rhythms themselves.

*On tape*  Ask individuals to describe what happens, and what they hear in the kitchen. Insist on structured sentences. Do not use any visual aid. Record the conversation and play back. Remind the class that they have to speak clearly and quite slowly and that they must keep their sentences short.

# Daily lesson 145

**Materials**
1 Tool cards as listed
2 Nursery rhymes as selected by the children
3 Tape recorder

**Procedure**
Ask the class to give as many words as they can beginning with the following sounds:
1 *n* for needle
2 *oa* as in oak
3 *o* as in otter
4 *p* as in picture
5 *q* as in queue

Ask the class in what way the following pairs are the same:

| | |
|---|---|
| 1 mouse and rat | 6 cat and tiger |
| 2 sugar and salt | 7 water and milk |
| 3 glove and mitten | 8 shoe and slipper |
| 4 fly and bird | 9 cow and horse |
| 5 tree and flower | 10 coat and dress |

Ask the class to give a word or words to describe the following:

| | |
|---|---|
| 1 knife | 6 hammer |
| 2 kettle | 7 nail |
| 3 plate | 8 saw |
| 4 table cloth | 9 wheelbarrow |
| 5 envelope | 10 lawnmower |

*Nursery rhymes*   Ask the class to think of their favourite nursery rhyme. Have individuals recite their selection to the tape recorder and play back.

**Materials**

1 Narrative pictures—pictures depicting television characters with which the children are familiar e.g. Dougal and Dylan of the *Magic Roundabout*, *Tom and Jerry*
2 Nursery rhyme—*Rub a dub dub, three men in a tub*

**Procedure**

Display the pictures and ask the class to identify them. Ask individuals about the characters' activities and antics. Have them describe the characters' personalities and get the class to verbalize their feelings about the characters. Do they think they are attractive, unattractive, silly or stupid in any way, kind or cruel, lovable or hateful?

Ask the class to say in what way the following pairs are different:

| | | |
|---|---|---|
| 1 mouse and rat | 6 | tree and flower |
| 2 cat and tiger | 7 | glove and mitten |
| 3 cow and horse | 8 | fly and bird |
| 4 water and milk | 9 | coat and dress |
| 5 sugar and salt | 10 | shoe and slipper |

*Nursery rhyme*  Teach *Rub a dub dub, three men in a tub* by reciting and analyzing; have the class join in when they can.

# Daily lesson 147

**Materials**
Tape recorder

**Procedure**
Explain to the class that you are going to read them a story called *Building a house* and that you want them to listen carefully to the story because you will ask them questions about it afterwards.

Building a house

It was Saturday. No school today. But it was raining heavily outside so no playing either. What to do? Tom and Diana stood at the window staring at the rain. What to do? What to do? 'Why not make a house?' thought Diana. 'Tommy, let's make a house,' she said.

'A house? What with?' asked Tommy.

'Oh, anything,' said Diana. 'We could use a blanket, some chairs—oh come on, let's see.'

They wandered through the house asking their mother if they could use this cushion, and this chair and a blanket from upstairs. Yes, they could use whatever they liked as long as they were careful and didn't use anything that could be broken.

Using the front of the settee as one side of the house they tried to lean a cushion against it for another wall. But it fell down. They tried several times but it always fell down. It wasn't firm enough. They would have to try something else. A chair! What about a chair? They pulled one over and pushed it against the front of the settee. There, that was two walls up. They pulled another chair over and placed it against the front of the settee too. Now what about a roof? The blanket? Yes. They folded the blanket twice and placed it gently across the top of the two chairs. There. All they needed now was a door. The clothes horse that mummy had in the cupboard. They remembered that when mummy folded away the clothes horse after using it to hang clothes on to dry, it was quite flat and easy to handle. It would do.

They ran to the cupboard, lifted out the clothes horse and carried it through to where the rest of their building was. It filled the doorway just neatly. So in they crawled, pulling their door shut behind them. Then they sat quietly, warm and cosy, wondering what to do, as the rain beat against the windows outside.

Ask the class if they enjoyed the story. Then ask the following questions:
1 What was the name of the story?
2 What were the names of the boy and girl in the story?
3 What was the weather like?
4 What did the children decide to do?
5 What did they use to make the walls of the house?
6 What did they use to make the door and the roof?

Ask the class the meaning of the following words:

| | | |
|---|---|---|
| 1 window | 3 blanket | 5 cushion |
| 2 house | 4 chair | 6 clothes horse |

*On tape* Ask the class to describe any attempts they made to build a house, either indoors or outdoors.

# Daily lesson 148

**Materials**
1  Tape recorder
2  Nursery rhymes—class selection

**Procedure**
Ask the class what they would do in the following situations. Encourage responses which emphasize personal initiative rather than those which indicate simply 'telling mother' or 'telling the teacher.' Say 'What would you do if . . .'

1  You couldn't find your coat on the pegs.
2  Your shoelace broke.
3  A page became detached from a book.
4  You were alone at home and the phone began to ring.
5  You knew your mother wanted sugar but had forgotten to ask for it.
6  You went to a shop to buy bread but the baker said he didn't have any left.
7  Your nose began to bleed.
8  You lost a ball belonging to a friend.
9  You wanted to go to the toilet during class time.

*On tape*  Using the tape recorder interview several of the class. Ask their name and age and what they like doing best in class. Accept general response such as 'drawing', follow up such responses by asking what they like to draw and why. Children will have difficulty verbalizing their feelings. Speculate upon the feelings of each individual child and verbalize these feelings for them if necessary, but in a neutral nonthreatening way.

*Nursery rhymes*  Recite and/or sing the class's selection of nursery rhymes.

# Daily lesson 149

**Materials**
Any three narrative pictures used earlier in the year

**Procedure**
Ask individuals to mime the use of the following tools. Encourage the use of both hands where appropriate. The remainder of the class have to guess what tool is being used. Insist on well structured sentences in response.

1  tap
2  jug
3  bottle
4  hosepipe
5  sewing machine
6  mirror
7  soap
8  packet of washing powder
9  towel
10  bath
11 sink
12  lightswitch
13  tray
14  box of matches
15  pencil sharpener

Explain to the class that you are going to display a picture that they have seen before. You will let them see the picture for just one minute and then ask them to name as many things or activities in the picture as they can from memory. Display the picture for one minute, cover it up and ask the class to respond from memory. Count the number of acceptable responses. Repeat the same procedures with two other narrative pictures. Compare the results on each picture.

# Daily lesson 150

**Materials**
1 Random selection of cards from every section
2 Nursery rhymes—revise a selection of short rhymes

**Procedure**
Ask the class to name as many words, or things as they can beginning with the following sounds:

1 *r* as in rock
2 *s* as in sound
3 *t* as in tin
4 *u* as in up
5 *v* as in van
6 *w* as in word
7 *y* as in you
8 *z* as in zip
9 *ch* as in cheese
10 *th* as in theirs

Ask individuals to give a sentence (simple but well structured) using the following two words:

1 paper, pencil
2 table, fork
3 cooker, pan
4 water, dishes
5 carpet, coffee
6 sun, water
7 mirror, hair
8 garden, cat
9 window, trees
10 clean, basin
11 hard, ball
12 playground, noisy
13 car, fast
14 write, book
15 telephone, speak
16 watch, late
17 dinner, hungry
18 pretty, smile
19 hand, plaster
20 sing, school

Display the cards to the class, all at one time. Invite one child to select any card and another to select a card belonging to the same group (animal, tool, occupation, clothing etc). Invite two more selections by other children until you have four examples of the same group. Change the group and continue until enthusiasm wains.

*Nursery rhymes*   Revise a selection of short rhymes.

# Daily lesson 151

## Materials
1 Tape recorder
2 Nursery rhyme—*Mary, Mary, quite contrary*

## Procedure
Ask the class to make a list of all the things they can think of that live or
are kept in the following places:
1 attic
2 nest
3 drawer
4 hole in the ground

Ask the class to listen carefully to the list of words you read. When they
hear a number they have to clap their hands three times.

| | | | |
|---|---|---|---|
| 1 | weight | 13 | nine |
| 2 | eight | 14 | bee |
| 3 | now | 15 | hive |
| 4 | said | 16 | five |
| 5 | tree | 17 | four |
| 6 | three | 18 | good |
| 7 | floor | 19 | heaven |
| 8 | blue | 20 | seven |
| 9 | two | 21 | lick |
| 10 | yes | 22 | fix |
| 11 | bless | 23 | six |
| 12 | mine | 24 | ten |

*On tape*   Ask the class to describe anything that they have ever seen or
heard at a zoo. Do not use visual aids but record the conversation on the
tape recorder and play back. Remind the class to speak clearly and slowly
and keep their sentences short.

*Nursery rhyme*   Teach *Mary, Mary, quite contrary*.

# Daily lesson 152

**Materials**
Tape recorder

**Procedure**
Explain to the class that you are going to tell them a story called *The school doctor* and that you want them to listen carefully to the story because you will ask them questions about it afterwards.

### The school doctor

The school doctor was visiting today. Tina looked forward to the time when it was her turn to go. She would wait quietly in the corridor just outside the medical room. As she waited she had her eyes tested. She stood at one end of the corridor and the nurse stood at the other. The nurse held up pictures of animals, birds, flowers and other things, and Tina had to tell her what she was holding up. She looked at the pictures with first the left eye covered and then the right eye covered. It was a super game.

Soon it was her turn to see the doctor. He was dressed in a white coat and had a funny thing clipped behind his neck and hanging down his front. This was called a stethoscope and he used it to listen to the heart beating and the lungs breathing. He was a very kind man, always smiling. He looked at Tina's teeth and asked her to say 'Ah' loudly, and that was easy. Then he looked behind her ears and at her hands to see if she had washed them today. The best bit was when he asked if he could listen to her heart beating. He placed the stethoscope on her chest and plugged one end into his ears. Then he listened. The stethoscope was cold and tickly. Then Tina was lucky—he let her listen to his heart beating. What a noise it made! *Thumpity thump thump; thumpity thump thump.*

He said 'thank you' and 'goodbye' and back Tina went to her classroom to get dressed. She thought, 'Wouldn't it be fun to be a doctor and listen to people's hearts through that stethoscope all the time!'

Ask the class if they enjoyed the story. Then ask the following questions:
1  What was the name of the story?
2  What was the name of the girl in the story?
3  Where did she wait?
4  What happened while she waited?
5  What sort of pictures did she look at?
6  How was the doctor dressed?
7  What did he have hanging round his neck?
8  What did he ask Tina to say?
9  What noise does a heart make?

Ask the class to give the opposite of the following words:
| | | |
|---|---|---|
| 1 quietly | 4 covered | 7 behind |
| 2 outside | 5 dressed | 8 front |
| 3 left | 6 white | 9 kind |

*On tape*   Ask the class to describe any visits they have made to the doctor, or any visits the doctor has made to their home. Play back a selection.

# Daily lesson 153

**Materials**

None

**Procedure**

Explain to the class that you are going to read them a story called *Easter eggs* and that you want them to listen carefully to the story because you will ask them questions about it afterwards.

Easter eggs

It was nearly Easter and time to prepare Easter eggs and a picnic. Kay and Antony asked their mother to help them. They got out a pan and filled it with water and their mother placed it on the cooker. Then Kay put her two eggs in the water and then mother lifted Antony up so that he could pop his eggs in too.

They waited, watched and listened as the water came to the boil and the eggs began to cook. They waited seven minutes, for that was how long it took before the eggs became hard enough. Then they stood at the sink in the kitchen and held the eggs under the running cold tap to get them cool. Now to decorate them. They had crayons, and ink and paint, all the colours of the rainbow.

Kay painted part of hers with dots and wavy lines, so that there was a lovely pattern at the finish. Antony tried to paint a face on his, just like Humpty Dumpty. The other one he coloured all in blue. They were left to dry.

Next day the family went off for a picnic in the park. Kay and Antony and mummy and daddy. They sat at the top of a slight hill and began to empty the baskets they had brought with them. They laid out a large white tablecloth and placed sandwiches and cakes and fruit and paper cups and plates on it. They had brought bottles of fruit juice and a flask of tea, too.

Now it was time to roll their eggs down the slope of the hill. Down and down the eggs rolled, faster and faster, bumpity bump, until they reached the bottom. Kay and Antony ran down to fetch them again. The shells had hardly cracked at all! So up they climbed with their eggs again.

Then they rolled them down the hill again, faster and faster, bumpity, bumpity, bump. They raced after them and reached the bottom almost as soon as the eggs did. The shells were beginning to crack now. Antony could recognize the face he'd drawn on one of his. One last time should do. So up again and down they rolled. At last the eggs landed at the bottom, their shells cracked, with large bits littered about the grass. What fun it was.

Then they strolled up the hill again to enjoy the rest of the picnic with their parents.

Ask the class if they enjoyed the story. Then ask the following questions:
1  What was the name of the story?
2  What were the names of the boy and girl in the story?
3  How did they first prepare their eggs before painting them?
4  How can we tell that Antony was only a little boy?

5 What did they do with the eggs after they were cooked?
6 How did Kay and Antony decorate their eggs?
7 Where did they have their picnic?
8 What did they bring with them to eat and drink?
9 How many times did they have to roll their eggs before they finally cracked open?
10 What did they do after that?

Ask the class to give the meaning of the following words:

| | |
|---|---|
| 1 pan | 6 fruit |
| 2 cooker | 7 cup |
| 3 tap | 8 flask |
| 4 park | 9 grass |
| 5 basket | 10 sandwich |

Ask the class to give the opposite of the following words:

| | |
|---|---|
| 1 help | 11 empty |
| 2 filled | 12 large |
| 3 cooked | 13 white |
| 4 hard | 14 down |
| 5 stood | 15 faster |
| 6 cold | 16 last |
| 7 cool | 17 sunny |
| 8 lovely | 18 pleasant |
| 9 dry | 19 tidy |
| 10 bottom | 20 tasty |

# Daily lesson 154

**Materials**
1 Animal cards as listed
2 Random selection of animal, tool, clothing and occupation cards
3 Nursery rhyme—*Cock Robin*

**Procedure**
Ask the class to solve the following riddles:
  1 What animal is the king of the jungle? (lion)
  2 What animal is known as bunny? (rabbit)
  3 What animal has puppies? (dog)
  4 What animal has cubs? (tiger, bear etc)
  5 What animal is known as Billy? (he-goat)
  6 What animal is known as Nanny? (she-goat)
  7 What kind of animal is Dougal? (dog)
  8 What kind of animal is Dylan? (rabbit)
  9 What kind of animal is Ermintrude? (cow)
 10 What kind of animal is Brian? (snail)
 11 What animal looks like a man? (monkey or chimp)
 12 What birds can learn to speak? (parrots)
 13 What bird has a red breast? (robin)
 14 What bird says 'te wit to woo'? (owl)
 15 What animal is sometimes known as Porky? (pig)
 16 What animal is known as Bambi? (deer)
 17 What animal is known as Woody? (woodpecker)
 18 What animal is known as Jumbo? (elephant)
 19 What animal is known as Bruin? (brown bear)
 20 What animal is known as Donald? (duck)

Display your random selection of animal, tool, clothing and occupation cards. Ask each child in turn to select any two and give reasons why they are alike, and then how they are different. If the child hesitates or pauses after giving a 'different' or 'similar' response, remind him that he is required to give another response.

*Nursery rhyme*  Tell the class the story of Cock Robin, analyze the story line quickly and casually and recite the rhyme again.

# Daily lesson 155

**Materials**
1 Pictures or models of fruit and vegetables
2 Nursery rhyme—*One misty moisty morning*

**Procedure**
Arrange the class in groups of six. Have the groups compete against each other in naming as many things as they can which they would see in the following places:

| | | | |
|---|---|---|---|
| 1 | a bus | 7 | çhemist |
| 2 | street | 8 | baker |
| 3 | a supermarket | 9 | butcher |
| 4 | the seaside | 10 | grocer |
| 5 | farmyard | 11 | shoe shop |
| 6 | harbour | 12 | sweet shop |

Display the pictures or models of fruit but not (at this time) models or pictures of vegetables. Revise the name given to each fruit and then elicit or teach that these are all fruits. Then go over each item of fruit saying, 'An apple is a fruit; an orange is a fruit' etc. Proceed in a similar way with the vegetables. Teach or elicit in what way fruit and vegetables are alike. ('They both grow, and they both are good for us. We eat them both.') Finally mix the fruit and vegetables together and have the class classify the items as fruit or vegetables as you select them.

Ask the class to listen for articles of clothing. They must clap their hands three times when they hear an article mentioned.

| | | | |
|---|---|---|---|
| 1 | blue | 16 | foot |
| 2 | shoe | 17 | heart |
| 3 | candle | 18 | hat |
| 4 | supper | 19 | coat |
| 5 | hurt | 20 | hand |
| 6 | shirt | 21 | glove |
| 7 | skirt | 22 | glue |
| 8 | mess | 23 | head |
| 9 | house | 24 | bed |
| 10 | dress | 25 | box |
| 11 | lock | 26 | socks |
| 12 | frog | 27 | shoot |
| 13 | frock | 28 | boot |
| 14 | match | 29 | bumper |
| 15 | jacket | 30 | jumper |

*Nursery rhyme*   Revise *One misty moisty morning.*

# Daily lesson 156

**Materials**
1 Tape recorder
2 Selection of animal, tool, occupation and clothing cards

**Procedure**
Ask the class to name as many things as they can which have:
1 fur
2 wheels
3 drawers
4 feathers
5 no legs
6 handle

Explain to the class that you are going to display four cards at a time, for just fifteen seconds. Then you will ask them to close their eyes and remove two of the cards. They have to guess which cards have been removed. Repeat as often as enthusiasm allows. Vary the number of cards displayed and the number which are withdrawn according to how easy or difficult the class find this task.

*On tape*  Ask all members of the class to tell the tape recorder their name, address, age, school and teacher's name. Have them speak in a slow clear manner and in one or two simple but well structured sentences. Play back immediately after each child has spoken and criticize or praise gently.

# Daily lesson 157

**Materials**

Nursery rhyme—*Tom, Tom the piper's son*

**Procedure**

Ask the class to name as many things as they can, that are:

1 brushed
2 washed
3 dried
4 heated
5 kept cool
6 cooked
7 driven
8 switched on and off
9 opened
10 shut

Ask the class to imagine that they have been out in the garden and seen something. Have them say which of the following items it might have been and which it couldn't have been. Have them explain why.

1 train
2 book
3 flower
4 sun
5 fire engine
6 television set
7 hedgehog
8 tiger
9 mantlepiece
10 worm
11 car
12 washing
13 tree
14 tractor
15 fish
16 typewriter
17 aeroplane
18 star
19 mouse
20 cow

Ask the class to play a variety of the game 'We went to market and we bought . . .' Say 'We went on a picnic and we brought . . .' Have each child memorize and repeat the list already spoken and add an item of his own.

*Nursery rhyme*   Teach by reciting or singing the nursery rhyme *Tom, Tom the piper's son*

# Daily lesson 158

**Materials**
Tape recorder

**Procedure**
Explain to the class that you are going to read them a story called *Going swimming* and that you want them to listen carefully because you will ask them questions about it afterwards.

### Going swimming

Maggie and John loved to go swimming. There was a big swimming pool in the town where they lived and most Saturday mornings they would go there, along with their father.

They'd wrap their costumes in their towels and off they'd go. A short trip on the bus soon brought them almost to the main entrance of the swimming pool. Then they'd rush in, pay at the desk, and dash down to the changing rooms as quickly as they could.

Their father waited for them at the edge of the pool. Sometimes he went into the water and sometimes he didn't. But he was always on hand in case Maggie or John or any other boy or girl got into difficulties in the water. Maggie and John knew how dangerous water can be and although they always enjoyed themselves they were careful and never clowned about.

Neither Maggie nor John could swim yet, but they were learning. They enjoyed learning but enjoyed splashing about too. They were quite proud that they could open their eyes under water and they could also float on top of the water for quite a long time. They had water wings, rings and sometimes a rope to help them swim, but they didn't really need them now.

After they had been in the water for about an hour, dad would ask them if they'd like to come out. Usually they were quite happy to come out, because they got cold after a while. They'd rush and get changed, shivering as they got into their warm clothes.

Then dad would meet them near the main entrance where there was a little shop that sold hot drinks and biscuits. Did they look forward to that! What a smashing way to spend Saturday mornings.

Ask the class if they enjoyed the story. Then ask the following questions:
1  What was the name of the story?
2  What were the names of the boy and girl in the story?
3  What did they like to do on Saturday mornings?
4  How did they get to the swimming pool?
5  How long did Maggie and John spend in the water?
6  What did dad buy them before they left the pool?

Ask the class the opposite of the following words. Explain 'opposite' and give examples. Preface each question with 'Give me the opposite of . . .'

| | | |
|---|---|---|
| 1 loved | 5 girl | 9 proud |
| 2 father | 6 difficult | 10 open |
| 3 go | 7 dangerous | 11 top |
| 4 short | 8 careful | 12 help |

*On tape*  Get the class to tell the tape recorder about their visits to a swimming pool. Play back a selection.

# Daily lesson 159

## Materials

1 Nursery rhyme—*One, two, buckle my shoe*
2 Shape cards as listed
3 Animal cards as listed

## Procedure

Play the nursery rhyme. Play it again and invite the class to join in. Then ask the class to mime the activities of the poem, prefacing each activity by the appropriate line of the rhyme. Say the poem again. Have the class count up to ten as quickly as they can. Have the class recite the poem slowly, and ask them to think about the activities described as they do so.

Ask the class where the following items are kept or live:

1 mouse
2 horse
3 pig
4 sheep
5 rabbit
6 tiger
7 owl
8 budgerigar
9 worm
10 octopus
11 otter
12 spider
13 ant
14 centipede
15 bee

Display the shape cards. Discuss the differences between the shapes and have the class copy the following—circle, square, triangle, diamond. Discuss the mistakes made especially in relation to the following:
circle—shape must be self contained and more circular than oval
square—discourage rectangle shapes and emphasize right angles
triangle—lines must meet at definite points with no extra corners
diamond—discourage 'squares on a point' or kite shapes

# Daily lesson 160

**Materials**
1 Nursery rhyme—*Monday's child*
2 Random selection of animal, tool, clothing and occupation cards

**Procedure**
Say the nursery rhyme to the class, explain the 'story' of the poem, say it again and invite the class to repeat it with you. Teach the days of the week again pointing out before you start that there are seven days.

Ask the class to name as many things as they can which are wholly or largely made of the following list of materials:

| | |
|---|---|
| 1 glass | 6 cloth or any man made fibre |
| 2 plastic | 7 paper |
| 3 leather | 8 brick, stone or concrete |
| 4 wood | 9 rubber |
| 5 metal | |

From your random selection display four cards at a time. Let the class see the display for seven seconds. Then ask them to close their eyes. Withdraw one card and ask which one is missing. Repeat as long as enthusiasm permits. Advise the class to name the cards to themselves quietly while they are on display—this will make their memory more effective.

# Daily lesson 161

**Materials**
1 Tool cards as listed
2 Animal cards as listed
3 Tape recorder

**Procedure**
Say to the class 'What do you call something which . . .'
1 tells the time and you wear it on your wrist (watch)
2 you dig with (spade)
3 you dry yourself with (towel)
4 you sew with, and is sharp (needle)
5 you stick things together with (glue)
6 you hang clothes out on (clothes line)
7 has teeth and you cut wood with (saw)
8 you measure things with (ruler or tape measure)
9 toasts bread (toaster)
10 you carry cups and saucers on (tray and trolley)

Ask the class to describe the following. Encourage definitions of objects in terms of function as well as physical appearance, and definitions of animals in terms of outstanding feature.

| | | | |
|---|---|---|---|
| 1 | letter | 11 | horse |
| 2 | star | 12 | albatross |
| 3 | refrigerator | 13 | goldfish |
| 4 | aeroplane | 14 | ladybird |
| 5 | sideboard | 15 | shark |
| 6 | hosepipe | 16 | hawk |
| 7 | telephone | 17 | ostrich |
| 8 | wheelbarrow | 18 | camel |
| 9 | tap | 19 | walrus |
| 10 | sewing machine | 20 | rabbit |

*On tape*   Have the class copy simple rhythms mouthed, tapped or clapped out by you. Initially make the rhythms simple and short becoming gradually more challenging.

*Nursery rhymes*   Ask individuals in the class to recite their favourite nursery rhyme. Record them.

# Daily lesson 162

**Materials**
1 Tape recorder
2 Nursery rhyme—*This is the way we . . .*

**Procedure**
Explain to the class that you are going to read them a story called *Painting the bedroom* and that you want them to listen carefully to the story because you will ask them questions about it afterwards.

### Painting the bedroom

Daddy decided that it was time the bedroom had a new coat of paint. What colour? He asked Patricia and Ken what they would like. 'Red?' 'No.' 'Green?' 'No.' 'What about blue?' 'Yes, a light shade of blue would be very nice.'

So out they went to the garage to see if there happened to be a tin of blue paint there. Yes, luckily there was. Dad carried in the pot of paint and Patricia and Ken each carried a brush. Dad then opened the pot and Patricia washed the brushes carefully. Upstairs they ran to get started.

Dad moved the bed and the dressing table and the chest of drawers out of the room just in case they got paint on them. And Patricia and Ken placed some old newspapers down on the carpet to protect it. Dad didn't have a ladder to stand on so he used a chair instead. Now they were all ready, so they got started—dad on one wall and Ken and Patricia on another.

They all concentrated very hard, being careful not to drop paint on the carpet and careful not to get any on their clothes. Paint makes an awful mess if it gets on your clothes.

They dipped the brush into the paint, then quickly onto the wall, spreading the paint up and down and across the wall. It was great fun. Time flew by and before they knew it the room was finished.

They called mummy up to show off their work proudly. She was pleased! How clean and bright the room looked, and how tidily they had worked. Not a spot of paint on the carpet. It would look even nicer once the doors and window frames were painted too! Dad looked at Ken and Patricia as if to say, 'Do you want to paint the doors and window frame now?' They decided not to do it today. Although they had enjoyed doing the walls, they didn't feel very much like doing any more. Not today, anyhow. Down they went to watch television, leaving poor dad to lift the old newspapers, put back the furniture and clean the paint brushes. There was always so much to do in a house!

Ask the class if they enjoyed the story. Then ask the following questions:
1 What was the name of the story?
2 What were the names of the boy and girl in the story?
3 What colour did they decide to paint the bedroom?
4 Where did they get the paint?
5 What had they to do before they started painting?
6 What did dad stand on?
7 Why did they not want to get paint on their clothes?
8 Did the three of them take long to paint the room?

9 Was mummy pleased?
10 What did she ask them to paint next?
11 Did dad and the children feel like doing it today?
12 Who cleared up after painting?
13 What did Ken and Patricia do?

Ask the class the meaning of the following words:

| | | | |
|---|---|---|---|
| 1 | garage | 6 | window |
| 2 | bed | 7 | clothes |
| 3 | newspaper | 8 | carpet |
| 4 | ladder | 9 | stairs |
| 5 | chair | 10 | bedroom |

Ask the class the opposite of the following words:

| | | | |
|---|---|---|---|
| 1 | new | 9 | down |
| 2 | light | 10 | careful |
| 3 | there | 11 | proud |
| 4 | luckily | 12 | tidily |
| 5 | opened | 13 | so much |
| 6 | carefully | 14 | quickly |
| 7 | upstairs | 15 | high |
| 8 | started | | |

*Nursery rhyme*  Have the class recite 'This is the way we paint the . . .' to the tune of *Here we go round the mulberry bush*. Include verses on doors, ceiling, walls and floor.

# Daily lesson 163

**Materials**
1 Means of transport pictures
2 Nursery rhyme—*This is the way we* . . .

**Procedure**
Display pictures individually and teach or elicit the name given to each. Teach or elicit the various uses of each, pointing out similarities or differences between them. Finally revise the entire list quickly, calling upon individuals to name them.

*Miming*    Ask individuals in the class to mime the following actions. Have the rest of the class guess what is being done.
1 brushing a pair of shoes
2 cleaning windows
3 getting into a car
4 opening a window
5 filling a cup with orange juice
6 slicing a loaf of bread
7 preparing a dish of food for a cat
8 sewing
9 knitting
10 skipping

*Nursery rhyme*    Have the class revise the rhyme *This is the way we* . . . using the activities above.

# Daily lesson 164

**Materials**

1 Means of transport cards
2 Nursery rhyme—*Monday's child*

**Procedure**

Revise the names and uses of the means of transport cards. Display all the cards together and ask children to select cards according to the following criteria:

| | |
|---|---|
| 1 fly in the sky | 8 carry goods |
| 2 sail on water | 9 carry both |
| 3 sail underwater | 10 haulage vehicles |
| 4 no wheels | 11 animals |
| 5 many wheels | 12 no engines |
| 6 two wheels | 13 uncommon vehicles |
| 7 carry people | |

Ask the class to think of as many things as they can to fit the following phrases:

1 a pair of . . .
2 a bottle of . . .
3 a tin of . . .
4 a packet of . . .
5 a pound of . . .

*Nursery rhyme*   Revise the rhyme *Monday's child* and the names of the days of the week.

# Daily lesson 165

**Materials**
1 Selection of animal, clothing, occupation and tool cards as listed
2 Tape recorder
3 Nursery rhyme—*Jack Sprat could eat no fat*

**Procedure**
Ask the class in what way the following items are alike:
1 banana and orange
2 carrot and cabbage
3 tea and coffee
4 saw and comb
5 ball and apple
6 paper and blackboard
7 TV and radio
8 donkey and bicycle
9 rain and snow
10 grass and flowers

From a selection of cards display three cards, two like and one odd. Call upon individuals to select the odd one out. Have the responder explain why he chose the card he did.

*On tape*    Have each individual think for a minute about what his favourite meal is. Then call upon each member of the class to tell the tape recorder his name, address and age, and favourite meal. Question them all about how the food they prefer is cooked.

*Nursery rhyme*    Teach *Jack Sprat could eat no fat*.

# Daily lesson 166

**Materials**
Nursery rhyme—children's selection

**Procedure**
Ask the class to discuss with you the sort of games they play in the playground—marbles, skipping games, ball games etc. Call upon several of the class to describe the rules of the games and find out from them which games are most preferred. Insist on clearly structured sentences and ask individuals to repeat any sentences that you have to correct in the usual, gentle, casual way.

Ask the class to name objects which come into the following categories:
1  things with one wheel
2  things with more than four wheels
3  things with four legs
4  things without legs
5  things which are round, or nearly so
6  things that are long, like a pencil
7  things that are square or rectangular
8  things that we eat, which grow in the ground or on trees
9  things that we eat, which must be cooked
10  things that are used to contain liquid

*Nursery rhymes*   Children's selection.

# Daily lesson 167

**Materials**
Tape recorder

**Procedure**
Explain to the class that you are going to read them a story called *The hairdresser* and that you want them to listen carefully to the story because you will ask them questions about it afterwards.

### The hairdresser

Jean and Alex had been to the hairdresser before when they watched their mother getting her hair cut or shampooed or perhaps set for a special occasion. But today instead of just watching her, they were going to get their hair cut and mummy would watch them. They had both had their hair cut before of course but mummy, or sometimes daddy, had done it. This was the first time that they would have it cut by a real hairdresser.

In they came with their mother and the hairdresser lifted them up into the chairs. There they sat, perched in the large, high chairs looking down on the handbasin and big clear glass mirrors in front of them. They felt very grown up and smiled to mummy. The hairdresser tied a white overall behind each of their necks to catch the hair as it fell and then asked them if they were both comfortable. 'Yes, thank you,' they said. Now all they could see of themselves in the mirror were their heads, sticking out of the hole in the sheet. They both thought they looked rather funny.

Then the hairdressers got busy. They began cutting. *Snip, snip, snip,* the children heard the scissors go, and clumps of hair began to fall around them. *Snip, snip, snip.* The hairdressers combed and cut, and smoothed and cut, turning the children's heads this way and that very gently but firmly. Neither of them wanted a short haircut, so it didn't take long. The hairdressers gave Jean and Alex a final brush and comb, and asked them how they liked what had been done to their hair. 'Fine,' said Jean. 'Yes, fine,' said Alex, rubbing his hand over the back of his neck. Mum was pleased too. The hairdresser untied the overalls and down Jean and Alex jumped. They felt very pleased with themselves.

Ask the class if they enjoyed the story, then ask the following questions:
1  What was the name of the story?
2  What were the names of the boy and girl in the story?
3  Had they been to a hairdresser before? What for?
4  Had they had their hair cut before? By whom?
5  What did they see before them as they sat in the chairs?
6  How did they feel?
7  What did the hairdresser do next? What was the sheet for?
8  How did they think they looked in the mirror?
9  What noise did the scissors make?
10  What else did the hairdresser use, apart from the scissors?
11  Were Jean and Alex pleased with their haircuts?

*On tape*  Ask the class to describe their last visit to the barber or hairdresser. Play back a selection.

# Daily lesson 168

**Materials**
Pictures or models of fruit and vegetables

**Procedure**
Revise the name given to each fruit and vegetable and revise the category into which each falls. Then ask in what way any pair are the same and how they are different. Accept any physical similarities but encourage also responses such as 'we eat them both', or 'they both grow'. Elicit and teach also how we eat the fruit and vegetables—fresh, frozen, tinned, cooked or uncooked.

Ask the class what is silly or odd about the following sentences. Have them correct the sentence and repeat it as it should be:
1 Carl closed the book and began to read a story.
2 Yvonne heard the telephone ringing, put it down and began to speak.
3 Christine had such a sore throat, that she couldn't walk properly.
4 Monica tried to be as noisy as possible because her mother was feeling unwell.
5 Janet pedalled her bicycle quickly up the stairs.
6 It had rained so heavily that the water ran up the walls.
7 The plums grew thick and heavy on the apple tree.
8 Jack went up and down, up and down, on the merry-go-round.
9 James switched off the television set and sat down to watch his favourite programme.

Ask the class to give the meaning of the following words:
| | | | |
|---|---|---|---|
| 1 | ball | 11 | cup |
| 2 | hammer | 12 | shoe |
| 3 | spoon | 13 | glue |
| 4 | hat | 14 | flower |
| 5 | dog | 15 | nail |
| 6 | pencil | 16 | hand |
| 7 | key | 17 | flask |
| 8 | telephone | 18 | drawer |
| 9 | book | 19 | knob |
| 10 | watch | 20 | window |

# Daily lesson 169

**Materials**
Pictures of, or examples of, sports and games equipment (work in the open or in the gymnasium or hall)

**Procedure**
Display the items of sports and games equipment one at a time. Elicit or teach the name of each. Then arrange the items in the following groups:
1 bats (cricket, tennis racquet, table tennis, hockey stick)
2 balls (football, rugby, cricket, tennis, shuttlecock, table tennis)
3 swimming gear
4 protective clothing
and demonstrate how each item within the group is used—emphasize that group one items are held in either one hand or two hands and are used for batting some of the items in group two. Group two items are hit by items in group one—which goes with which and which items in group two are kicked? Demonstrate the use of the swimming gear and protective clothing.

Play 'This is the way we . . .' calling on the children to demonstrate two handed cricket stroke, one handed tennis stroke, football kick and swimming strokes. Have the class play reasonably freely with the material but under close verbal guidance. Advise 'use one hand', 'use two hands', 'throw it hard' etc.

# Daily lesson 170

**Materials**
1 Tape recorder
2 Nursery rhyme—*Mary, Mary, quite contrary*

**Procedures**
Ask the class what or who would live in the following situations:

| | |
|---|---|
| 1 a hole in a wall | 6 a hotel |
| 2 a nest | 7 a box of straw |
| 3 a hole in a tree | 8 a field of corn |
| 4 a cave | 9 a forest |
| 5 a caravan | 10 a jungle |

*On tape* Ask the class what would they do in the following situations, and why. Record their response and play back a selection:
1 They see a two year old baby wandering in the street.
2 They see a cat jump into a pram in which a baby is sleeping.
3 They see a three year old little girl playing with empty milk bottles on the doorstep.
4 They find a bird injured in the garden near their home.
5 They see a little field mouse in their kitchen at home.
6 They see an old lady laden with a shopping bag, struggling to get onto a bus.
7 Mummy feels unwell at home.
8 They see a cat apparently trapped on the roof of their house.

*Nursery rhyme* Revise *Mary, Mary, quite contrary*.

# Daily lesson 171

**Materials**
None

**Procedure**
Take the class for a walk, no more than 400 yards from the school. Explain to them that you want them to walk slowly and keep their eyes wandering above, below and to the side, looking at everything around them. As you walk with them stop and bring their attention to anything that might interest them but which they have become accustomed to pass by without a second glance or moment's thought e.g. goods being delivered to a shop, an animal sniffing around the street, puddles drying up etc. Take note of the different shops and public institutions and kinds of houses you pass. When you return to the classroom take the children through the walk again in chronological order, calling upon individuals to tell what happened next. They may like to make a book of drawings of the walk.

# Daily lesson 172

**Materials**
Tape recorder

**Procedure**
Explain to the class that you are going to read them a story called *The building site*, and that you want them to listen carefully to the story because you will ask them questions about it afterwards.

### The building site

On the way from their home to their school Christine and Bill often passed a building site. Sometimes they stopped to watch the workmen building houses.

It was a very noisy place. There were lorries with loud engines, belching smoke, loading and unloading bricks. There were smaller trucks, splattered with mud, carrying bags of cement. There were small lifts carrying tiles from the ground to the roof tops where men were working.

Everywhere there was thick, heavy, dark brown mud. It clung to the tyres of the lorries, it clung to the working boots of the workmen, and here and there Christine could see deep holes in the ground filled with thick mud.

There were only two houses being built. Both looked as if they were nearly finished. The walls, built with yellow bricks the colour of straw, were all finished. The glass windows in the downstairs and upstairs rooms were all in. They could see that the front and side doors were in position too, although they hadn't yet been painted. Most of the work being done on the houses was on the roof. Christine and Bill could see men kneeling on the roof fixing the brown coloured tiles in place with a hammer and nails. The men chattered and laughed and joked as they worked.

After a little while Christine and Bill moved on home. And as they walked they decided that when they got home they would build some houses just like the workmen. Christine would build with her Lego and Bill with his wooden bricks. They couldn't wait to get home and start.

Ask the class if they enjoyed the story. Then ask the following questions:
1 What was the name of the story?
2 What were the names of the boy and girl in the story?
3 What were the large lorries carrying?
4 What was being carried in the lifts?
5 What covered the lorries' tyres and workmen's boots?
6 How many houses were being built?
7 What were the windows made of?
8 What were the doors made of? Were they painted yet?
9 What were the workmen doing on the roof?

Ask the class the opposite of the following words:

| | | | |
|---|---|---|---|
| 1 noisy | 4 up | 7 here | 10 furnished |
| 2 loading | 5 thick | 8 deep | 11 downstairs |
| 3 smaller | 6 heavy | 9 same | 12 front |

*On tape*  Ask the class to describe any building sites they have seen—What did they see? What did they hear?

# Daily lesson 173

**Materials**
Colour cubes

**Procedure**
Ask the class to give the opposite of the following words. Explain 'opposite' and give examples. Preface each question with: 'Give me the opposite of...'

| | | | |
|---|---|---|---|
| 1 | high | 11 | pleasant |
| 2 | pretty | 12 | dead |
| 3 | hard | 13 | long |
| 4 | good | 14 | wide |
| 5 | sour | 15 | a lot |
| 6 | happy | 16 | far away |
| 7 | smile | 17 | over there |
| 8 | round | 18 | under |
| 9 | dark | 19 | before |
| 10 | white | 20 | up |

Distribute colour cubes. Revise names of colours and have the class select appropriate colours to match colours displayed by you, and to match verbal instructions. Then ask the class to form colour chains according to verbal instructions. Insist on their working from left to right. Begin with two colour chains, working up to three and four colour chains. Take care that the children do not merely copy the chain made by their neighbour. Have them learn to rely on their own memory and understanding of your verbal instructions.

Ask the class to supply the missing word:
1 The ball bounced _____ the wall. (against)
2 He jumped _____ the chair. (off)
3 The cat climbed _____ the tree. (up)
4 The dish was placed _____ the table. (on or under)
5 The boat sailed _____ the bridge. (under, or into, or towards)
6 The horse jumped _____ the fence. (over)
7 The car went _____ the road. (off, along, or onto)
8 They drank _____ the cup. (out of)
9 He poured water _____ the cup. (into)
10 The water ran _____ the tap. (out of)
11 She put the scissors _____ the drawer. (into)
12 Monday comes _____ Tuesday. (before)
13 They went to school _____ breakfast. (after)
14 They walked _____ the floor. (across)
15 The cat walked _____ the branch. (along)

# Daily lesson 174

**Materials**
Tool cards as listed

**Procedure**
Have individuals in the class mime the use of the following tools. Insist on their using two hands where appropriate. The rest of the class have to guess what tool is being used. Display the appropriate tool card after it has been guessed correctly:

1 axe
2 spade
3 take
4 wheelbarrow
5 lawn mower

6 garden shears
7 scissors
8 vacuum cleaner
9 long handled brush
10 short handled brush

Ask the class, 'What is odd, or funny, about what I say?' Have the class correct what is odd, in a well structured sentence.
1 Daddy put some water onto the fire to make it burn.
2 The sun shone brightly last night.
3 She sat down to milk the horse.
4 She saw she had four thumbs and one finger on her hand.
5 He went to the baker to buy some meat.
6 She drank her soup quickly, using a knife.
7 They boiled their eggs in the kettle.
8 They sat down in front of the telephone to watch their favourite programme.
9 They hammered the nails in with the screwdriver.
10 They sawed at the tree with a heavy spade.

Tap out rhythms with your hands or with a pencil and have the class copy them. Begin with simple rhythms and make them increasingly challenging. Use words and phrases to help the class catch the rhythms and then practise without the aid of words. E.g. Push me quickly, along the road (long long short short sh-short long long).

# Daily lesson 175

**Materials**

1 Random selection of animal, tool, clothing and occupation cards
2 Nursery rhyme—*See saw Margery Daw*

**Procedure**

Explain to the class that you are going to display three cards for just ten seconds. You will then ask them to close their eyes, and you will take one card away. They have to guess which card has been removed. As the class become more skilled at this, increase the number of cards displayed to four.

Ask the class to give you a word that rhymes with the following words. Explain 'rhymes with', giving examples:

| | | | |
|---|---|---|---|
| 1 | sing | 11 | hoot |
| 2 | moon | 12 | much |
| 3 | feet | 13 | said |
| 4 | song | 14 | toes |
| 5 | tin | 15 | foot |
| 6 | play | 16 | bold |
| 7 | only | 17 | you |
| 8 | task | 18 | tub |
| 9 | came | 19 | fall |
| 10 | cup | 20 | me |

Ask individuals to mime the use of the following tools. Insist that they use both hands if necessary. The remainder of the class have to guess what tool is being used. Insist on a structured sentence in response:

| | | | |
|---|---|---|---|
| 1 | shovel | 6 | newspaper |
| 2 | watch | 7 | rubber (eraser) |
| 3 | alarm clock | 8 | tape measure |
| 4 | pen | 9 | drawer |
| 5 | typewriter | 10 | tin opener |

*Nursery rhyme* Teach by reciting, singing and repetition *See saw Margery Daw*.

# Daily lesson 176

**Materials**
1 Cards as listed in activities
2 Nursery rhyme—*Ding dong bell*

**Procedure**
Ask the class to solve the following riddles:
1 What has a head and a handle, and cleans the floor? (brush)
2 What has a face and two hands and tells the time? (watch)
3 What has teeth and cuts wood? (saw)
4 What has a head and a handle and chops wood? (axe)
5 What has a spout and a handle and heats water? (kettle)
6 What has a head and a handle and knocks in nails? (hammer)
7 What is made of rubber and makes things disappear? (rubber)
8 What has one eye and mends clothes? (needle)
9 What are white and we have about thirty of them in our mouth? (teeth)
10 What has four fingers and a thumb? (hand)

Ask the class to place the following items in their appropriate categories. Use 'sense' categories e.g. television set would be placed in the 'eye' and 'ear' categories; sugar would be in the 'taste' category, a tool in the 'hand' category etc. Some items may fall into more than one category.

1 towel
2 soap
3 clock
4 daffodil
5 fruit
6 jam
7 newspaper
8 perfume
9 pencil
10 radio
11 food
12 scissors
13 garden
14 book
15 music

Ask individuals in the class to describe the following objects. Encourage as many short simple sentences as the child is capable of, especially sentences describing physical features such as shape, size, colour, weight; sentences describing characteristic features or idiosyncrasies and function.

1 ball
2 chalk
3 button
4 penny
5 sweet
6 spoon
7 shoelace
8 ribbon
9 glasses (spectacles)
10 handkerchief
11 door handle
12 coat hanger
13 light switch
14 bicycle
15 dog's collar

*Nursery rhyme* Teach and have the class learn and enjoy the nursery rhyme *Ding dong bell, pussy's in the well.* Discuss the morality of the two actions described briefly.

# Daily lesson 177

**Materials**

Tape recorder

**Procedure**

Explain to the class that you are going to read them a story called *The butcher's shop* and that you want them to listen carefully to the story because you will ask them questions about it afterwards.

## The butcher's shop

Jenny often went shopping with her mother to the butcher's shop. They would go early on Saturday mornings before the shop became too crowded and busy. That way they usually got served quickly.

Mummy made a list of things that she wanted and wrote them down on paper. When they reached the shop she would hand the list to the butcher who then rushed to collect together all the things she wanted. What a lot of things there seemed to be, and Jenny wondered, 'Gosh, do we eat all this?'

The butcher prepared a pound of mince first of all and Jenny watched as he fed a large piece of red meat into a mincing machine. Then he switched on the machine. Jenny could hear a loud buzzing sound and a few seconds later the large piece of meat disappeared in one end and reappeared at the other end chopped up into tiny little bits. Jenny always liked to watch this.

The butcher then took a long, sharp looking knife from a hook on the wall and began hacking away at another piece of meat. He was cutting off six chops. The knife must have been very sharp because he didn't take long to do this. Jenny was frightened in case he cut off one of his fingers, and she did notice that he must have cut himself sometime because he wore a plaster on his thumb.

Then the butcher rushed to yet another piece of meat and began to slice thin pieces off it. And as he sliced he placed each piece on a sheet of paper. Then he placed the whole lot onto the weighing machine, looked for a second at a needle which told him how heavy it was, and finally parcelled it all up neatly.

All this time, while he was preparing her mother's order, Stacey noticed he chatted about this and that—how cold it was getting, how busy he was and yes, how expensive everything seemed. Jenny wondered how he could do so many things at once.

Jenny heard him say, 'That will be two pounds then, altogether' and her mummy handed over the money. She waited for her change then said, 'Thank you and bye bye.'

'Good morning and thank you, Mrs Baxter,' said the butcher and off she and her mother went, home with their shopping.

Ask the class if they enjoyed the story. Then ask the following questions:

1 What was the name of the story?
2 What was the name of the girl in the story?
3 Where were the girl and her mother going to shop?
4 When did they usually go and why?
5 What did Jenny's mother do before leaving the house?
6 How did the butcher make mince?

7 What did the butcher use to cut off the six chops?
8 Why did Jenny think it must be very sharp?
9 What did the butcher do as he prepared the order?
10 How much did the meat cost, and did Jenny's mother get any change?

Ask the class the opposite of the following words. Explain 'opposite' and give examples. Preface each question with 'Give me the opposite of . . .'

| | | | |
|---|---|---|---|
| 1 | early | 11 | end |
| 2 | crowded | 12 | long |
| 3 | quickly | 13 | sharp |
| 4 | reach | 14 | thin |
| 5 | eat | 15 | heavy |
| 6 | first | 16 | neatly |
| 7 | large | 17 | cold |
| 8 | loud | 18 | expensive |
| 9 | few | 19 | good morning |
| 10 | disappear | 20 | went |

*On tape*   Have the class describe to the tape recorder the butcher's shop that they are familiar with.

# Daily lesson 178

**Materials**
1 Miscellaneous objects from the classroom
2 Nursery rhyme—*I love little pussy*

**Procedure**
Distribute the objects to each member of the class. Have the class arranged in groups of four, three, two and individuals, both boys and girls, standing alone. The object of this procedure is to teach and practise the use of *mine, his, hers, ours, theirs* etc. Demonstrate to the class examples of each and then ask each individual pair, couple or group to verbalize similarly thus 'This piece of chalk is mine; that book is hers' and so on.

Ask one child to think of a small object, name it and describe it. The next child has to chose an object which is bigger, name it and describe it, and so on until four children have contributed. Begin at either extreme of height, weight, length or width until every member of the class has had a turn.

Ask the class to say exactly what you say. Repeat words and numbers at a rate of one per second. Ask the class as a whole, groups and individuals to respond.

| | | |
|---|---|---|
| 1 two—four—eight | 11 seven—two—three—four |
| 2 pencil—table—book | 12 pig—house—duck—tractor |
| 3 five—two—nine | 13 nine—two—six—three |
| 4 ship—car—horse | 14 ear—pencil—hair—eye |
| 5 six—three—four | 15 five—two—six—seven |
| 6 knife—pot—cup—green | 16 now—hand—knock—watch |
| 7 three—six—eight—one | 17 eight—five—seven—one |
| 8 you—and—hard—roof | 18 green—ink—round—hat |
| 9 four—three—eight—one | 19 four—two—nine—six |
| 10 window—floor—ceiling | 20 yes—paper—pin—top |

*Nursery rhyme*   Revise *I love little pussy* and any other rhymes about cats with which the class are familiar and which they enjoy.

# Daily lesson 179

**Materials**
1 Tape recorder
2 Nursery rhymes—teacher's selection from early lessons

**Procedure**
Ask the class to follow your instructions:
1 Put your finger to your lips.
2 Stand at attention.
3 Touch your knees.
4 Put your hands on your hips.
5 Put your fingers in your ears.
6 Touch your toes.
7 Put your hands over your eyes.
8 Put your feet together.
9 Stand on tip-toe.
10 Put your hands over your ears.

*On tape*   Ask the class to tell the tape recorder their full name and address, the name of their school and their teacher's name. After four children have been recorded, play back and ask the class to be critical (but gently so) of the efforts. Were these recordings too quick perhaps or too slow? Were the words clear enough to be understood by an outsider?

'Ask individuals to finish the following sentences any way they like. Insist on a short, simple, but well structured sentence. Correct, if necessary, and ask the child to repeat:

| | | |
|---|---|---|
| 1 I like... | 4 I hate to go... | 7 Every day... |
| 2 I like to go... | 5 I would like... | 8 Tomorrow... |
| 3 I hate... | 6 I would not like... | 9 Yesterday... |

*Nursery rhymes*   Recite and sing along with the class your favourite nursery rhymes. Explain to the class why you like them and ask the class if they agree or disagree with your reasons for liking them.

# Daily lesson 180

**Materials**
Tape recorder

**Procedure**
Have the class name as many things as they can that have:

1 lids
2 hair
3 handles
4 tails
5 switches
6 points

Ask the class to tell the tape recorder what they would see and hear at a building site. Do not use a visual aid. Insist on simple short structured sentences. Remind the class that they should speak clearly and slowly.

Ask the class where they would have to go to

1 eat out
2 see a film
3 see fire engines
4 see railway engines
5 see lots of books
6 see a play
7 see aeroplanes
8 watch football
9 see cows
10 go for a boat ride

Ask the class to give you words that rhyme with the following:

1 train
2 bike
3 far
4 flick
5 ten
6 three
7 whip
8 hay
9 merry
10 head
11 won
12 town
13 sack
14 mean
15 mind
16 not
17 play
18 find
19 sun
20 hate

# Daily lesson 181

**Materials**
None

**Procedure**
Take the class for a walk lasting no more than twenty minutes. Encourage the class to keep their eyes peeled for the common, everyday sights, sounds and happenings that children tend to ignore. Bring such things to their attention on the walk, verbalizing for them what they see and hear but tend to ignore. When you return to the classroom run through the trip in chronological order, calling upon every individual to contribute to the story. You may wish to record what was seen on the walk in a book of drawings.

# Daily lesson 182

**Materials**
Tape recorder

**Procedure**
Explain to the class that you are going to read them a story called *The kitten* and that you want them to listen carefully because you will ask them questions about it afterwards.

## The kitten

Anne and Harry were on their way home from school. They lived very close to their school and so didn't usually take long to get home. But today they were going to take longer than usual because something was going to hold them up. And that something was a kitten.

They first saw the kitten near the bottom of a large tree which stood in a garden near their own house. The kitten looked as if it were trying to climb the tree but then Harry saw that all it was trying to do was catch a moth that was fluttering around bushes at the bottom of the tree. The kitten was tiny with black, soft, shiny fur and little white patches on its tummy, nose and each of its four little paws. Its eyes were bright and moving about quickly as they followed the moth. Its ears and whiskers twitched and its mouth half opened and shut many times ready to pounce and catch the moth with its teeth. It had small sharp teeth too.

Anne and Harry stopped to watch. The kitten stopped too and watched them. Then it padded over miaowing. They stroked it but had to be careful not to get scratched or bitten because it jumped about so much.

Soon, though, the kitten seemed bored and returned to playing in the bushes. Anne and Harry watched for a second and then began to walk home again. They were only a little way along the road when they heard the kitten miaowing close behind them. They petted it and lifted it up, but it struggled and scratched them. Then they took it back to its garden.

It followed them again. And again they took it back. Finally the lady who owned it saw them from the window and came out to meet them. 'Oh, thank you,' she said. 'He's such a playful rascal, and I'm never sure where he is. Thank you for bringing him back.'

And off Anne and Harry went. They'd be late home tonight. But they had enjoyed playing with that kitten—even although they'd got scratched.

Ask the class if they enjoyed the story. Then ask the following questions:
1. What was the name of the story?
2. What were the names of the boy and girl in the story?
3. Why didn't they usually take long to get home?
4. What was going to hold them up today?
5. Where did they first see the kitten?
6. What was the kitten trying to do?
7. Describe the kitten.
8. What did the kitten do when they stopped to watch it?
9. What did they do when it came over to them?
10. What did the kitten do when they began to walk home?
11. How often did it follow them?

Get the class to give the opposite of the following words. Explain 'opposite' and give examples. Preface each question with 'Give me the opposite of . . .'

| | | | |
|---|---|---|---|
| 1 | close | 11 | bright |
| 2 | didn't | 12 | quickly |
| 3 | first | 13 | open |
| 4 | near | 14 | sharp |
| 5 | bottom | 15 | stop |
| 6 | large | 16 | bored |
| 7 | tiny | 17 | behind |
| 8 | black | 18 | sure |
| 9 | soft | 19 | later |
| 10 | shiny | 20 | tonight |

*On tape*   Have the class tell the tape recorder of an experience they have had with an animal which they did not own or know well. Play back a selection.

# Daily lesson 183

**Materials**

Narrative pictures—pictures depicting characters and scenes of famous nursery rhymes

**Procedure**

Ask the class to complete the following sentences:

 1  In winter it is cold; in summer it is _____ . (hot)
 2  A brother is a boy; a sister is a _____ . (girl)
 3  A dog has hair; a bird has _____ . (feathers)
 4  A lion is fierce; a dog is _____ . (tame)
 5  A bird flies; a fish _____ . (swims)
 6  A car goes on the road; a boat sails on _____ . (water)
 7  A dog has paws; a bird has _____ . (claws)
 8  Stockings are long; socks are _____ . (short)
 9  Boys wear trousers; girls wear _____ . (dresses)
10  A wasp flies; a caterpillar _____ . (crawls)
11  A car is made of metal; a house of _____ . (bricks)
12  A book is made of paper; a table is made of _____ . (wood)

Display the narrative pictures of the nursery rhyme characters and scenes. Have the class identify each character and describe in detail the physical characteristics, idiosyncrasies and the antics and events with which he is associated in the nursery rhyme. Have the class recite the nursery rhymes depicted.

Ask the class to complete the following phrases with as many appropriate responses as possible:

 1  a bottle of _____
 2  a cupboard of _____
 3  a house full of _____
 4  a garden of _____
 5  a forest of _____
 6  a book of _____
 7  a field of _____
 8  a case of _____
 9  a bucket of _____
10  a sack of _____
11  a room full of _____
12  a box of _____
13  a drawer full of _____
14  a nest of _____
15  a collection of _____

# Daily lesson 184

**Materials**

1 Occupation cards as listed
2 Animal cards as listed
3 Nursery rhymes—children's selection

**Procedure**

Ask the class to say exactly what you say. Do not accept any alterations or omissions.

1 Mary drank her milk slowly through a straw.
2 Gerry tied his shoelaces very carefully and slowly.
3 Margaret hung her coat and hat up on the pegs.
4 Elizabeth placed the vase of flowers on the window ledge.
5 Alfred sat down and began to play the piano quietly.
6 Janet and Jill played with their own dolls all morning.
7 Michael tried to climb up the stairs quickly but fell down.
8 Eleanor helped her mother dry the dishes each morning.
9 As the sun came out, the wet streets began to dry.
10 The wind blew the leaves off every branch of the tree.

Ask the class where the following people would work:

| | |
|---|---|
| 1 teacher | 9 nurse |
| 2 pilot | 10 housewife |
| 3 traffic warden | 11 mineworker |
| 4 lollipop man | 12 janitor |
| 5 slater | 13 baker |
| 6 bricklayer | 14 bank clerk |
| 7 typist | 15 milkman |
| 8 clerk | |

Ask the class to clap their hands three times when they hear you say the name of an animal:

| | |
|---|---|
| 1 horse | 14 bee |
| 2 house | 15 big |
| 3 mouse | 16 pig |
| 4 tear | 17 habit |
| 5 fair | 18 rabbit |
| 6 hare | 19 lovely |
| 7 how | 20 arrow |
| 8 cow | 21 sparrow |
| 9 frog | 22 towel |
| 10 log | 23 owl |
| 11 dog | 24 carrot |
| 12 can't | 25 parrot |
| 13 key | |

*Nursery rhymes*   Recite and sing the children's selection of nursery rhymes.

# Daily lesson 185

**Materials**

Nursery rhyme—*Oranges and lemons*

**Procedure**

Ask the class the following questions:

1  What furniture do we sit on?
2  What heats our homes?
3  What do we wear on our heads?
4  What do we wear on our hands?
5  What do we wear on our feet?
6  What tells us the time?
7  What do we live in?
8  What shines in the sky at night?
9  What shines in the sky during the day?
10  What do we speak with?
11  What do we hear with?
12  What do we see with?
13  What do we taste with?
14  What do we smell with?
15  What do we breathe with?
16  What do we pick things up with?
17  What do we write and draw with?

Ask individuals to mime using the following tools. The remainder have to guess what is being used. Insist that the mime involves both hands where necessary. Insist also on a structured sentence to describe the mime:

1  knife and fork
2  spoon
3  kettle
4  toaster
5  teapot
6  cup and saucer
7  sugar bowl
8  salt cellar
9  telephone

*Nursery rhyme*   Revise *Oranges and lemons* and the traditional song that accompanies it. Add as many verses as the class can take.

# Daily lesson 186

**Materials**
Selection of animal, tool, occupation and clothing cards

**Procedure**
Ask the class to follow the following instructions:
1 Stand up straight, with your hands by your sides.
2 Bend down slowly so that your knees stick out at the side and there is a big hole between your legs.
3 Stand up straight again.
4 Stretch your hands high up in the sky.
5 Take your arms slowly down to your sides.
6 Roll your head round and round, to the left.
7 Roll your head round and round, to the right.
8 Touch your toes and stand up straight three times.
9 Shake your hands quickly and loosely.
10 Flap your arms like a bird flying.

Have individuals in the class mime the following actions, while the remainder of the class guess what they are doing:
1 filling a kettle
2 setting a table
3 making a bed
4 moving a heavy piece of furniture
5 planting a bush
6 pouring a cup of tea
7 opening a bottle of lemonade
8 completing a jigsaw
9 spinning a top
10 throwing snowballs

Display the selection of cards. Then explain that you are going to ask each of the class to bring you four from the selection and they have to say when they bring them, 'I have brought you a_____ , a_____ , a_____ and a_____ .'

*Nursery rhyme* Use the tape recorder to let a selection of the class record their favourite nursery rhyme. Play back after each child has recorded and gently criticize on the basis of whether the rhyme was clear to the ear, too fast or too slow, or not enough expression.

# Daily lesson 187

**Materials**
None

**Procedure**
Explain to the class that you are going to read them a story called *Leaves* and that you want them to listen carefully to the story because you will ask them questions about it afterwards.

### Leaves

It was autumn. Katherine and James were on their way home from school. It wasn't quite dark yet but the sky wasn't very bright, either. The air was slightly cold and damp. They wore their hats, overcoats and gloves.

On the corner of the street where they lived stood a huge tree. In the summer time the tree was laden with green leaves. So many and growing so thickly together that you couldn't see the sky if you looked up from underneath the tree. But now that it was autumn the leaves had begun to change colour, die and float gently down to the ground. The ground below the tree was thick with leaves of all different colours—yellow, brown, light green, orange.

Katherine and James had great fun scraping their feet among the leaves. The leaves made a lovely rustling noise as the children marched through them. Katherine and James would pile up the leaves in heaps too, using their feet to scrape them together into small piles, then carrying these piles in their arms to form bigger heaps. The leaves stuck to their coats and gloves and were quite dirty, but the dirt and the leaves were quite easily brushed off. So they played.

All of a sudden—out of the corner of her eye—Katherine thought she noticed something moving jerkily. She stood very still and turned her head towards the trunk of the tree. She saw nothing at first but just a few seconds later there was the movement again. It was so dark under the tree that she couldn't make out what it was at first. Then she realized what it was: a squirrel, a little grey fluffy tailed squirrel.

'James,' she whispered, as loud as she dared, 'James, look, a squirrel. Don't move, you'll frighten it away.'

James couldn't see it. So he moved ever so slowly and quietly over to where Katherine was. 'On the trunk,' said Katherine quietly. 'Wait a minute and you'll see it move.' And so it did, jumping and climbing quickly round and up the tree trunk until it disappeared high up among the dark branches. They lost sight of it.

What excitement! They'd never seen a squirrel before, although they had seen pictures of them at school and on television. They rushed home to tell mummy.

Ask the class if they enjoyed the story. Then ask the following questions:
1 What was the name of the story?
2 What were the names of the boy and girl in the story?
3 What time of year was it?
4 What was the weather like?
5 Was it dark or light?
6 How were Katherine and James dressed?

7  What stood at the corner of the street where they lived?
8  What did the tree look like in summer?
9  What happened to the tree in autumn?
10  How did Katherine and James play with the leaves?
11  Were the leaves dirty?
12  Why did Katherine suddenly stand still?
13  Why couldn't she see what had moved?
14  What happened when James came over to Katherine?
15  Had they ever seen a squirrel before?

Ask the class the opposite of the following words:

| | | | |
|---|---|---|---|
| 1  dark | | 11  together |
| 2  cold | | 12  bigger |
| 3  damp | | 13  dirty |
| 4  thickly | | 14  first |
| 5  many | | 15  later |
| 6  underneath | | 16  away |
| 7  gently | | 17  slowly |
| 8  thick | | 18  tiny |
| 9  different | | 19  high |
| 10  quietly | | 20  disappear |

Ask the class the meaning of the following words. Insist on a clear explanation. Elaborate and structure every response and ask the class to repeat:

| | | |
|---|---|---|
| 1  hat | | 6  trunk |
| 2  gloves | | 7  umbrella |
| 3  tree | | 8  shoes |
| 4  eye | | 9  house |
| 5  squirrel | | 10  school |

# Daily lesson 188

## Materials
Tape recorder

## Procedure
Explain to the class that you are going to read them a story called *The sweet shop* and that you want them to listen very carefully because you will ask them questions about it afterwards.

### The sweet shop

Victoria and Edward stood in the sweet shop waiting for their turn to be served. They always used the same sweet shop because it was small and quiet and because the lady who worked there was usually very pleasant to them. She always gave them plenty of time to make up their minds about what they wanted to buy. She never seemed in a hurry. And of course Victoria and Edward were never in a hurry because half the fun of going to the shop was deciding what to buy.

There was such a lot to choose from. There were dozens of glass jars filled to the brim with sweets covered in paper wrappers. There were liquorice sticks stuck in a jar on the counter. They looked like black flowers without leaves or petals. There were many different kinds of bars of chocolate—different sizes, different shapes, even different coloured chocolate.

Although there was so much to choose from and although Victoria and Edward always spent time thinking about what they would buy, they almost always bought the same thing—a packet of Smarties. Or sometimes they bought them in a tube. But it was always Smarties. Why? Well, you got such a lot for only a few pence. And they made such an exciting noise when you shook the bag or tube, just like a rattle. And there were so many different colours—red, blue, yellow, green, orange, brown—all the colours of the rainbow. Yes, they sounded and looked so attractive. And didn't they taste smashing! You could eat them singly or a whole lot at a time!

Victoria and Edward did enjoy going to the sweet shop and they did enjoy their Smarties.

Ask the class if they enjoyed the story. Then ask the following questions:
1  What was the name of the story?
2  What were the names of the boy and girl in the story?
3  Why did they always come to the same sweet shop?
4  Was Victoria or Edward in a hurry?
5  What kinds of sweets were there to choose from?
6  What did they always choose?
7  What was it about the sound that they liked?
8  What was it about the colours that they liked?
9  How did Victoria and Edward like to eat them?

Ask the class to give the opposite of the following words. Explain 'opposite' and give examples. Preface each question with, 'Give the opposite of . . .'

| | |
|---|---|
| 1  sweet | 11  black |
| 2  same | 12  without |

| | |
|---|---|
| 3 small | 13 noise |
| 4 quiet | 14 attractive |
| 5 lady | 15 pretty |
| 6 pleasant | 16 lucky |
| 7 half | 17 often |
| 8 going | 18 hard |
| 9 buy | 19 smiling |
| 10 lot | 20 good |

*On tape*  Ask the class to tell the tape recorder about their favourite sweets. Get them to describe colour, shape, texture, taste and how they are wrapped. Play back a selection.

# Daily lesson 189

**Materials**
Colour cubes

**Procedure**
Ask the class to say in how many different ways we use the following materials:
1 water
2 plastic
3 paper
4 glass

Ask the class to follow the following instructions:
1 Put a white cube on top of your desk.
2 Put a black cube underneath your desk.
3 Put an orange cube on the back of your left hand.
4 Put a green cube in the palm of your left hand.
5 Put a brown cube on top of your desk.
6 Put a yellow cube on top of this brown cube.
7 Put a red cube on the back of your right hand.
8 Put a blue cube in the palm of your right hand.
9 Put a red cube on top of your seat.
10 Put a yellow cube beside this red cube.

Ask the class to make the following chains, using your verbal instructions. Remember, have the class work from left to right. Increase the number of cubes in the chain if the class can manage them.
1 blue, orange, red, green
2 yellow, white, brown, red
3 black, green, red, blue
4 white, blue, yellow, black
5 white, blue, brown, red

Have one child think of an object and ask another to describe it. The latter will then think of an object and in turn ask someone else to describe it. Continue until each child has had a turn.

# Daily lesson 190

**Materials**
Nursery rhymes—children's selection

**Procedure**
Ask the class to say in what way the following three things are the same:
1  rose, tree, carrot
2  shoe, slipper, boot
3  newspaper, comic, book
4  crayon, pencil, pen
5  cup, mug, glass
6  frying pan, saucepan, oven
7  water, soap, towel
8  chair, bench, sofa
9  ball, skipping rope, bicycle
10  coat, jacket, hat

Ask the class to list as many things as they can that live or could be kept in the following:
1  pocket
2  school bag
3  tree
4  wardrobe
5  attic

Ask the class to listen for the name of an animal or a tool and when they hear it they have to clap their hands three times:

| | | | |
|---|---|---|---|
| 1 | by | 14 | heard |
| 2 | fly | 15 | bird |
| 3 | cry | 16 | mitten |
| 4 | tie | 17 | monkey |
| 5 | telephone | 18 | scissors |
| 6 | table | 19 | orange |
| 7 | label | 20 | match |
| 8 | house | 21 | rabbit |
| 9 | horse | 22 | happy |
| 10 | like | 23 | puppy |
| 11 | nose | 24 | greedy |
| 12 | letter | 25 | sparrow |
| 13 | pencil | | |

*Nursery rhymes*   Revise rhymes according to children's selection.

# Daily lesson 191

**Materials**
Nursery rhyme—*Goosey goosey gander*

**Procedure**
Ask the class to repeat exactly what you say.
1 five—six—three
2 four—eight—one
3 two—nine—six
4 three—ten—four

Then explain that instead of just repeating what you say, they have to say the numbers backwards. For example, when you say four—two they must say two—four; when you say two—four—six, they have to say six—four—two.

| | |
|---|---|
| 1 five—three | 11 one—ten—six |
| 2 eight—seven | 12 two—nine—seven |
| 3 two—nine | 13 three—eight—five |
| 4 one—eight | 14 four—seven—six |
| 5 three—five | 15 five—ten—eight |
| 6 two—five—one | 16 six—five—one |
| 7 three—eight—four | 17 seven—four—ten |
| 8 eight—one—two | 18 eight—three—nine |
| 9 three—six—one | 19 nine—two—one |
| 10 four—five—three | 20 ten—six—three |

Ask the class to tell you in simple, well structured sentences what sounds they would hear in the following places. Have the responders explain what would make the sounds:
1 swimming baths
2 restaurant
3 classroom
4 farmyard

Ask the class to imagine that their mother has just come in from the street saying she has seen something just outside the door. Ask the following list of 'Could it be . . .' asking them to explain why it could or couldn't be:

| | |
|---|---|
| 1 a horse | 9 a ship |
| 2 an aeroplane | 10 a tractor |
| 3 a policeman | 11 a bus driver |
| 4 a mirror | 12 a dentist |
| 5 a meat mincer | 13 a nurse |
| 6 a telephone | 14 a motorcycle |
| 7 a car | 15 a submarine |
| 8 an elephant | |

*Nursery rhyme*   Revise *Goosey goosey gander*

# Daily lesson 192

**Materials**

1 Tape recorder
2 Narrative picture—the birthday party
3 Nursery rhyme—*There was an old woman who lived in a shoe*

**Procedure**

Ask the class to give you words to rhyme with *hat, me low* and *tie*. Then ask them to give rhyming words according to the following instructions. Say 'Give me the name of . . .'

1 an animal that rhymes with fig
2 a flower that rhymes with nose
3 a colour that rhymes with head
4 a bird that rhymes with arrow
5 something that sails on the sea, that rhymes with coat
6 something that sails on the sea, that rhymes with lip
7 something we have two of that rhymes with cries
8 an animal that rhymes with keep
9 a bird that rhymes with beagle
10 an insect that rhymes with tie

*On tape* Ask the class to tell the tape recorder what they would see and how they would feel at a birthday party. Do not use a visual aid and do not prompt the class or individual with questions unless absolutely necessary. Even then ask neutral questions like 'what else?' Children may have difficulty verbalizing freely without a visual aid, and without the stimulus of direct questioning. The aim of this procedure is to teach them that they can verbalize freely, and to give them practice in so doing. Summarize what they have verbalized, using the tape as 'evidence', then display the narrative picture of the birthday party. Compare what they have said with what they could have said and point out omissions.

Play a variation of the game 'We went to market and we bought . . .'; play 'We went to a birthday party and we saw . . .' Have the class stand, giving each child five seconds to think of an additional item to add to the previous list. The nonresponding child should sit down. The game is over when only one child remains.

*Nursery rhyme* Revise *There was an old woman who lived in a shoe.*

# Daily lesson 193

**Materials**

None

**Procedure**

Explain to the class that you are going to tell them a story called *The vegetable shop* and that you want them to listen carefully to the story because you will ask them questions about it afterwards.

### The vegetable shop

Amanda and Stephen were walking home with their father. They had just been to feed the ducks. On their way home they passed the vegetable shop. Outside the shop, on the pavement, they could see buckets filled with freshly cut flowers and row upon row of wooden trays filled with fruit and vegetables. They thought, 'Wouldn't it be nice to buy some flowers for mummy, just as a surprise?' So in they went.

There was no one in the shop except the shop assistant—a smiling, helpful lady, wearing a green overall. Daddy and Amanda and Stephen looked around. There was every kind of vegetable you could think of— cauliflowers, lettuces, potatoes, tomatoes, cress, onions, carrots. There was only one kind of flower, daffodils, because it was springtime. But there were different kinds of bulbs and seeds to plant. There were many different kinds of fruit displayed: grapefruit, bananas, oranges, apples and lemons.

Father couldn't remember if they had any fruit or vegetables at home so he said, 'I'd better buy some, just in case. What should I buy?' he asked Amanda and Stephen.

'Get some bananas,' said Stephen.

'and grapefruit,' added Amanda. 'Mummy would like a lettuce, I think,' said Stephen.

'And a cauliflower too?' questioned daddy. 'Yes.' So they bought a pound of bananas, four grapefruit, a lettuce and a cauliflower.

'Is that everything?' asked the shop assistant.

'Yes, I think so,' replied daddy, and he handed over a pound to pay for them.

'Thank you,' said the shop assistant, giving him change. 'Thank you,' said Amanda and Stephen, carrying out the vegetables.

They had hardly reached the door of the shop when Stephen stopped in his tracks. 'Gosh, daddy, we forgot to buy some flowers for mummy!' Of course! How funny, they'd only gone into the shop to buy flowers and here they were laden with vegetables but no flowers. Daddy hurried back and bought a lovely little bunch of yellow daffodils. Wouldn't mummy be pleased!

Ask the class if they enjoyed the story. Then ask the following questions:

1 What was the name of the story?
2 What were the names of the boy and girl in the story?
3 Where had they been and who was with them?
4 What did they see outside the vegetable shop?
5 Who was in the shop?

6 What did she wear?
7 What kind of vegetables did they see?
8 What kind of fruit did they see?
9 What kind of flowers did they see?
10 Why only one kind of flower?
11 What did they buy?
12 What did they remember to buy at the last minute?

Ask the class the meaning of the following words, most of which will present little difficulty. The children will probably know the meaning. However they have some difficulty in expressing what they want to say. Accept any reasonable response but elaborate, clarify and structure, asking individuals to repeat what you say:

| | | | |
|---|---|---|---|
| 1 | home | 6 | banana |
| 2 | shop | 7 | orange |
| 3 | bucket | 8 | door |
| 4 | potato | 9 | window |
| 5 | daffodil | 10 | bag |

Ask the class the opposite of the following words:

| | | | |
|---|---|---|---|
| 1 | outside | 6 | everything |
| 2 | buy | 7 | lovely |
| 3 | smiling | 8 | stopped |
| 4 | daddy | 9 | pleased |
| 5 | remember | 10 | funny |

# Daily lesson 194

**Materials**

None

**Procedure**

Ask the class to finish each sentence. The questions may be repeated and posed to children who did not respond the first time round.

1  Snow is cold; fire is _____ .
2  Snow is white; coal is _____ .
3  You kick with your feet and throw with your _____ .
4  In winter it is cold; in summer it is _____ .
5  In the daytime it is light; at night it is _____ .
6  A dog walks, but a bird _____ .
7  A bird has wings; a boy has _____ .
8  A bird flies; a fish _____ .
9  A cat has kittens; a dog has _____ .
10  A cat's ears are short; a rabbit's ears are _____ .

Ask individuals to confirm or correct the following sentences. Insist on their responding in a structured fashion as in the responses given to questions one and two. Have the class elaborate their response.

1  Is a window made of glass? (Reply: Yes, a window is made glass and of wood also.)
2  Does a dog have two legs? (No, a dog doesn't have two legs, but a bird has two legs.)
3  Can fish fly?
4  Can you bounce a tin can?
5  Do you sit on a table?
6  Is the sky green?
7  Do elephants sing?
8  Can you see through glass?
9  Do rabbits have short ears?
10  Do trains run quickly?

Acting as a guide ask the class to act out the following instructions. Have them respond to verbal instructions initially. Demonstrate only when the majority do not appear to understand the verbal instructions and always accompany demonstrations with verbal instructions.

1  Reach for the sky (emphasize words like high, stretch, up).
2  Curl up into a ball (tightly, round).
3  Pretend it is cold and you are shivering (teeth chattering, arms flapping, knees knocking).
4  Pretend it is hot and you are sweating (panting, drooping).
5  Hop like a rabbit (tail bobbing).
6  Pretend you are a pussy cat wanting to come in (miaowing, scratching at the door, stretching up, scraping).
7  Pretend you are an elephant (lumbering, trunk swinging, slowly).
8  Pretend you are a spider (quietly, swiftly, stopping, starting).
9  Lie flat on your backs and listen to the wind outside howling (insist on absolute silence in the room).

# Daily lesson 195

**Materials**

1 Narrative poster—winter
2 Tape recorder
3 Nursery rhyme—*Here we go round the mulberry bush*

**Procedure**

Display picture and ask the class to analyze it. Emphasize that this season is called winter, and elicit the activities and events associated with winter —cold weather, falling snow, icy roads, blocked roads, burst pipes, snow-men, snowball fights, slides, sledging, absence of flowers or leaves on the trees, heavy clothing, warm fires, ice patterns on the window etc.

*On tape*   Having analyzed the picture and structured the points mentioned above, have some of the class tell the tape recorder what they like best and what they like least about wintertime.

*Nursery rhyme*   Finish by singing *Here we go round the mulberry bush.*

# Daily lesson 196

**Materials**
1 Animal, tool and occupation cards as listed
2 Nursery rhyme—*Pussy cat, pussy cat, where have you been?*

**Procedure**
Ask the class to repeat exactly what you say. No omissions or alterations are acceptable.
1 Mummy pulled open the drawer and took out a knife and a spoon.
2 Daddy opened the cupboard door and looked for a hammer.
3 Emma put her head on the pillow and fell asleep immediately.
4 The little puppy pulled on its lead and then sat down.
5 Richard sat down on the floor and spread the comic out flat in front of him.
6 Brian tied knots in the skipping rope to make it shorter.
7 Mummy searched in her handbag for the key of the door but couldn't find it.
8 Jane handed her pennies over to the ice cream man and waited for her change.
9 They played in the bath with an empty lemonade bottle and a boat.
10 It was springtime and the grass began to grow longer and thicker.

Display the pictures as below and ask the class to pick the odd one out. Ask each child the basis upon which he made his selection. Insist on a well structured sentence, mentioning the three cards e.g. 'Well, the cow has four legs, and the cat has four legs, but the bird has only two'.
1 cow, mat, sparrow
2 tiger, lion, dog
3 elephant, giraffe, mouse
4 pig, sheep, deer
5 python, cobra, worm
6 fly, bee, wasp
7 slippers, pyjamas, boots
8 milkman, baker, policeman
9 hammer, cup, plate
10 watch, alarm clock, soap
11 snake, insect, soap
12 cow, milk jug, teapot
13 scissors, saw, paper
14 mirror, comb, pen
15 letter, book, spade

Ask the class to finish the following sentences:
1 An aeroplane flies in the sky; a motor car runs _____ . (on the road)
2 You wear slippers inside the house; you wear boots _____ . (outside)
3 A monkey can move fast, but a snail moves _____ . (slowly)
4 Jam is sweet; vinegar is _____ . (sour)
5 A cow has four legs; a sparrow has _____ . (two)
6 In the summer it is hot; in the winter it is _____ . (cold)
7 A cat miaows; a lion _____ . (roars)
8 You sit in a chair; you lie on a _____ . (bed)
9 A table has four legs; an eagle has _____ . (two)
10 An octopus has eight legs; a camel has _____ . (four)

*Nursery rhyme*   Revise *Pussy cat, pussy cat, where have you been?*

249

# Daily lesson 197

**Materials**
1 Narrative picture—spring scene
2 Nursery rhyme—*Ding dong bell*

**Procedure**
Ask the class to name as many things, or say as many words as they can beginning with the following sounds:

1 *b* as in ball
2 *sh* as in shoe
3 *st* as in step
4 *r* as in run
5 *c* as in cup
6 *n* as in needle
7 *t* as in table
8 *h* as in horse
9 *s* as in stay
10 *w* as in window

Ask the class to supply the missing words.

1 a bottle of _____
2 a pair of _____
3 a herd of _____
4 a flock of _____
5 a flight of _____
6 a bowl of _____
7 a roll of _____
8 a book of _____
9 a packet of _____
10 a bag of _____
11 a cage of _____
12 a field of _____
13 a bunch of _____
14 a wardrobe of _____
15 a sheet of _____
16 a box of _____
17 a pint of _____
18 a ton of _____
19 a bucketful of _____
20 a flask of _____

Display clearly and analyze the foreground, middle ground and background of the picture. Emphasize the weather, the activity of nature etc. Structure and summarize the picture quickly at the end.

*Nursery rhyme*   Have the class listen to, learn and recite *Ding dong bell*.

# Daily lesson 198

**Materials**
1  Fruit and vegetables—pictures or plastic models
2  Nursery rhyme—*There was a crooked man*

**Procedure**
Display pictures or models of fruit and vegetables one at a time. Elicit or teach the name of each. Have the class describe the object in terms of colour, shape, size and, if possible, texture. Ask also how they taste. Do we usually eat them raw or cooked? Do we, in this country, eat them fresh, frozen, tinned or what? Revise the list quickly, having the class name the fruit and vegetables.

Ask the class to stand on the left foot, to see if there are children who are still confused. Correct those who are. Ask the class to stand on the right foot—again check, correct and confirm. Explain that you are now going to play a game which uses a lot of left and right directions, so the class will have to be very alert.
  1  Raise your left hand.
  2  Stand on your left foot.
  3  Touch your left knee with your left hand.
  4  Touch your left ear with your left hand.
  5  Touch your left eye with your left hand.
  6  Touch your left hip with your left hand.
Say, 'So all down this side is your left side, isn't it?'
  7  Raise your right hand.
  8  Stand on your right foot.
  9  Touch your right knee with your right hand.
10  Touch your right ear with your right hand.
11  Touch your right eye with your right hand.
12  Touch your right hip with your right hand.
Say, 'So all down this side is your right side, isn't it?' And all down this side is your left side. Left side and right side.' Give some more simple instructions, alternating left and right.

*Nursery rhyme*  Teach *There was a crooked man* by the usual method.

# Daily lesson 199

**Materials**
1 Tape recorder
2 Nursery rhyme—*Bobbie Shaftoe*

**Procedure**
Ask the class to say what things you could carry in the following containers.
Encourage them to name items which are not usually kept in the containers
but which in theory could be e.g. paint in a bottle, or buttons in a matchbox.
Discuss the feasability of each suggestion.

| | | | |
|---|---|---|---|
| 1 | bottle | 7 | aeroplane |
| 2 | basket | 8 | bus |
| 3 | car | 9 | cigarette packet |
| 4 | tin can | 10 | shoe box |
| 5 | matchbox | 11 | hat |
| 6 | drawer | 12 | glove |

*On tape* Ask individuals in the class to describe to the tape recorder what
they did last night between getting home from school and going to bed.
Insist on simple, well structured, lucid sentences and the use of words such
as 'then', 'afterwards', 'at first', 'finally'.

Play a variation of the game 'We went to market and we bought . . .' Ask
the class to say what they would see at the following places. Each child lists
the items previously mentioned in the game and adds one of his own:

| | | | |
|---|---|---|---|
| 1 | airport | 4 | hospital |
| 2 | harbour | 5 | fairground |
| 3 | cinema | 6 | library |

*Nursery rhyme* Sing the nursery rhyme *Bobbie Shaftoe*. Explain the
meaning of the poem casually (e.g. silver buckles on his knee) and play
again. Invite the class to join in.

# Daily lesson 200

**Materials**
None

**Procedure**
Take the class for a walk, no more than 400 yards from the school. Explain to them that you want them to walk slowly and keep their eyes wandering above, below and to the side, looking at everything around them. As you walk, stop and bring their attention to anything that might interest them but which they have become accustomed to pass by without a second glance or moment's thought e.g. goods being delivered to a shop, an animal sniffing around the street, puddles drying up etc. Take note of the different shops and public institutions and kinds of houses you pass. When you return to the classroom take the class through the walk again in chronological order, calling upon individuals to tell what happened next. They may like to make a book of drawings of the walk.

# Index

Bernstein, Basil 12
  language styles 12ff

chaining 76, 89, 110, 120, 131, 149, 158, 167, 222, 241
classification 15, 31, 41, 42, 45, 46, 49, 87, 97, 99, 108, 126, 148, 155, 162, 198, 204, 209, 216, 218, 225, 242, 249
class lessons 33ff
  aims 25
  arrangement 25
  principles 28
  role of teacher 26–27
colour 54, 61, 66, 76, 87, 89, 92, 97, 108, 126, 148, 155, 162, 198, 204, 209, 216, 218, 225, 242, 249
colour cubes 21, 54, 61, 66, 76, 89, 92, 97, 99, 104, 110, 120, 131, 132, 149, 158, 167, 222, 241
comprehension 77, 84, 103, 133, 136, 137, 138, 143, 174, 180, 185, 196, 220, 230, 234, 235

days of the week 77, 109, 138, 209, 214
deaf-mute children 15
definitions 65, 83, 105, 112, 130, 135, 146, 151, 157, 160, 166, 173, 178, 184, 185, 195, 202, 212, 218, 225, 237, 246
descriptive exercises 31, 46, 54, 71, 85, 88, 92, 94, 99, 110, 115, 120, 125, 126, 142, 144, 149, 164, 169, 181, 182, 186, 187, 193, 210, 225, 233, 241, 248, 251, 252
differences 31, 50, 70, 75, 82, 87, 99, 116, 136, 167, 176, 181, 194, 203, 218
drama 29, 35
drawing 29–30, 35, 51, 58, 60, 69, 87, 99, 115, 122

elaborated code 13

family relationships 30, 36, 39, 121
following instructions 31–32, 49, 59, 71, 92, 104, 109, 132, 138, 161, 176, 179, 181, 229, 236, 241, 247, 251
fruit (plastic) 21–22, 70, 87, 204, 218, 251
Furth, HG 15

Kendler, HH and TS 11
  experiment 11–12

language codes
  effect on schooling 14
linguistic ability 5
Luria, AR 7
  role of language 7–10

manikin 22, 35, 39, 49, 69, 141
materials 17ff
memory 93, 119, 142, 143, 149, 156, 163, 170, 175, 191, 197, 205, 209, 220, 224, 228, 230, 234, 249, 253
mime 31, 46, 65, 82, 94, 99, 102, 110, 125, 133, 164, 197, 213, 223, 224, 235, 236

narrative pictures 20, 55, 58, 59, 71, 88, 99, 110, 115, 122, 126, 142, 149, 158, 164, 169, 186, 191, 194, 197, 233, 244, 248, 250
nonreversal shift 11, 12
nonsense 30–31, 40, 45, 105, 156, 180, 218, 223
number 66, 99
nursery rhymes 22–24, 28, 33, 34, 35, 36, 39, 41, 42, 45, 46, 49, 50, 54, 55, 56, 57, 60, 61, 66, 72, 77, 79, 83, 84, 87, 88, 94, 98,

104, 109, 114, 118, 128, 137, 138, 140, 143, 148, 149, 150, 153, 155, 156, 157, 161, 162, 163, 164, 170, 173, 174, 175, 180, 181, 182, 185, 186, 188, 193, 194, 196, 198, 199, 203, 204, 206, 208, 209, 210, 212, 213, 214, 215, 216, 220, 224, 225, 228, 229, 233, 234, 235, 236, 242, 243, 244, 248, 249, 250, 251, 252

opposites   15, 38, 44, 48, 53, 57, 62–63, 68, 73–74, 80, 81, 86, 91, 96, 101, 106–107, 112, 118, 124, 130, 135, 146, 151, 158, 160, 166, 172, 178, 184, 200, 202, 212, 221, 222, 227, 232, 238, 239–240, 246

picture cards   17, 33, 34, 50, 54, 58, 60, 155, 157, 198, 204, 218, 225, 251
  animals   17, 39, 40, 41, 45, 49, 75, 88, 93, 97, 108,ʼ116, 119, 128, 131, 137, 148, 162, 167, 170, 176, 179, 181, 203, 205, 208, 209, 210, 215, 224, 234, 236, 249
  clothing   17–18, 34, 35, 39, 49, 99, 136, 148, 162, 167, 168, 176, 179, 205, 209, 215, 224, 236
  family relationships   18, 36, 39, 121, 148
  food   42
  furniture   19, 46, 98, 148
  house   19, 98, 148
  ʼhow to doʼ   46, 92, 104, 125
  institutions   18, 81
  number   19, 66
  occupations   18, 42, 45, 64, 83, 120, 132, 148, 167, 168, 185, 203, 205, 209, 215, 224, 234, 236, 249
  public entertainments   18
  shape   18–19, 58, 122, 208
  shops   18, 42, 45, 78, 114, 148

sports   20, 219
tools   19, 45, 65, 72, 83, 94, 105, 119, 128, 133, 138, 143, 144, 148, 162, 167, 168, 170, 173, 176, 179, 181, 193, 203
transport   20, 82, 119, 128, 213, 214
utensils   19, 45, 65, 72, 94, 128
plurals   153
posters   20
puppet   21, 27, 33, 34, 36, 39, 40, 41, 42, 45, 50, 55, 61
  role of   21, 27–28

relationships   50, 58, 93, 99, 108, 228
repetition   143, 149, 153, 174, 224, 230, 244
restricted code   13
reversal shift   11, 12
rhyming   78, 116, 141, 155, 174, 224, 230, 244
role of language   7ff

self expression   28–29, 33, 36, 39, 44, 48, 53, 59, 67, 74, 81, 82, 86, 88, 91, 96, 97, 99, 101, 103, 107, 110, 112, 113, 114, 115, 125, 126, 130, 133, 135, 136, 140, 141, 146, 147, 149, 151, 152, 153, 154, 160, 163, 170, 172, 174, 178, 184, 186, 190, 191, 192, 194, 195, 196, 199, 200, 202, 215, 216, 217, 220, 227, 229, 230, 232, 238, 240, 241, 243, 244, 248, 252, 253
self identity   29, 34, 36, 113, 121, 153, 175, 180, 188, 205, 215, 229
sentence completion   65, 75, 102, 121, 147, 156, 176, 188, 161, 162, 164, 222, 229, 233, 247, 249
sentence formation   152, 157, 164, 187, 198
shapes   22, 51, 58, 122, 208
sounds   30, 40, 115, 137, 192, 243

sources   20–21
stories   37, 43, 47, 52, 56, 62, 67,
73, 79, 85, 90, 95, 100, 103, 106,
111, 113, 117, 123, 127, 129,
134, 144, 145, 150, 154, 159,
165, 171, 177, 183, 189–190,
195, 200, 201, 207, 211, 217,
226–227, 231, 237, 239, 245

tape recorder   22, 33, 34, 39, 41,
42, 44, 47–48, 50, 53, 54, 57, 67,
71, 74, 81, 82, 86, 91, 96, 97, 99,
101, 103, 107, 110, 112, 113,
118, 121, 124, 128, 130, 210,
212, 215, 217, 220, 221, 227,
229, 230, 232, 240, 244, 248,
252
teacher preparation   6
*Treasure Chest for Teachers*   21

vegetables (plastic)   21–22, 87,
204, 218, 251
vocabulary   28, 33, 34, 35, 36, 39,
40, 41, 42, 45, 46, 49, 51, 55, 58,
64, 65, 69, 70, 75, 81, 82, 83, 84,
87, 88, 98, 99, 104, 105, 112,
114, 116, 119, 120, 122, 125,
126, 130, 131, 132, 135, 136,
137, 138, 141, 146, 151, 166,
168, 172, 178, 179, 182, 184,
185, 195, 202, 204, 206, 210,
212, 213, 214, 218, 219, 238,
250
Vygotsky, LS   10, 15
relationship between speech
and language   11

Watson, J B   14
Whorf, B L   14